THE POLITICAL IDEAS OF
THORSTEIN VEBLEN

THE POLITICAL IDEAS OF THORSTEIN VEBLEN

Sidney Plotkin and
Rick Tilman

Yale UNIVERSITY PRESS
New Haven & London

Published with assistance from the foundation established in memory of Amasa Stone Mather of the Class of 1907, Yale College.

Yale University Press books may be purchased in quantity for educational, business, or promotional use. For information, please e-mail sales.press@yale.edu (U.S. office) or sales@yaleup.co.uk (U.K. office).

Set in Galliard Old Style and Copperplate 33 types by IDS Infotech, Ltd.
Printed in the United States of America.

Library of Congress Cataloging-in-Publication Data

Plotkin, Sidney.
   The political ideas of Thorstein Veblen/Sidney Plotkin and Rick Tilman.
     p. cm.
   Includes bibliographical references and index.
   ISBN 978-0-300-15999-8 (pbk.: alk. paper) 1. Veblen, Thorstein, 1857–1929—Political and social views. 2. Political science—Philosophy. I. Tilman, Rick. II. Title.
HB119. V4P56 2011
320.092—dc22

2011008451

A catalogue record for this book is available from the British Library.

This paper meets the requirements of ANSI/NISO Z39.48–1992 (Permanence of Paper).

10 9 8 7 6 5 4 3 2 1

CONTENTS

FOR MARJORIE LYNN GLUCK, 1962–2009

ACKNOWLEDGMENTS

        This book originated in conversations between the authors when they first met at the 2004 meeting of the International Thorstein Veblen Association (ITVA), at Carleton College, Veblen's alma mater. ITVA emerged in the 1990s as a convivial group of scholars sharing an interest in Veblen, his life and thought, its origins and relevance to contemporary social theory and political economy. The late Arthur Vidich, for many years a distinguished professor of sociology at the New School, founded ITVA in 1994. Urging on a distinguished cadre of scholars, including Franco Ferrarotti, John Diggins, Clare Eby, and Rick Tilman, Art perceptively saw the end of the Soviet era as a moment ripe with opportunities for rediscovery of Veblen. In the face of a neoliberal ascendancy and the rightward drift of the Democratic Party, and with the appeal of Marxism fading, Art insisted that Veblen's work offered an untapped reservoir of insights relevant to understandings of the current situation. It was high time for an organization to help mobilize possibilities for Veblen research. Beginning with its first meeting in 1994 and throughout subsequent biennial sessions, ITVA's vibrant and remarkably warm and collegial intellectual milieu helped to rekindle interest in Veblen. It also provided an indispensible forum for development of this work.

Rick Tilman had written extensively on Veblen and American thought prior to 2004. Sid Plotkin was new to Veblen studies, having spent the majority of his career working on issues of public policy and political power. Though trained in political theory, Plotkin was introduced to Veblen's writing in the course of his dissertation research on American land policy. It was the late Bob Engler who provocatively suggested that a careful look at *Absentee Ownership* might be a useful way to learn something about the politics of American development. Spurred by Engler's encouragement, Plotkin looked to Veblen as an important source in his work and teaching on American politics. But it was not until the early 1990s that he decided to explore in a serious way the explicitly political dimensions of Veblen.

A crucial moment in this decision was a fortuitous invitation from Sondra Farganis to comment on a work in progress on Veblen by Art Vidich, delivered at the New School. Because the link between that invitation and this study could not be more direct, our gratitude to Sondra is substantial. For Plotkin's meeting with Art Vidich led to his membership in ITVA and a growing confidence that following a political lead into Veblen's thought made sense. More than anything else, though, it was Rick Tilman's idea that careful study of Veblen's political ideas had merit and that we should collaborate on it.

Every venture in intellectual cooperation has its own peculiar contours. This one has been a special pleasure throughout. Most of the writing is Plotkin's, drawing on his own research as well as on earlier articles and books that Tilman had written. Throughout the writing, Tilman made numerous bibliographic and editorial contributions to Plotkin's work in progress. Because the authors' minds run in the same channels on the subject of Veblen's political thought, very little revision of the completed draft was needed. Stylistically and organizationwise the study reflects Sid Plotkin's design, although its main themes and the way they are developed is fully a joint product, with the senior author (in age only!) nevertheless playing an important secondary role.

The authors are deeply indebted to a host of supportive and generous colleagues and friends. Art Vidich's and Franco Ferrarotti's early encouragement was especially invaluable. Russ Bartley provided an unusually comprehensive and penetrating reading of the manuscript for Yale University Press. The work is considerably better for his commentary and we owe him abundant thanks. Sid Plotkin's many conversations with Jim Farganis about the themes in this study proved to be an endlessly stimulating source of ideas and criticisms, echoes of which appear throughout.

Bob Prasch, Ross Mitchell, Steve Edgell, Larry Van Sickle, and William E. Scheuerman Jr. gave generously of their time, reading various parts of the emerging manuscript and offering valuable criticism and insights. We are also grateful to Tom Veblen, Thorstein's grandnephew, for letting us see his engaging family biography of the Veblens prior to its publication. Beth McCormick, secretary of Vassar's Political Science Department, graciously assisted in copying more than a few versions of the manuscript. In addition, Sid Plotkin enjoyed the help of an exceptional corps of student assistants, especially Allie Merriam and Marianne Kies. The manuscript also benefited from the many inquisitive Vassar students who dared take Thorstein Veblen and the Politics of Capitalism, a course that has been a principal testing ground for many of the ideas developed here. Plotkin is also most fortunate to work in a political science department whose members share a broad, rich, and imaginative sense of the political. That they welcomed Plotkin's scholarly detour back to Veblen and political theory made work on this project infinitely easier.

Sid Plotkin had the good fortune of meeting Jean E. Thomson Black, Yale's science and medicine editor, at Vassar College's Publisher's Day event. After reading a draft of the first chapter, she generously guided our initial introduction to Yale University Press and to our editor, Bill Frucht. We are deeply grateful to both for their faith in and support for this project, and to Ann-Marie Imbornoni for her able copyediting.

In the end of course, it is family that bears the greatest burden of a writer's hours at the keyboard. For Rick Tilman, Ruth Porter-Tilman's constant love and support have eased Rick's way. Sid Plotkin's children, Joanna, Rachel, and Sam, bore the burden of Dad's hours at the screen with good cheer, gifting him with love, humor, and a recurrent sense of reality (pecuniary and otherwise!) as this work progressed. For Sid, Aura Goldberg has been an invaluable source of love and care in the later stages of the manuscript's preparation. And through good times and bad over the years, Jeff Stein, Bill Scheuerman, Steve Rock, and Iva Deutchman have consistently displayed comradely friendship and love in their best and truest sense. ·

But above all, Sid's late wife, Marjorie Lynn Gluck, to whom this work is dedicated, was its chief inspiration and support. Without her faith, help, counsel, and love Plotkin could not have mustered the courage to risk such a drastic change in scholarly focus. Her presence, through twenty-three years of marriage, family building, and work, was the rock on which the Plotkin/Gluck clan made its way. Marjorie displayed to all who knew and loved her the lesson of how to wage a courageous fight against cancer without sacrificing for a moment the qualities and virtues of a good and caring life. Marjorie did not live to see this work published. She passed away quietly on August 3, 2009, eighty years to the day after Veblen's death. But she remains vivid and alive for us. Every reference to Veblen's concept of "fullness of life" reflects her generous and brilliant spirit and her affirmation of a life lived in dignity, kindness, humility, and virtue.

Several chapters in this volume appeared in earlier versions under Sid Plotkin's authorship. These include: "Thorstein Veblen and the Sabotage of Democracy," in *Thorstein Veblen and the Revival of Free Market Capitalism*, ed. Janet T. Knoedler, Robert E. Prasch, and Dell P. Champlin (Cheltenham, U.K.: Edward Elgar, 2007), 170–201; "The Critic as Quietist: Thorstein Veblen's Radical Realism," *Common Knowledge* 16, 1 (Winter 2010): 79–94; "Thorstein Veblen and the Politics of Power," in *Thorstein Veblen, Economics for an Age of Crisis*, ed. Erik S. Reinert and Francesca Lidia Viano (London: Anthem, 2011). We gratefully acknowledge permission to use this material.

We offer the usual authorial apologies, and assume full responsibility, for any errors.

A NOTE ON CITATION

In addition to his seven books, Veblen produced many important essays, some technical, others more journalistic or polemical. As a whole they represent an indispensible part of his output and a source of valuable clues to his thought, political and otherwise. These essays are available in two collections. The first is *The Place of Science in Modern Civilization and Other Essays*, published in New York in 1919 by B. W. Huebusch. A later edition of this volume appeared in 1969, published in New York by Capricorn Books, under the title *Veblen On Marx, Race, Science and Economics*.

The other collection, edited after Veblen's death by his friend Leon Ardzrooni, appeared first in 1934, under the title *Essays in Our Changing Order*, published by Viking Press. In 1964 Augustus Kelley republished the volume in hardcover. In 1998, Transaction Publishers, which has republished all of Veblen's works in paper editions, brought out a new edition of Ardzrooni's collection, with a new introduction by Scott Bowman.

In the text throughout, we cite from the Capricorn 1969 edition of *The Place of Science in Modern Civilization and Other Essays*. Citations refer to the year of publication of the collection, 1969; the year of publication of the original essay is included at the relevant entry in the reference list. Lowercase letters following 1969 refer to an alphabetical ordering of the essays included in the bibliography.

For *Essays in Our Changing Order*, we cite from the 1964 Augustus Kelley edition and use the same format as above.

1

INTRODUCTION: POWER AND POLITICS

IN VEBLEN

This is a study of the political ideas of Thorstein Veblen. It may be hard to imagine a less provocative sentence. But Veblen is not a thinker to whom political scientists routinely turn for insight. A political theory canon that includes such familiar European names as Marx, Weber, Tocqueville, Foucault, or Habermas generally ignores the American mind of Thorstein Veblen. Conventional scholarly wisdom casts Veblen outside the class of important political writers. The popular view runs something like this: Veblen earned his reputation for impressive contributions to sociology and economics, but politics did not interest him, and so he has little of value to say about it. Veblen's early books, the works that made his name—*The Theory of the Leisure Class* and *The Theory of Business Enterprise*—are justly celebrated studies. One opens the door on the social psychology of class; the other penetrates crisis tendencies in finance capitalism. These works tell us much about contemporary patterns of consumption and the chronic turbulence of financial markets, but they hardly mention politics. The subject is all but invisible in *The Theory of the Leisure Class*, and Veblen avoids government in *The Theory of Business Enterprise* until late in the study, offering only a seemingly dry formal essay on "Business Principles in Law and Politics."

In fact, there is considerably more politics in these early studies than meets the casual eye; Veblen's later writings are even richer in political thought. In *The Theory of the Leisure Class*, for example, Veblen based his radical critique of economic inequality on a theory of power that he called "exploit." And "Business Principles in Law and Politics" amounts to more than a sterile catalogue of juridical principles. Veblen charts there the beginnings of what will emerge in later works as a fuller-blown theory of the warfare state, a theory that resonates all too closely with contemporary international relations, U.S. foreign policy, expansion of executive power, and dangers for democratic institutions. In fact, considering the whole of Veblen's works, the many books and essays that he regularly brought out in the period of enormous social change between 1892 and 1923, it becomes hard to ignore Veblen's increasingly focused observations on the importance of political institutions. And at the heart of his growing interest in politics, matters of war, executive power, and democracy loom large.

It is certainly true that Veblen accented the economic power of giant corporations and their political influence. He fully understood, indeed, perhaps exaggerated, how much contemporary democracy owes to the power of "substantial citizens" and giant corporations. But for all his emphasis on economic power, Veblen held that the state is, in its genesis, history, and development, a fundamentally political institution, preoccupied with its own political power and prestige in relation to other states. Modern states were born in a precapitalist crucible of violent international competition. Veblen believed this historic birthright had lasting, cumulative impacts on modern governments, especially by shaping the character and direction of aggressive executive power in ways that render it inimical to democracy.

Thorstein Veblen read international relations through a cold realist lens. Leaders who succeed in the political arts of diplomacy and war must be skilled in wily ways of duplicity, dissimulation, and secrecy, traits uncongenial to democratic openness. Foreign policy and war, the real sport of kings, poison commitments to transparency, truth, and candor, elements essential to any democracy worthy of the name. Modern democratic chief executives are not kings, of course, but Veblen believed, as did many early American republicans, that the institution of executive power favors kingly habits of secrecy, subterfuge, and war making.[1] Institutions shape their leaders. Above all, he believed that chief executives inherit suspicions of democracy because ordinary people prefer honesty and peace to duplicity and war. War thus requires political salesmanship of a high order; the passion to fight does not come naturally. It demands calls to national conceit, patriotism, and fear, a host of emotional appeals that erode claims of reason. For Veblen, democracies cannot continue to make war without insult to candor and authenticity. By the same token, he held that it is hard for democracy, caught up as it is within the international state system, to subsist as a form of state without bending toward war. In short, democracy makes its peace with war by accepting an increasingly autonomous executive. "All this trading on the national integrity," as he once put it, "is carried on as inconspicuously as may be, quite legally and morally under democratic forms, by night and cloud, and is covered over with such decently voluble prevarication as the case may require . . . such a volume and texture of prevarication as may serve to keep the national left hand from knowing what the right hand is doing, the left hand in these premises being the community at large, as contrasted with the Interests and the official personnel."[2]

Reading Veblen can seem like a chilling tour of recent history. Besides war, he regularly examines a raft of familiar and crucial matters: the political influence of corporate power; irrationalities of loan credit, financial speculation, and economic crisis; political salesmanship and the politics of dissimulation; a troubling reliance on antique constitutional rules for answers to current needs; and perhaps most insidiously, an ominous tendency of power motives to entrap leaders and states in self-defeating imperial projects. Veblen would surely have been impressed by the election of the nation's first African-American president; but the fact that Barack Obama's election and administration turned on matters of financial crisis, economic stagnation, and war would not have surprised him at all. People are mostly governed by habit, Veblen insisted, including their worst, most self-injurious, barbaric habits.

Politics, Power, Habit, Time

Among Veblen's great contributions as a thinker is the way he teaches us to see how seemingly decrepit values and habits bleed into contemporary institutions and patterns of thought, continuing to influence much of the irrationality of modern political economy, the violence of international relations, and attenuated forms of democracy. We moderns live consciously with the idea of our steadily increasing freedom and rationality, our emancipation from the irrationality and arbitrariness of the past.

In Max Weber's famous formulation, the modern world is disenchanted, shorn of its old faiths, its traditional beliefs, its preoccupations with magic, belief in luck, devotion to mysterious spirits, the embrace of invisible gods. Modernity, said Weber, weds us to icy hard quantitative thinking, matter-of-fact science, to an iron cage of administrative routine. Or, as Marx observed, once-solid bonds of tradition and faith vanish into thin air. Tocqueville made comparable points about democracy. Modernity marked a chasm, a more or less decisive break with the past, with tradition and with obscurantism. Latter-day postmodernists show less optimism about human rationality, but many retain beliefs in freedom and expansive democratic possibility.[3]

Veblen surely recognized the high "place of science in modern civilization." And he firmly believed that "it is the frame of mind of the common man that makes the foundation of the modern world."[4] But apart from the fact that he had doubts about the unqualified benefits of science and even more about the strength of democracy, he gave more credit than Weber, Marx, or Tocqueville to persistence of archaic belief within ostensibly modern settings. We cling to old faiths and shibboleths, to a host of premodern presuppositions. Quasi-feudal habits of mind and belief still shape much of our behavior. We admire prowess and seek charismatic leaders; we hope for luck; we remain enchanted by illusion and flock to manufactured spectacles. As a people, Americans, especially, like to think of themselves as young and brash in spirit and outlook. Veblen understood that heady American spirit, but he also saw how old the American mind could be, how the past haunts it in ways that Marx, Weber, and Tocqueville underestimated. Veblen's modernity is not so disenchanted; it is resplendent with primitive belief, hoary myth, aged illusion—all kinds of irrational attachments to old patterns of thought and atavistic institutions.

Because we tend not to appreciate these enduring legacies, because we think ourselves so thoroughly modern and enlightened, we often blindly replay barbaric scripts, repeating mistakes of the past. For Veblen, this is not a question of history repeating itself. Nor is it a matter of Nietzsche's "eternal recurrence." Veblen does not think that history has any particular ordering logic at all. Involved here is something else: a chronic failure to gauge how many crusty ideas populate our cool, modern brains. Three major implications follow, implications that resonate all too clearly with visible patterns in contemporary life.

First, our persistently high valuation of exploit means that conspicuously wasteful display of elite prowess still absorbs large shares of the
community's industrial output. Those who run economy and state see
to it that much of what the working class produces goes for monuments
to power, to gothic-like castles and soaring office towers, to vast estates,
luxurious garb, lavish festivals, inordinately expensive vehicles, as well as
investment in the arms necessary to protect it all. That such tribute exacts
heavy prices in ecological destruction and impoverishment of much of the
species confirms Veblen's appraisal of the immense social cost of living by
wasteful habits of exploit and emulation, our rush to imitate the practices
and lifestyle of the rich, famous, and powerful.

Second, because ruling classes monopolize trappings of honor, the truly
indispensible human activities of labor and production still unfold in an
opaque, darkened background of material culture. Labor remains tainted,
devalued by its association with dirty nature, mundane industry, and an
ill repute entailed by subordination. Workers, their activity, and their very
forms of apolitical life, still slip unassumingly into the shady, remote back-
stage of culture, its foreground filled with grand theatrics of elite action.
Labor remains subaltern activity; we have learned to think of it as irksome
rather than life affirming. We continue to value power over work.

Thus, finally, while many patterns of violent exploit passed into history,
habits of modern exploit and predation thrive. Yes, the West went from
"mediaeval to modern times . . . but all that had gone before was not lost
. . . Many things were carried over."⁵ War, for example, and the honorifics
of military power, along with such celebrations of formidability and the
strong hand as America's exaltation of college and professional football,
or basketball's "slam dunk." Or consider the society's raining of disproportionately large shares of national income, prestige, and assorted perks
of success on investment bankers and Wall Street traders, segments of the
business elite furthest removed from grimy factory floors; this even after
Wall Street demonstrably failed to master the magic of its own highly
engineered markets.

Veblen guides readers through the self-deceptive, confounded mental
terrain of early twentieth-century America, a terrain that has changed less
than we may think. A queer cohabitation in our minds of modern and
premodern outlooks still percolates through today's governing institutions,

policies, and rituals. Veblen urges us toward an uncomfortable truth: we postmodern citizens of the information age live anthropologically in a darker past; we still genuflect to patterns of exploit that leave us acutely vulnerable to machinations of fraud and force. Bernard Madoff followed Charles Ponzi, but one day a craftier scoundrel yet will better Madoff. "There is . . . no occasion for levity in so calling to mind these highly significant works of human infatuation, past and current," Veblen once observed, for "when all is said and done, they rest . . . on the same ubiquitously human ground of unreasoning fear, aspiration and credulity."[6] In other words, we like to pretend that today can be the first day of the rest of our lives, preferring to ignore how vulnerable we remain to old modes of self-delusion. Henry Ford famously said, "History is bunk." Veblen unforgettably pummels us with the message of our anachronism. And the consequences are dire.

Qualifications and Caveats

Scholars of many stripes have commented on the social, economic, and anthropological dimensions of Veblen's thought, so much so that its critique of power—its political core—is unjustifiably obscure. Though his gaze focused only intermittently on the subject matter of orthodox political science, Veblen's thought was political because its whole point was to indict the corrosive effects of predatory power. This is why we question the conventional wisdom on Veblen's indifference to political matters. His work is throughout an examination of the material fate of underlying populations when the cultures in which they live ritualize and reward "comparison of the abilities of different agents . . . to put forth evidence of power."[7] Following the lead of this guiding principle illuminates political themes that pervade Veblen's many works. Taken together, these ideas furnish valuable contributions to understanding today's political economy and its failures. But we do not want to overstate the case; our argument has important limits and qualifications.

First, Veblen was not a political theorist and we make no claim that he was. Certainly, he did not think of himself as a political scientist, and he held little regard for political studies. For Veblen, political theory and political science offer "worldly wisdom," practical knowledge of expediency, the instrumental rationality that helps predatory classes to control institutions and underlying populations. Veblen did not want to make exploitation easier, nor did he want to help predatory institutions work any better than they already do. The point of an independent social science should not be to assist power-driven institutions or to offer sage advice to rulers. It should be to analyze critically the norms, purposes, and direction of the going institutional behavior, and to weigh the implications for a greater potential fullness of human life, a potential governed by the material and intellectual resources available to the community.[8]

The search for such critical knowledge is hampered, Veblen insisted, if scholars bind themselves to the logic and criteria of prevailing institutions. Detachment from popular beliefs, however difficult or attenuated, is indispensable to rigorous analysis of social life. This stance helps, in part, to explain why Veblen did not address the raging party politics of his day, or such familiar theoretical issues as authority, power, freedom, community, the state, democracy, absolutism, or revolution—at least not within a context of primary concern for the performance of political institutions, the state, public life, or citizenship. His many works are full of reflections on these classic subjects of political theory. But they often emerge from the shadow of a focus on the interplay of cultural and material factors in the evolution of human institutions.[9] He was concerned with how such factors established a context for institutions of power and politics, democratic or otherwise.[10] Although Veblen was impressed by the influence of political motivations on human behavior, he did not believe that politics or the state could be understood unless they were seen within cultural and material frames that lent content and direction, habit and point-of-view, to the power motivations of political life. He placed much less stock in the formal arrangement of government institutions than he did on their cultural surroundings. It could, of course, be said that Veblen's political ideas are matters less of political science than of political anthropology. Perhaps so, but they are no less political for that.[11] We treat political themes here, within this Veblenian frame of interest, in the anthropological, cultural, and material context of politics.

A second qualification is in order. Because Veblen steered away from studies of formal political institutions, many of his most useful or impressive observations about these arrangements come in fragmentary, discontinuous, or incomplete form. His political discussions are often unfinished or under-developed. In many instances, we can understand or evaluate them only by tracing connections across multiple works covering quite different subjects. Veblen's key political categories and analyses will tend, for this reason, to stimulate among many students of politics that very sense of "chronic dissatisfaction" that he lamented for conspicuous consumption. Too often, promise exceeds delivery. Tantalizing leads abound, but it is fair to say that Veblen frequently leaves stimulating observations dangling in midair, discon-nected from the sustained or systematic argument necessary to make them theoretically cogent or persuasive. We do not believe that there is a resolution to this recurrent sense of dissatisfaction. It is, as Veblen might say, a defect of his virtue. Veblen is in many ways the most elusive of writers, never more so than when he crosses political terrain.

Third—and this is less a qualification than a general guide to our approach—we try to encompass the range and scope of Veblen's political ideas as they emerge, change, and develop throughout his work as a whole. We attempt to clarify how these ideas embrace more than issues of economic power and technological influence, or the impact of business enterprise and the machine process on American culture, themes that scholars have most frequently linked with his political ideas. When Veblen's thought focuses most explicitly on politics, it concerns itself above all with the state as an engine of warfare, as a threat to democracy, or as resource for the advantage of business enterprise. Obviously, Veblen offers no final words on these subjects, but his works provide rich and untapped perspectives for radical critiques of politics. In this sense, we hope to remedy an undervalued aspect of an important thinker's work.

At the same time, we realize that Veblen did not get everything right; he was not always clear; sometimes he was inconsistent; portions of his work are, as we have noted, unfinished or undeveloped—there was much that he left unexamined and unsaid about politics and other things. Critics who have made such arguments have a point. We believe that it is incumbent upon us to indicate weaknesses as well as virtues in Veblen's work. We approach Veblen in the spirit of sympathetic but critical readers. This means that we remain alert to deficiencies, weaknesses, and problems. Obviously we admire him; we think that he made major and underappreciated contri-butions to social science and social theory. But we are not acolytes.

This means, among other things, that when we think that critics make a legitimate point, or that Veblen fails to develop his own argument effectively, we are prepared to say so. On this score, we offer no apologies. Frankly, for a study as sympathetic to Veblen as ours, we would prefer to be charged with being overly fair to Veblen's critics than with being excessively sympathetic to Veblen himself. Still, if our major claim has merit, the general lack of attention to Veblen's political ideas is problematic. After all, we do not have to dig very deep to find the strongly political undercurrent in his work.

Locating the "Political" in Veblen

As early as *The Theory of Business Enterprise*, Veblen said the big pressures constraining capitalism stemmed from the most dynamic forces that it encouraged: the rationalizing tendencies of the machine process, and imperialism, which in turn stimulated "the aggressive politics and aristocratic ideals" of militarized warfare states. As imperial politics gathered strength, Veblen held that the "logical outcome is an abatement of those cultural features that distinguish modern times from what went before, including a decline of business enterprise itself."[12] In other words, he identified the two most potentially hostile forces threatening the future of capitalism as the development of technology and the warfare state. Veblen's writings feature various and repeated formulations of these themes; they did not originate, as some have argued, in the corpus of Veblen's later, most overtly political works, *Imperial Germany and the Industrial Revolution*, *The Nature of Peace*, and *Absentee Ownership*. If, as Michael Spindler has justly claimed, Veblen analyzed war "as part of a system of invidious emulation between nations," we should also recognize the deep historical connections between emulation and political behavior and understand that Veblen described the violent implications and potentials of predatory emulation in 1899, in *The Theory of the Leisure Class*.[13] Another recent commentator on Veblen offers even more stimulating hints of Veblen's deeper political preoccupations, observing that the whole "leisure class thesis was predicated on deep class polarity and on the absolute power of the master classes."[14] Once again, if Louis Patsouras is right to suggest that Veblen held class relations to reflect claims of mastery and power, a logical implication is to explore the work for its clues to the relationship between political motivation and economic exploitation. In similar ways, James K. Galbraith reminds us that Veblen criticized "the leisure class" because its members do not work. They "hold offices . . . perform rituals . . . enact deeds of honor." Thus if "the relation of overlords to underlings is that of predator to prey," it is also a conspicuously and primarily a political relation of dominator and dominated.[15]

These preliminary observations are only suggestive. But they help to amplify our point that Veblen's famous distinction between industry and exploit is at heart a political distinction, or at least it is a distinction that invidiously separates political from economic activity. If anything, Veblen's idea was that political institutions, in thrall to expansive business interests, exploit and contaminate the fruits of workaday economic life processes, turning technological advances toward warlike and exploitative ends. This is precisely why Veblen pairs technology and war as prime threats to capitalism: war potentially empowers the state over business interests, while a robust technology undermines market needs for scarcity, driving corporations to sabotage production in order to preserve the status quo. In either case, power motivations loom larger than material ones. As John Gambs pointed out many years ago, proffering a clue that students of politics have not followed, Veblen's critique of the market system centered on its latent political character, that is, on differential powers of class coercion. As Gambs insightfully acknowledged, "the word 'political' . . . might be better" suited to an understanding of Veblen's critique of the market system "than either 'pecuniary' or 'coercive.' " Unfortunately, Gambs retreated from this fruitful suggestion, fearing that it "would probably be confusing."[16] So strong has been the compulsion for writers to treat Veblen in economic terms that even readers sensitive to his political emphasis have been remarkably reluctant to shed the orthodox view.

Of course, some writers have seen political significance in Veblen's ideas. Jonathan Nitzan, for example, follows Veblen's lead when he argues that "the absentee owner . . . seeks higher profit, not in order to buy *more goods and services*, but in order to assert . . . *differential* power."[17] A few, like Gambs, have even traced the source of those political implications to the foundations of his thought. But what has remained more obscure in the Veblen literature is how we might take such ideas to have an inherent logical and thematic unity, one that derives from the greater unity of Veblen's thought as a whole.

The political character and unity of Veblen's thought rest largely on his claims that power and prestige motivations lie behind human exploit; Veblen's materialism was highly mediated. Modern cultures are organized around human self-understandings that still fall prey to the magnetism of power. But there is an equally substantial politics in the antipolitics of Veblen's theory of savagery, especially in its relationship to anarchy, feminism, and insubordination, themes at the center of his ideas about commonwealths, democracy, social equity and justice, and the industrial republic. As the distinguished Veblen scholar Franco Ferrarotti commented several years ago, "Veblen is essentially a political thinker, dealing with central issues of social fairness and power."[18] And those preoccupations with "social fairness and power" emerge precisely within Veblen's evolutionary analysis of fundamental antagonisms between power motivations and anarchistic sensibilities, each still vivid in the political life of contemporary institutions. The trouble is that Veblen's discontinuous, fragmentary style of theorizing and writing frequently obscures the political core of his work.

Impediments of Style and Focus

First among these difficulties is the fact that for reasons we noted above, Veblen tended to write about the most overt, formal features of politics—the state, democracy, political parties, the executive, public opinion, and law—in frustratingly fragmented, abortive, and disconnected ways. But this defect has a kind of virtue, for it invites attention to the unity of Veblen's political thought, which lies in his consistently critical approach to power. Veblen treats exploit as a generalized social phenomenon, refusing to reduce it to a distinctively economic or political meaning. As far as he is concerned, the diffuse social character of exploit and power undermines the neat disciplinary boundaries of university departments in the social sciences. In essence, Veblen studies exploit and power like he studies everything else: in multidisciplinary, cross-disciplinary, and evolutionary ways. Veblen is, in his distinctive fashion, an unheralded patron saint of contemporary multidisciplinary studies.

For Veblen, the problem of power precedes the rise of the state and is never coterminous with government. The state offers but one locus in his wide survey of the quality and consequences of power. This helps to explain why his political reflections appear not as a considered whole but as discontinuous, often painfully unfinished discussions. His main reflections on war and the state, for example, spread over at least four separate texts, and his richest discussions of anarchic forms appear in three different books. And Veblen pauses for revealing observations about democracy in a chain of essays and books that appear as early as 1892 and that culminate in *Absentee Ownership*, three decades later. He offers similar explanations for the origins of predation in several early essays as well as in *The Theory of the Leisure Class*, while a comparable but curiously different account appears in *The Instinct of Workmanship*.

Confronted with this fractured and discontinuous body of work, many students of Veblen, even those as careful as John Diggins, conclude that Veblen "seldom wrote about politics" and "made no observations about political institutions."[19] Still, the evidence of Veblen's concentrated political focus in works such as *The Nature of Peace* and *Imperial Germany and the Industrial Revolution*, or in his early critiques of, say, Marx's theory of revolution, makes such claims puzzling. We can find rich veins of political observation and theory in Veblen, but to locate them we need to see power and exploit as key aspects of his sustained point of view. And then comes the task, as Hal Draper has said of his own study of Marx's scattered political writings, of working "out an answer that is at least consistent with the assembled evidence."[20]

The issues facing interpreters of Veblen's political ideas are both perplexing and enticing, and they go beyond problems of discontinuity. Especially intriguing and challenging is his pronounced tendency to place politics in the cloudy background of his most important early works. Especially if we take politics, as Diggins does, to encompass formal political institutions or efforts by social groups to influence the state, it is certainly true that Veblen gives these subjects only passing notice in the books for which he earned his greatest intellectual credit. It is as if he exacts revenge on conventional historians' preoccupation with politics by turning this focus inside out, putting politics in the rearview mirror of an intellectual focus on the primacy of material and social activity. In this sense, Veblen anticipated the shift toward history as the study of everyday life.

For example, the first chapter of Veblen's single most famous work, *The Theory of the Leisure Class*, explains how "the point of view of the fight"—in effect, the political point of view—became characteristic of barbaric culture. But then he proceeds to virtually ignore the state in the rest of the book. He discovers the symbolism of exploit in all kinds of activities, from the taking of women as slaves to the ownership of eccentric-looking dogs. Perhaps he thought that political exploit was too obvious to study, but he does not bother looking for it in government. Likewise, Veblen's observations on "Business Principles in Law and Politics" highlight the general argument of *The Theory of Business Enterprise*. But the analysis comes late in the book, and he tends to mute it by stressing contradictions between the machine process and business civilization.

Examples multiply of Veblen's habit of cloaking politics with his cultural and material preoccupations. We can discover analysis of such political forms as matriarchal anarchy and the warfare state in *The Instinct of Workmanship*, but the material is packed densely into chapters on "The Contamination of Instincts in Primitive Technology" and "The Era of Handicraft." By the same token, Veblen offers the provocative idea of a popular "spirit of insubordination," but to find it one needs to follow a trail into "Supplementary Notes" tucked in at the end of *Imperial Germany and the Industrial Revolution*. Veblen leaves it to careful readers to discover the rich political material here almost by accident or surprise. Only with the later war-centered studies of *Imperial Germany* and *The Nature of Peace* does Veblen really begin to bring out the state's importance as an institution worth study in its own right. We can see the heightened political emphasis clearly in his last major work, *Absentee Ownership*. After a brief introduction, Veblen devotes two substantial chapters to unambiguously political themes: "National Integrity," a classic statement of his theory of the warfare state, and "Handicraft and Natural Right," a look at the role of liberal values and ideals in the ideological evolution of early business enterprise and liberal democracy. Clearly, by 1923, Veblen held the state to be a key institution in the organization and legitimation of modern society and economy.

Nevertheless, the fractured quality of his political arguments suggests that Veblen never intended to produce nor did he ever write a systematic study of politics and government. There is no dispute about that. But another point remains equally important. Behind the whole of Veblen's critique of war, exploit, and capitalism there is a unifying point of view, a consistently critical standpoint on humanity's evolving cultural absorption with phenomena of power and conflict, which are at the crux of politics. Veblen's critical theory is fundamentally a narrative about the enduring habits, institutions, and costs of a barbaric adoration of power. Even as western civilization supposedly matured and became increasingly peaceable, the barbarian's love for competitive "aggression" remains among the most valued and esteemed forms of human action. We believe that this consistency of viewpoint permits us to synthesize Veblen's discontinuous political ideas. His view of power, as the antagonist of industry, unifies the work. Veblen's theory of the state shows the point perfectly.

The contemporary state is a capitalist *state* because it preserves so much of what it was *before* capitalism: a legally legitimate institution for perpetrating and honoring capacities to inflict violence. Its chief social function in the age of business is to secure and to legitimate the rights and powers of absentee ownership, itself a mechanism for predatory control of industry. But the business state persists as an institution whose potential for violence remains central to its character, norms, and behavior. Thus Veblen consistently views the state as the most dangerous contemporary expression of barbarism, more dangerous even than corporate exploit itself, because in the end, it is the state, not capital, that makes and legitimates war. And war remains the most ominous enemy of democracy.

An Antipolitical Animus

Why then do orthodox political scientists generally see so little politics in Veblen? Perhaps the main reason is the most obvious one: Veblen's contempt for the political led him away from systematic studies of political systems and political behavior. But in an important sense, this answer only begs the question. After all, Veblen did not care for absentee owners and business executives either, yet he wrote whole books and many essays about their activities. The salient question is then, why did Veblen give more systematic attention to financial than political power?

Part of the answer centers on Veblen's primary intellectual and moral concern for the economic life process of human beings, the question of how human beings go about doing the work necessary to live. Through its control of investment in productive industry, finance capital has immediate, tangible material implications for economic life. Financial dealings directly pervert the economic life process, generating waste and abuse of vital material resources and human prospects. Veblen's critical concept of absentee ownership highlights how corporate executives run the business economy for their own pecuniary purposes, leaving much "undone" in respect to "the material interests of the underlying population."[21]

In contrast, ceremonial politics is twice removed from real, material life. For one thing, the system of business enterprise bars states from engaging in substantial productive or industrial activity; for another, the class of "substantial citizens" insists that governments serve above all the cause of financial and pecuniary exploit. Veblen privileged the study of financial over political power because its ramifications touched current material life more directly. Recent events suggest that he was on to something.

At the same time that capitalists pursue the status to be found in money, however, the old honorifics of military and political domination never died off. Veblen's condemnation of the state rests on the fact that, even in the face of and sometimes because of quasi-peaceable capitalism, statesmen and politicians continue to refight old battles, all too often recalling for us how "the highest honors within human reach may, even yet, be gained by an unfolding of predatory efficiency in war, or by a quasi-predatory efficiency in statecraft."[22] One has only to remember a recent president's landing on the flight deck of a U.S. aircraft carrier, resplendent in the garb of a warrior pilot, to understand Veblen's point. Or we might just as well recall the longtime leader of the western hemisphere's only communist state, who entertained a preference for a soldier's uniform.

The point is that in his own politics Veblen was prepared to be as caustic about self-proclaimed revolutionaries as he was about democratic leaders in hock to business interests. He slapped reform and revolution with equal skepticism. In this respect, his sympathetic portrait of David Hume might well stand as an epitaph that he never wanted written for himself.[23] Like Hume, Veblen "was not gifted with a facile acceptance of the group inheritance . . . of his generation." His gifts ran in another direction: toward "an alert, though somewhat histrionic skepticism touching everything that was well-received."[24]

A Man from Mars?

Mention of Veblen's skepticism raises the question of the man himself and his controversial place in the pantheon of American thinkers. Put simply, Thorstein Veblen is reputed to be one of the strangest oddballs in the history of American thought, a "man from Mars," the iconic outsider.[25] Veblen is the proverbial weird professor, mumbling his way through classes, forever claiming that his biting criticism is simply dispassionate science, all the while skewering "the vested interests," "elder statesmen," and "captains of erudition." Veblen's was a brilliant, complex, and ironic mind. Surely, he was no ordinary man; but he was hardly a "man from Mars." In his life he avoided conspicuous consumption, but firsthand reports suggest that Veblen and his family lived in reasonable comfort. Jacob Warshaw, a professor of Romance languages who befriended Veblen during his years at the University of Missouri, describes a colleague who, in contrast with the extraterrestrial visitor of academic legend, was an amiable host to close friends:

> He could be whole-heartedly congenial, as the few persons who visited in his home could testify. Lounging about in his loose dressing gown and looking not nearly as anemic and fragile as in his street clothes, he reminded one, with his drooping mustaches and Nordic features, of nothing so much as a hospitable Viking taking his ease at his own fireside. At such times, he was at his best, pouring out curious information, throwing off a little malicious gossip which, in view of his seclusiveness, he must have picked miraculously out of the air, mixing picturesque slang with brilliant phrases of his own coinage, solicitously watching out for his guests' comfort, and in general behaving like a "regular guy." An evening with him—when you were fortunate enough to get one—was as good as a French salon or an eighteenth century London coffee-house. When it was over you wished that you had a Boswellian memory and eye.[26]

Warshaw described Veblen's "smile [as] one of the features that I best remember him by. It was a kindly, amused, rather Olympian smile, and thoroughly genuine," one that appeared most often as they enjoyed "rambles over the golf links." Warshaw tells also of Veblen's remarkable gift with languages—Greek, Latin, the Romance languages, Dutch, and the various Scandinavian tongues, including Icelandic—and of his reputed ability to "read two columns of print simultaneously."[27] Veblen could work with his hands too. Growing up on a Minnesota farm, he learned carpentry skills from his father. Later in life he designed and built cabins and furniture for himself. One cabin was in the hills overlooking Palo Alto, near Stanford, and another was on Washington Island, Wisconsin, where he frequently summered with his family.[28] How then did this gifted, multitalented man become the legendary eccentric of academic lore?

Veblen's image as iconic American oddball stems most of all from Joseph Dorfman's important, still quite useful, but significantly flawed book *Thorstein Veblen and His America*.[29] Published just five years after Veblen's death, in 1934, Dorfman's volume has influenced scholarly impressions of Veblen the man for seven decades. Through Dorfman, generations of readers have come to know Veblen as a model of the estranged intellectual. And the alienation was reputed to be more than personal. It reflected, claimed Dorfman, nothing so much as an embittered and twisted reaction against the harsh ethnic, social, and economic circumstances of the Veblen family. Its intellectual expression was Veblen's social theory: "alien . . . convoluted . . . misleading."[30]

Veblen's hardscrabble Norwegian immigrant background, his childhood spent on Wisconsin and Minnesota farms in the 1860s, said Dorfman, explains his later detachment from prevailing institutions. Even beyond the specific ethnic conditions of rural Minnesota, Dorfman claimed, "the cultural isolation of the Norwegians was intensified to an extent never surpassed in any large immigrant group in this country."[31] Such "cultural isolation" motivated Veblen's unceasing drive to lacerate and punish American culture with the sharp knife of his ironic wit. Thus it was that Thorstein Veblen became for Max Lerner and many others, in words that reflected Dorfman's influence, a "strange 'Norskie' boy among Americans, with a scanty knowledge of English, lacking money and social standing," an intellectual outlier on the American scene, a bitter genius who got his revenge not by living well but by writing with a pen dipped in acid.[32]

Toss in Thorstein's alleged entanglements with faculty wives and admiring female students, and his refusal to conform to such norms of

university life as grading, and one begins to understand why presidents
of such prestigious institutions as the University of Chicago and Stanford
fired him.[33] Or why as sympathetic an observer as C. Wright Mills could
conclude that if Veblen was "the best critic of America that America ever
produced," his most distinctive trait "is not alienation; it is failure." So
much so that "There is no failure in American academic history quite so
great as Veblen's."[34]

The Veblen legend is a familiar fixture in American academia. But it is
largely the stuff of myth born of misrepresentation. Recent scholarship
reveals that Dorfman's reductionist portrait of Veblen is problematic at best.
Files at Columbia University, recently opened, show that the biographer had
access to information about the family's experience from Andrew Veblen,
Thorstein's older brother, that bears little resemblance to the portrait of an
isolated family dangling at the margins of American life. Andrew's account
also clashes with Dorfman's picture of Thorstein as a child, ill at ease with
others and unfamiliar with English or with American mores and habits.
He was apparently a curious, bright, precocious prankster, who loved to
toy with language, including English, frequently inventing clever names
for family and friends. Moreover, according to Andrew, as well as other
evidence now at hand, the Veblen family enjoyed amicable relations with
nearby farmers of various ethnic backgrounds.[35] And Thorstein's sister
Emily recalled that the family "early became very patriotic Americans and
were glad we were born in America."[36] Veblen's father, Thomas Anderson
Veblen, was a first-rate farmer, "his brain nimble and precise," said Andrew.
Thorstein once told a student at Chicago that "the basic ideas in *The Theory
of the Leisure Class* came from boyhood talks with his father."[37] His mother,
Kari Bunde Veblen, was exceptionally intelligent too, and with her husband
deeply committed to getting their children a higher education at a time
when college was a rarified social privilege indeed.[38]

Whatever sources fired Veblen's critical imagination, his penetrating
insights into American institutions did not come from a spiteful sense of
exclusion from American institutions. The Veblen family was intimately
involved in the mainstream of the American farming business and well
respected in their community. Thorstein Veblen himself was admitted to
and taught at some of America's best colleges and universities. And when
Thorstein married Ellen Rolfe, he joined a wealthy railroad family that

was itself tied into one of the most dynamic sectors of American enterprise. Indeed, it is hard to square the image of Veblen as a loner with his salacious reputation as a womanizer.[39] Loners make awkward romantic companions. In point of fact, late nineteenth-century America was not foreign to Thorstein Veblen nor was he foreign to it.

Thorstein Veblen: A Biographical Sketch

Veblen was born in 1857 in Manitowoc County, Wisconsin, part of the American agricultural heartland. He grew up not very far from his birthplace, in the rural quiet of cold Minnesota winters and hot prairie summers, his evenings lit by candlelight and oil lamps. He died in August 1929 as America's industrial cities crackled with the tumult of auto horns, telephones, radio sets, and wire tickers. As Stephen Edgell put it, Thorstein Veblen came into a world on the precipice of "the most turbulent period of civil disorder" in U.S. history. The great national crisis of slavery exploded. Industrial capitalism upended the society. A nation of farmers gave way to a humming network of "machine-made cities and towns."[40] During his seventy-two years, America became a startlingly different place. Veblen described this American passage with a luminous sense of the unfolding drama.

He experienced childhood in a state of "moderately advanced savagery," learning the rigors of life on a successful working farm. He came into adulthood as a rising regime of absentee owners mobilized newfangled credit arrangements to promote corporate enterprise, their laggard political system still prone to war and unable to corral looming forces of financial chaos. Populist, labor, women's, peace, and temperance movements challenged this new order, their "unrest and revulsion" suggesting, as Veblen put it, that ordinary folks "are better adapted to life under conditions radically different from those" under which they lived.[41] In this light, as Edgell reasonably observes, it was probably not Nordic isolation that shaped Veblen's contribution so much as the big sweep of American industrialization, just as British industrialization had served as Marx's reference point fifty years before.[42] Indeed, as he moved from "country town" Minnesota to academic life in some of the nation's major urban centers—Baltimore, Chicago, the San Francisco Bay area—then back to the "country town" setting of Columbia, Missouri, with brief late stays in Washington, D.C.,

and New York City, Veblen's own life roughly traced the nation's trajectory of change.

Veblen spent his early years in northern Midwest rural communities, mainly
in central Minnesota, not far from Northfield, where he lived until he entered
graduate school at Johns Hopkins in 1880.[43] Thorstein was one of twelve
children, the fourth son of upwardly mobile immigrant farmers, who sent their
children to nearby Carleton College. Although Thomas Veblen "was sharply
criticized" by neighbors for putting on Yankee airs by gifting his children with
a higher education, he was not a man to live in fear of neighborly complaint.
If the children were to make a better American life for themselves, higher
education was imperative, regardless of what the neighbors said.[44] Thorstein's
sister, Emily, was likely the first woman to graduate from a Minnesota college,
while Thorstein himself was fortunate to be taught at Carleton by the brilliant young economist John Bates Clark, the first of a series of conservative
professors from whom he would receive valuable support and encouragement.

Following graduation from Carleton, Veblen taught mathematics for an
unhappy year at Monona Academy in Wisconsin. The school's religious
character and spirited theological debates were hardly to his liking, nor was
mathematics his chosen field. Encouraged by his older brother Andrew, who
planned to enroll in mathematics study at Johns Hopkins, Veblen agreed
to join his brother, though Thorstein's plans centered on studies in history
and political economy. At Hopkins, Thorstein took courses with, among
others, the noted historian Herbert Baxter Adams, the up-and-coming
economist Richard T. Ely, and in philosophy, the brilliant young Charles
Peirce. In need of additional financial aid, spurred by a growing interest in
philosophy, and, according to Dorfman, "anxious to be away from supervi-
sion of his brother Andrew," Thorstein shortly left Baltimore for Yale.[45]

For his doctorate in philosophy at Yale, Veblen wrote a dissertation
on Kant, under the direction of the Reverend Noah Porter. Notably,
Veblen also impressed Porter's main campus adversary, the preeminent
social Darwinist William Graham Sumner.[46] Though Veblen would invert
the lessons of Sumner's social Darwinism, the latter's influence on the
younger man's evolutionary naturalism was substantial. Having achieved
his doctorate, but ill, probably with malaria, according to Andrew, Veblen
returned to Minnesota, living with relatives or in-laws, occupying his days
with reading, reflection, and study.

As he recovered, teaching positions proved hard to come by. Thorstein's religious skepticism probably complicated his job search, but even apart from religion, "the 1880s were an extremely uncertain period in American academia, and particularly so for historians and economists."[47] In any case, a PhD dissertation on Kant was of little value in the great farming country of the American Midwest. Still Veblen made a consequential personal decision in this period: in 1888, he wed Ellen Rolfe. She was the niece of Carleton's president and the daughter of a prominent Midwest entrepreneur, whose ties to regional capitalist enterprise furnished a convenient perch from which Veblen could observe the workings of American business. Before the marriage, his future father-in-law apparently made unsuccessful efforts to get the young man a job as an economist with the Santa Fe Railroad. But while he remained aloof from the labor market, Veblen's seven postdoc years in Minnesota became a time of further reading and reflection, an interregnum during which he was likely germinating some of the major ideas and themes that would fuel his emerging social theory.

Veblen decided to make another run at academic life, in 1890, this time as a PhD candidate in constitutional history, political science, and economics at Cornell, where he quickly impressed the eminent conservative historian and economist James Laurence Laughlin.[48] Laughlin was so taken by his new student that when he moved to the University of Chicago, in 1892, he took Veblen with him, appointing the junior scholar managing editor of the prestigious *Journal of Political Economy*. Seven years later, Veblen delivered *The Theory of the Leisure Class* to the reading public, immediately gaining the notoriety that goes with a widely read and controversial new book. *The Theory of Business Enterprise*, which followed in 1904, revealed a shift from a pungent satire of American consumption to a sober, relatively humorless critique of corporate finance and its governance of the production system.

Success at Chicago did not last. Ellen Rolfe's inability to have "normal conjugal relations" aggravated their private tensions, whose ramifications percolated up to the university president's office.[49] In addition, Veblen's radicalism, coupled with his failure properly to "advertise" the university, further offended Chicago's president, William Rainey Harper. Soon enough he was fired, moving to Stanford for a three-year stay.[50]

Similar difficulties followed him to the Bay Area, along with his estranged wife, whose charges of "womanizing" again helped to torpedo his position.⁵¹ After months of unemployment, Veblen reluctantly headed back to the Midwest, landing at the University of Missouri in 1911 and finally divorcing Ellen a year later. He taught at Missouri until 1918, a sojourn that turned out to be an enormously productive period in his career. *The Instinct of Workmanship*, a book that Veblen considered his best, appeared in 1914. It was followed in short order by two of his most explicitly political works, *Imperial Germany and the Industrial Revolution*, published in 1915, and *An Inquiry into the Nature of Peace and the Terms of Its Perpetuation*, two years later. Veblen's time in Missouri also turned out to be a happier period in his personal life, as he wed Ann Bradley (Babe) Bevins in 1914. A radical, with two young daughters from an earlier marriage, Bevins' progressive habits and values nicely dovetailed with Veblen's own, and Veblen warmed to his new role as father.

Feeling increasingly isolated after several of his closest friends left and one, Robert Hoxie, committed suicide, Veblen departed Missouri in 1918, a year that also finally saw the publication of *The Higher Learning in America*, an attack on "the conduct of the university by business men." The book had originally been written in his dark days at Chicago in 1904, under the more incendiary title "A Study in Total Depravity." After a brief stint at the Department of Agriculture in Washington,⁵² Veblen moved to New York City, where he coedited the radical journal *The Dial*. Veblen's service on *The Dial*'s editorial board spawned some of his most polemical and accessible writing, including a host of essays that culminated in one of Veblen's best known and undervalued collections, *The Vested Interests and the Common Man* (1919), and *The Engineers and the Price System* (1921), this last perhaps his most widely criticized book. Many of the best *Dial* essays also appear in *Essays in Our Changing Order* (1934)—an indispensible volume that spans his career, edited by a former student and close friend, Leon Ardzrooni. *The Place of Science in Modern Civilization*, a collection of important earlier essays on science, economics, and socialism, appeared in 1919. Veblen's academic life closed with his role as one of the founders of The New School for Social Research. The year 1923 saw the publication of his last work of political economy, *Absentee Ownership: Business Enterprise in Recent Times: The Case of America*. His final published work was a pure labor of love, a well-regarded translation of Norwegian folk tales, *The Laxdaela Saga*, in 1925.⁵³

In the late '20s, Veblen returned to northern California, where he died quietly, in August 1929, a few months shy of the economic crisis whose onset he anticipated in *Absentee Ownership*.

Throughout his academic life, Veblen supported radical causes, showing special sympathies for feminists, the Industrial Workers of the World, and the conscientious objectors who resisted service in World War I.[54] Publicly, however, Veblen did not make for a loud or challenging presence in American politics; he led no political movement or party to advance progressive agendas, nor did he lend his name to any sectarian program of social change. Indeed, he rarely voted.[55] Overall, he played little active role in conventional or subversive politics. He might well be an exemplar of the twenty-first-century tenured radical, except that Veblen paid the price of his views in substantial job insecurity, showing no willingness to change his opinions in order to preserve employment. His outspoken criticisms did considerable harm to his academic career, probably at least as much if not more harm, in fact, than the colorful legend of amorous liaisons. Though he did not act aggressively in politics, Veblen's radical political voice strengthened in the years during and after World War I. But to anyone who bothered to listen, that political voice was clearly audible before the war.

Though he was never militant, Thorstein Veblen did have a strong political voice, its claims advanced in an impressive series of books and essays that penetrated the mysteries of the human situation. "In a low sarcastic mumble of intricate phrases," wrote John Dos Passos, "subtly paying out the logical inescapable rope of matter-of-fact for a society to hang itself by," Veblen produced the most penetrating critique of American society that has yet been achieved.[56] With incisive wit, a sure sense of irony, and the wake-up logic of a cold-water bath, Veblen disassembled the seemingly solid foundations of conventional society to expose the self-delusions at its core. As his student Wesley Mitchell once put it, Veblen practiced "vivisection upon his contemporaries" but without benefit of "anaesthetic."[57]

To read Veblen is to become acquainted with a reservoir of rich and original radical thinking. Students of society and the economy can certainly consult his work on issues of consumption, technology, the business cycle, corporate behavior, and waste. But politically interested readers can profit from study of his work too. That is the central contention advanced here.

2

SOCIAL SCIENCE AND POLITICS

That Thorstein's Veblen's ideas inspire political criticism from all quarters suggests the political significance at their core. His writings are so enmeshed in criticism of American society, that "it is," as David Riesman once said, "a measure of Veblen's strength as a social critic that no rounded judgment of his work can be made that is not also a judgment of American society, now as well as then."[1] As Riesman suggests, scholars may have trouble separating their thoughts on Veblen's critique of America from their own ideas about the society and its prospects for change. So, liberals and conservatives charge him with overstating the wrongs and weaknesses of American institutions while remaining blind or indifferent to America's virtues and strengths. Marxists, by contrast, often see substantial value in Veblen's criticism of the business order. But many are impatient with his reluctance to offer a full-blown theory of labor exploitation and proletarian revolution. The most sophisticated critics find ways of reinforcing their own views by connecting Veblen's failings with the imperfections of his evolutionary method and its related categories.

Of course there are plenty of reasonable intellectual grounds for questioning Veblen's work. There is its frequently ponderous style and evasive language; its clever denial of values in the face of transparent moral judgments; its Darwinian cast, instinct biology, and dependence on century-old psychology and anthropology; its criticism of neoclassical economics and the state, coupled with agonizing silence on alternative forms of economic calculation or the positive uses of political power. Such concerns are entirely legitimate. Still, it is hard to miss an unusual vehemence in many of the charges hurled at Veblen. More than the quality of intellectual work seems to be on the line, more than mere flaws of scholarship or theory. Much intellectual disenchantment with Veblen appears to betray an acutely political and ideological impatience, a temper that cannot abide his distancing from politics and ideology.[2]

Many of Veblen's critics seem to sense in his work an uncomfortable challenge to their own political assurance. His political hesitation disturbs them. Veblen sees no definitive outcome to history: not the triumph of democracy, the vindication of markets, or the success of the proletariat. The open-endedness of his evolutionary naturalism undermines— sabotages, he might say—the coherence and rationality of familiar political theories. The one thing that ideologically minded writers have in common, after all, is ideology itself, belief in the truth and power of political ideas. Confidence is a hallmark of popular political writing; uncertainty is less satisfying. Consider such disparate political thinkers of the last generation as Milton Friedman, John Kenneth Galbraith, or Herbert Marcuse. Their works resound with levels of political confidence nowhere to be found in Veblen. Friedman was certain about the rationality of market forces; Galbraith harbored few doubts that the liberal state could muster countervailing power against big business; and Marcuse rejected capitalism root and branch.

Veblen's thought is rich in its own value judgments; its unsparing point of view is as obvious as it is cutting and critical. Its thorough debunking quality easily justifies the claim that Veblen is a serious ideological critic of capitalism and its antidemocratic tendencies. But on a fundamental issue in all ideology—one's political stance toward change—Veblen remains stubbornly, stalwartly, and defiantly . . . agnostic.[3] His thought is perhaps most recalcitrant and unorthodox in its refusal to capitulate to certainty on matters of change or direction. As a theorist of ceaseless change amidst anachronistic institutions, Veblen felt absolutely no compulsion to take a political position on questions of direction or action; indeed he consistently avoided questions of political action and program. Even as his oppositional standpoint was unmistakable, he felt entirely justified on scientific and scholarly grounds to remain silent on strategic questions. As far as political action is concerned, he has little or nothing to say. America values democracy

and celebrates hope; Veblen refused to validate either. This is not a stance
well suited to the winning of popularity contests, political or intellectual.

The Question of the Engineers

Consider, for example, Veblen's most notorious book, *The Engineers
and the Price System. The Engineers* has consistently vexed and perplexed its
critical readers. They have debated its purpose and message at length.[4] Many
interpretations of Veblen as a "technocratic" or "scientific" collectivist are
based heavily, if not exclusively, on this work. For this is the book in which
Veblen points most clearly to an ideal economy, an industrial republic,
run by apolitical technicians, experts, and engineers. His "soviet of engineers" legitimizes technocracy, but just because it does, it conflicts directly
with Veblen's egalitarian and libertarian sympathies, especially his affection
for insubordination, masterless men and women, and local anarchistic
communities.[5]

But even if, indeed especially if, it is read as a serious call to replace
capitalism with a "soviet of technicians," the book has no answers to
basic questions of strategic political action. How will engineers politically
organize themselves for revolution? How, if at all, will they connect their
revolution with popular organizations such as unions, social movements,
or a revolutionary party? How will they defeat the businessmen, elder
statesmen, and generals of the warfare state? And, even putting aside hard
questions of a technocratic alternative to market calculation, what kind of
state will the engineers lead? How will the "industrial republic" represent
popular aspirations or secure civil liberties and civil rights? And above all,
who will hold the elite of engineers responsible for their uses of power?
Will the people choose the technocrats or will the technocrats choose
themselves? Veblen ignores all these big questions.

Could a writer as sensitive to issues of power as Veblen really believe
that apolitical rule by experts would solve riddles of power? If one takes
Veblen's call for a "soviet of technicians" as an authentic expression of his
political views—rather than as a satire of business rule, or as an outrageous
hypothesis about the improbability of revolutionary change—the omission
of anything approximating mature political discussion is astounding.[6] But
a more telling criticism, one suggested throughout the critical literature,

is that Veblen's errors of political omission in *The Engineers and the Price System* reflect qualities of political indifference and unsophistication that mar his work as a whole.

There can be little doubt on this central point: if qualification for inclusion in the canon of serious political thinkers requires an explicit position on questions of the direction or morality of political action, Veblen fails the test, and he fails it badly. For many of Veblen's critics, some such test seems indeed to be the qualifier for consideration as a serious political thinker. On this point of omission, his output has infuriated conservatives, liberals, and radicals alike. Theorists of the right condemn Veblen's subversion of business enterprise. The liberal left cannot abide his skepticism of reform and the positive state, while many Marxists see in Veblen a man whose critique of capitalism empties radical thought of its animating passion and ideological direction.

Veblen surely grasped the politics in all these schools of thought, but he offered none of his own, at least not in the sense of urging a substantive political practice of reform or revolution. With the exception of a handful of policy proposals advanced late in his career, when he briefly worked for the Wilson government, Veblen would not yield to urgings that he make his work politically useful. And even in these instances, Veblen's suggestions—for example, to increase the available labor pool during World War I by heavily taxing wealthy employers of servants, by releasing from socially unnecessary commercial tasks those currently engaged in "wasteful duplication," and by engaging the services of the Industrial Workers of the World to work the farms—did not exactly conform to the boundaries of the politically possible.[7]

In this respect, there are not many miles between Veblen's standpoint and that of the Frankfurt School, an attitude memorably expressed by one of its founding members, Max Horkheimer. As Horkheimer put it, "There now exists a human attitude which takes the society itself as its object. It is not merely oriented towards the removal of particular abuses, for the latter appear to it as necessarily bound to the whole arrangement of the social structure. Although this attitude has arisen out of social structure, it is no concern either of its conscious intention or of its objective significance that anything in this structure should function any better than it does."[8] But while Horkheimer and critical theory were as indifferent to reform as Veblen, critical theorists were more or less hopeful that revolution was still possible. Thus critical theorists also joined the larger condemnation of Veblen's technocratic outlook, especially Theodore Adorno, who insisted that this American-bred radical was utterly incapable of seeing beyond the existing order.[9] In fact, Veblen was pervasively critical in his work of what he called "pragmatic" or instrumental political thinking. He rarely, if ever, urged practical political reforms. His very abhorrence of instrumental or practical thinking in politics helps to explain why he so often inspires the wrath of more optimistic liberals, such as David Riesman or Daniel Bell. At stake here is a key issue: Veblen's understanding of the relation between science and pragmatism.

Science versus Pragmatism

Much of intellectual work, especially the work of political theory, broadly conceived to include the politically normative implications of economics and sociology, is indeed, in Veblen's sense, thoroughly "pragmatic." Horkheimer's yearnings for revolution were in this sense as hopelessly instrumental as Milton Friedman's claims for free market rationality. A hallmark of the pragmatic attitude, as Veblen understood it, is the attempt to work out relationships between preconceived norms, theoretical principles, and political action "to the agent's preferential advantage," be that agent an individual, a group, or a class.[10] This attitude can express itself in the institutional advice of reformers, the programs of revolutionaries, or the political reservations of conservatives. Such views share a belief in the theorists' capacity for practical insight, a spirit of worldly political wisdom that is built on, but that also departs from, purely theoretical considerations. "The pragmatists," Veblen once wrote, "value themselves somewhat on being useful as well as being efficient for good and evil." Their standardized terms "of human nature, of human preference, prejudice, aspiration, and disability" are all put in evidence to inform strategic political questions of action or policy.[11]

For pragmatists of whatever ideological stripe or allegiance, the point is not merely to understand the world; it must be to secure it, to reform it, or, as Marx demanded, to change it root and branch. In contrast, Veblen's "skeptical spirit" does not stop at the frontier of politics. His ever-present doubt and constant probing extend into, indeed permeate, his attitude toward politics, including democratic politics, consistently underscoring his refusal to be politically useful in matters of "good and evil."

"Pragmatism," said Veblen, "creates nothing but maxims of expedient conduct. Science creates nothing but theories." Inspired by "idle curiosity" to pursue knowledge, the scientist undertakes "disinterested inquiry." In this pursuit, she is—or ought to be—free of practical political concern. Scientific work has an ongoing, unfinished, incomplete theoretical character. Its conclusions are tentative, not absolute. This fact alone, Veblen suggests, should inhibit theorists from promoting bold policy recommendations, at least in their role as scientists.[12] Effective political action depends on confident assertions of rational connections between means and ends. Theory, however, is not about action. It consists of claims about likely or probable relations between cause and effect. Theoretical statements carry candid reservations of caution. The work of scientific theory, for Veblen, is like the movement of history or evolution itself. Both are ongoing, open-ended, and cumulative; they are equally forever works in progress, their outcome indefinite. The last thing theorists can promise is certainty.[13]

Clearly, Veblen drew broad distinctions between science and pragmatism, or instrumental knowledge. Like Max Weber (1949), he well understood that science rests on unproven presuppositions. So while he greatly respected such obviously ideological or pragmatic thinkers as, say, Locke, Hume, Smith, or Marx and valued their theoretical insights into the logic and bias of cultural institutions, he did not value their political advice. For Veblen, the line between science and pragmatism may be difficult to sustain, but it is discernible. The scientist, and Veblen clearly saw himself—albeit in his own distinctive way—as a scientist, should strive hard to stay on the actively skeptical, critical side of the line.[14] For "wherever canons of expediency are intruded into or are attempted to be incorporated in the inquiry, the consequence is an unhappy one for science, however happy it may be for some other purpose extraneous to science. The mental attitude of worldly wisdom is at cross-purposes with the disinterested scientific spirit, and the pursuit of it induces an intellectual bias that is incompatible with the scientific spirit."[15] It is important to be clear that our focus here is not on the relation between facts and values. It is rather the distinction between the rationality of analysis and belief in the rationality of action. However, because the fact-value distinction is a highly problematic aspect of Veblen's approach to social science and also a key element in his satiric style, it may be helpful to say a few words about these matters before returning to the relation between science and action.

Fact and Value, Science and Power

On the fact-value distinction, Veblen's position was ambivalent. A consistent sociologist of knowledge, he held that social facts reflect prevailing social values, habits, interests, and powers. They are intrinsically value laden. The social scientist, a product of institutions and habits herself, will therefore find it hard at best to isolate her own values from studies of ongoing institutions. This is the familiar Weberian position on the difficulty of achieving objectivity in the social sciences. Veblen believed that scientific curiosity might ease this challenge a bit.

Scientists, he held, are likely to possess an above average proclivity toward idle curiosity. They are insistently skeptical about conventional explanations of things, especially when anomalies and problems appear in orthodox explanations. The theorist's impatience with unresolved questions motivates intellectual activism, a willingness to push through and beyond established explanations to arrive at more-complete, coherent answers. Yet further inquiry is likely to prove such results incomplete. All scientific results remain tentative, subject to revision. In this way idle curiosity leads to an endless search for deeper and more comprehensive theoretical insight into the nature of things. This is Veblen's answer to Max Weber's famous question concerning why the scientist devotes her life to proposing answers that she knows will be challenged and rejected down the road.[16] The desire to know creates compulsions that can be resolved only by quests to seek better answers. Thus "the enterprising skeptic alone," Veblen observed, "can be counted on to further the increase of knowledge in any substantial fashion."[17] In this way, active curiosity can lead scholars or theorists to emancipate themselves, however incompletely, from the boundaries of conventional thought. But they pay a heavy price—psychological disquiet, or the "loss of that peace of mind that is the birthright of the safe and sane quietist." This is a main theme of Veblen's essay "The Intellectual Pre-eminence of the Jews."[18]

Though Veblen appreciated how hard it is to acquire an "exemption from hard and fast preconceptions," he believed the effort to do so is vital for the growth of knowledge and the development of theory. Moreover, Veblen made frequent and strong claims for his own work as distanced, objective, and value neutral. But his habit along these lines was characteristically ironic; indeed, some would say it was downright confusing or contradictory. Nonetheless, throughout his writing, Veblen regularly appends to his critiques immediate apologies for an unfortunate and unintended "air of finding fault." Veblen's silence in respect to any corrective course of political action quickly reinforces the sense of unintended—but still conspicuous—fault finding. Here in essence is the Veblen style: claims to objectivity, piercing criticism, political silence. One way to appreciate what holds these elements together is to see how they reflect the relations among science, satire, and power in Veblen's thought.

There is a sense in which Veblen's peculiar style operates as a kind of mimetic inversion, a subversive mirroring, of the duplicitous operations of power. Holders of legitimate power everywhere claim to be in service to norms and to be bound by morality. Yet everywhere they operate in deference to their own strategic imperatives. This is above all the case for "the elder statesmen" of international politics, but then "the shadow of external politics covers also the management of domestic affairs."[19] In Veblen's words, "All is fair in war and politics . . . [Politics,] being in the nature of an enterprise in chicane and coercion, is necessarily furtive, runs forever on sharp practice, carefully withholds 'information that might be useful to the enemy,' and habitually gives out information with intent to deceive . . . It is a game of force and fraud. There is said to be honor among thieves, but one does not look for such a thing among statesmen."[20]

Stated more formally, power claims to be normative; as authority, it stands subjectively for the right and it respects the law. In fact, Veblen insists, power will do whatever is necessary to perpetuate and enlarge its domain and prestige. To further their objectives, the powerful will abrogate the very norms in whose name they speak. Orwell's newspeak is the classic literary exposure of the power-language relation. Legitimation in word, amorality in action: the ends do not so much justify as obscure the nefarious methods of politics. Machiavelli caught the fundamental dualism in his distinction between the Prince's appearance and reality; Samuel P.

Huntington captured it in his advice to the powerful to crave darkness; Hans Morgenthau described it with his insight into the slave's yearning for mastery more than freedom; and Reinhold Niebuhr recognized it with his memorable reference to "moral man and immoral society."[21] Thorstein Veblen approaches power with the same caustic sense of political reality. Within practices of exploit and predation, legitimation and amorality coexist. They form the contradictory schematics of power. Though distinct, each is entangled with the other, so closely inosculated and interwoven that to treat them as distinct is to confuse and misunderstand the dualism that forms the essential nature of the phenomenon of power itself. As Veblen would say, "It lies in the nature of the case, unfortunately."[22] Power succeeds in its Janus-faced operations only by dint of evasions, exceptions, duplicities, illusions, and hypocrisies. A whole battery of concealments, including self-delusions, stands to shield from exposure its amoral ways.

Veblen confronts this duality of power with a literary style that uses the equally double-sided quality of scientific objectivity as its satirical weapon. Objectivity and critique, far from being opposites, come together. To be dispassionate about power, Veblen suggests, is to fall helplessly into the pose of critic. Science is committed to but one value: truth. A central truth of power is its habit of deceit. The intellectual servants of power will conceal this truth. The truth-telling scientist has no choice but to reveal it. In this way, Veblen's ironic style uses the claims of science to turn the operations of power inside out. Where power claims to be dedicated to values, Veblen claims to be free of any value save commitment to truth. As his science aims for an approximation of the truth, when it comes to revealing the truths of power, even approximations sting. Thus Veblen adds angular, critical strokes to his meandering sentences, his satirical observations sticking sharply out of the dispassionate claims. He regularly interrupts his heavy prose and ponderous sentences with lightning flashes of irony. And yet these flashes seem less a surprise than bursts of candor required for a full disclosure of the facts, as if they cannot be contained if truth is to prevail. Factual accounts cannot help but seem critical. They juxtapose power's claims to stand for right with the evidence of hypocrisy. Or as President Harry Truman famously put it, "I don't give them hell. I just tell the truth and they think it is hell." It is just this strategy that led C. Wright Mills to say that "Veblen was a profoundly conservative critic of America," for he attacked American power with American values.[23] For similar reasons Samuel P. Huntington might add that Veblen is solidly in the American critical tradition, for exposure of "the gap between political ideal and political reality is a continuing central phenomenon of American politics."[24]

Veblen's own claim is that science can't help itself; empirical candor leads to an appearance of finding fault; straight talk makes power look bad. He repeatedly apologizes for stating the obvious, but he adds that the obvious is sometimes too embarrassing to notice—naked emperors and draft-evading warrior presidents come to mind. This is especially so because ordinary language is not completely given to laggard preconceptions favorable to power. "The colloquial speech of our time," Veblen suggests, "carries a note of disallowance and disclaimer in all that it has to say of holdovers; which is an unfortunate but inherent defect of language, and which it is necessary to discount and make one's peace with." Matter-of-fact usage can reflect a "human intelligence that has not yet gone into abeyance," a "human speech . . . in continued process of remaking."[25] Veblen's favored critical words—workmanship, industry, need, efficiency, and productiveness—seem so ordinary, so dry, plain and matter of fact. But when he uses them they shout accusingly out of the narrative.

Veblen's reference to "remaking" of language is particularly striking in this regard, for it hints at the duplicity of his shrewd methodological strategy as well as his anti-power ethic. First, the notion of "remaking" recalls the evolutionary structure of Veblen's thought and the way it accents the historical quality of human experience and consciousness. Social change creates possibilities that can help to liberate repressed or thwarted dispositions in favor of a more truthful, complete explanation of things, all this reflected in new, evolved, or "remade" forms of expression. Consider what it meant in the '60s, for example, to say, "let it all hang out," or how today's hip-hop artists use harsh street jargon to tear away at social hypocrisy. The idea of a remade language also refers to one of Veblen's most familiar themes: the cultural lag of archaic ideas. Ordinary language, Veblen suggests, may keep pace with technology better than institutions, which invariably look backward. Conventional conceptions, like private property, for example, straggle behind progressive technologies, such as the capacity of computers to reproduce music and art in endless digital recombinations. When the young copy music files freely, corporations call it theft. Teenagers understand the same act in terms of a freer technological possibility. And they express it with a techno-socialist lingo of "downloading," "shareware," and "borrowing."

Veblen's literary style bridges his science, his criticism, and his political reticence. He poured the vinegar of his satire out of a bottle called science. But his claims for science were never more than tentative. Thus for all that he made his own critical views obvious through satire, Veblen never presumed that his views or theory provided a rational basis for action. How could they? The logic of science and the logic of strategic action pulled in completely different directions. This is why Veblen's work was evaluative and critical without being directive. He was fully prepared to indict institutions for failing to meet standards that he believed indispensable to the survival of the species and the generic well-being of humanity. As Russell and Sylvia Bartley note, "Whereas Veblen readily offended social convention and excoriated institutionalized religion as well as its clerical minions, he was raised in the ethical teachings of the Scriptures and embraced those that seemed to have enduring merit."[26]

Such standards often find religious expression, but as he insisted in different places, the basic principles of ethics are in fact a complex amalgam of primitive human experience, evolution, and biology. In *The Theory of the Leisure Class*, for example, Veblen described the broadest human values as enhancement of human life on the whole and furtherance of the life process taken impersonally.[27] He called the source of these generic human values "economic conscience." In the later *Instinct of Workmanship*, Veblen offered a biological basis for our moral sense, attributing its origin to a native disposition that he called the "parental bent." And in "Christian Morals and the Competitive System," he argued that Jesus's injunction to turn the other cheek originated in a brutal political situation. The early working-class believers in Christ, who "had been beaten to a pulp by the hard-handed, systematic, inexorable power of the imperial city," learned to value renunciation as a means of survival.[28]

Clearly, Veblen believed that humans can and do make important moral value judgments. And he used what he regarded as a scientific method to advance such claims. His studies of anthropology, psychology, and biology afforded a reasonable basis for saying that the basis of moral judgment is generic and intersubjective. Veblen never stated, however, nor did he believe, that he could prove such claims beyond a reasonable scientific doubt. Veblen believed that science can take us toward the truth, but it never carries us all the way there.

As Morton White argues, Veblen made judgments. But he carefully refrained "from judging . . . whether we ought to abolish" institutions that sabotage the life process taken impersonally.[29] That is, while Veblen was prepared to make judgments, quite political judgments in fact, he did not believe that he had scientific warrant to declare his arguments unimpeachably valid or true. To counsel action would be to presume an invidious distinction of superiority between his theory of judgment and others'. As a social scientist, Veblen saw no basis for making such a claim. He simply did not believe that he was competent as a social scientist to suggest political action that would rest on invidious comparisons between his judgments and those of orthodoxy. In White's view, using the critique of conspicuous consumption as an example,

> what [Veblen] refused to do was to compare the lack of value of conspicuous consumption to society as a whole with its apparent value to those who indulged in it. At this point he stopped his analysis for one of several possible reasons . . . Either he felt that it was exceedingly difficult to compare these two value estimates—that of society and that of individual members of the leisure class—or he may have wanted to suggest that, whereas true value statements express empirical knowledge, the decision what to do when two valuations conflict is not a matter of empirical knowledge. Veblen was undoubtedly at the brink of a difficult problem, but we cannot say that valuation was not scientific for him.[30]

Difficult indeed! White's first alternative suggests the curious implication that while Veblen criticized much of the theoretical structure of neoclassical economics, he accepted its argument against the possibility of a rational basis for intersubjective value judgments. We can see plenty of evidence for this idea in Veblen's repetition of the cliché that there is no disputing taste. On the other hand, to insist on the normative standpoint of generic well-being presupposes abilities to see the life process impersonally, that is, objectively, apart from interpersonal comparisons. This claim would seem to disqualify White's first alternative. But White's second possibility, the principle that practical conclusions may not be derived scientifically in cases where "two valuations conflict," points to the key issue. For while Veblen may have believed that his evolutionary naturalism supplied reasonable theoretical grounds for statements about economic conscience or the parental bent, he still felt constrained by the belief that any scientific theory, including not least his own, is part of the flow of cultural change, the slow advancement of understanding. It can only be tentative, a contingent social product.

Scientific conclusions are subject to modification, contradiction, or invalidation down the road. Scientific knowledge is always, once again, less than absolute. In short, Veblen put more confidence in the rigorous *procedures* of science than in its results at any given moment, a position far removed from Marx's confidence in the substantive political lessons of scientific materialism. Coupled with his acute skepticism about the nature and uses of power, especially political power, Veblen's scientific reluctance to pass from criticism to action begins to be understandable, if still unsatisfying, to more confident political minds.

Reinforcing Veblen's formal sense of the limits of scientific certitude, the substance of his evolutionary naturalism also prohibited anything more than hypotheses about future trends. "Veblen's general theory of evolution," as William Dugger has observed, "was clearly an open one. He never argued in support of predetermined or teleological ends. Instead, he inquired into the possibilities of different evolutionary paths."[31]

Furthermore, because his theory of action emphasized the impact of cumulative cultural, technical, and economic forces on the shaping of human decision, not to mention the resistance of vested interests, Veblen had significant epistemological reasons for doubting the efficacy of conscious policy changes.[32] Indeed, Veblen's action theory is the cornerstone of his theory of cultural lag. He firmly held the view that innovations in social and political practice proceed much more slowly than advances in technology because our social and political choices are burdened by value commitments based on habit and veneration of the past. In fact, important social changes are much less likely to be the result of conscious choice than the product of late-breaking, quasi-tropismatic reactions to accumulating problems, what modern policy analysts describe as policy "stability . . . punctuated with periods of volatile change."[33]

Veblen's skepticism of such halting and abrupt changes is clear. As he writes in a typical passage: "any resulting revision of the principles of conduct will come in as a drift of habituation rather than a dispassionately reasoned adaptation of conduct to the circumstances of the case. It appears always to be a matter of 'forced movements' rather than an outcome of shrewd initiative and logical design—even though much argument may be spent in the course of it all."[34] One has only to consider humanity's reluctant adaptation to the onset of global warming, or the problem of nuclear weapons proliferation, to understand what Veblen is getting at.

If Veblen's ideological stance, supposing we call it that, ceases at the point of advocacy, the reason goes right to the heart of his social theory. This is a demurral based on more than political timidity. Veblen condemns abuses of power committed by elder statesmen and absentee owners, but he refuses to tell us what to do about social evils. The ever-taciturn radical, he delivers blistering insights into the workings of power but remains mute about political alternatives and responses. Why then shouldn't we insist that the critic owes us more than diagnosis? As even Clarence Ayres, a theorist sympathetic to Veblen's work, once put it, Veblen vigorously attacks orthodox political economy, but his "controversial articles . . . give little or no clue to what other concepts Veblen would lay down as fundamental, let alone how he would build up from them a systematic understanding of industrial society."[35] Veblen's answer is that he did not believe social scientists were physicians. Rejecting all such Platonic analogies between philosopher and physician, Veblen understood social scientists at their best to be critical analysts, not dispensers of civic wisdom to political systems that do not operate on the basis of rationality in any case. "Veblen," Dorothy Ross has insightfully noted, "wanted science to provide critical insight into the course of evolution, not become a tool to control it."[36] There are many other candidates for service to action. Let the scientist tend to her portion; politics is governed by other motives than those of science and enlightenment. Certainly Veblen did not believe that he possessed any worldly wisdom to offer a predatory world and its guiding pragmatic minds. Yet for all his doubts about political action, Veblen never told activists and radicals to shrink from insurrection. If anything, his works are full of sympathy for radical labor and the feminist and peace movements. Just as obvious is his exasperation at the failure of American farmers and workers to fight collectively and militantly for their interests. But there is more to the political criticism of Veblen than hostility toward his prescriptions for scientific quiescence.

Against the Ideological Grain

Not only did Veblen question prevailing institutions and practices without showing how to change them; he did so in ways that cut across the grain of conventional political expectation. His thought, and not least in its political aspects, harbored principles that were, at once, an infuriating mix of conservative, liberal, and radical themes. Veblen was eclectic in his association of seemingly opposite ideas. For example, his high estimate of the staying power of ancient beliefs and habits, and of the stubborn willingness of people to venerate institutions outmoded by standards of science and technical progress, made him dubious about prospects for enlightenment. Liberals and radicals have been especially prone to attack Veblen's weighting of the power of atavistic institutions as a main source of his cultural and political pessimism. Yet few radicals have understood the potential political power of conservatism better than Veblen. His appraisals of institutional endurance are anything but celebratory, however, and this realization draws conservative fire.

Indeed, Veblen's suspicions of irresponsible or excessive institutional power came from liberal and anarchistic sources, and the resulting criticism of institutions led to his repudiation by conservative critics. Veblen's pronounced sympathies for individual workmanship, for the spirit of insubordination, for free-ranging curiosity and learning, for communal self-regulation, for impersonal law, and for a social minimum of authority suggest many liberal debts and influences and are elements of his thought that have drawn rebukes from conservatives and radicals alike. For intellectuals of the left, Veblen's embrace of the virtues of "live and let live," quiet industry, and "idle curiosity" bespeak a political cowardice and anachronism that offends the revolutionary spirit, even as his uncompromising critique of the going institutions horrifies conservatives.

Yet however much Veblen stressed the power of tradition and prized classic liberal liberties to live, work, and learn freely, his critique of institutions always accentuated the heavy traces of class exploit and predatory power that distorted social life. And he found such distortions in so many different places: in habits of dress and fashion, in spectacles of sport and religion, in the contrived corporate sabotage of markets, consumption, technology and the higher learning, and in the patriotic bluster that rallies the public will to support war. Veblen never lets us forget the raw violence, outright seizure, and harsh coercions that social institutions try to mask. Here, with its pervasive, penetrating, and uncompromising focus on exploitation, lies Veblen's radical root, his biting contempt for vested interests, power, and domination, his steadfast refusal to accept the claims of the past as a suitable norm for evaluating contemporary human needs and prospects.

Most of all, Veblen draws from radical traditions his antisectarian preoccupations with the generic interests of humanity as a species, a species endowed by its history with a seemingly bottomless reservoir of skills to do violence and injustice to itself and its environment. Veblen understood such endowments to be both profoundly cultural and deeply resilient. This view led him toward an essentially tragic sensibility about the human prospect. Veblen offers us a kind of radical realism that is as piercing in its diagnosis of institutional power as it is adamant in its refusal to offer reassurances or panaceas. He shows us the potential human madness for what it is, but he promises no ready strategy for its relief. In this contradiction between radical diagnosis and strategic reticence—a basic characteristic of his thought as a whole—the Veblen who refused the role of prophet armed his critics for attack. As John Dos Passos wrote, he dissected society "with a scalpel so keen, so comical, so exact, that the professors and students ninetenths [*sic*] of the time didn't know it was there."[37]

Considered in this light, Veblen's gravest political sin is to deny what Harry Kariel once called "the promise of politics."[38] For classic conservatives, such a promise is bound to the state's venerable traditions of community, authority, patriarchy, patriotism, and religion. Liberals, meanwhile, find it in the rule of law, in open processes of negotiation and compromise, in markets, in balances of power, in institutions of free and open political competition, and in popular sovereignty. And for Marxists, of course, political promise lies in proletarian revolution and rational economic planning.

Veblen's problem for all these prevailing orthodoxies of political thought is that he unhesitatingly and radically deconstructs their shared limitations.

He undermines their confidence, certitude, and hopes. This is painful, unpopular work. Among the important early twentieth-century precursors of postmodernist political skepticism, Veblen tore ideological veils away from traditionalism and pluralism, without ever abandoning his distrust of revolution.[39] Such tendencies lead us to conclude that Veblen is most credibly understood as a radical realist, the critic of power who, virtually everywhere in his work, reminds us of the incapacity of science or politics to offer convincing theories of progress or transcendence.

Veblen is the critic without a definitive political project. Or, if one wants to take the project of *The Engineers* as seriously intended, it is a project that reflects a supremely immature and even dangerous political sensibility. No complaints are more frequent in the Veblen literature than these: Veblen is politically naïve and unsophisticated, even ominously so.[40] But a study of Veblen's ideas about the nature of power suggests a considerably more mature and tough-minded political sensibility than many previous critics have been prepared to acknowledge.

The Place of Politics

Controversy about Veblen's political relevance goes beyond questions of quiescence, action, and ideology. There is the substance of the thought itself and what it says about the place of politics not only in relation to the economic realm but also in relation to culture more generally. This study is concerned with the substance and quality of Veblen's immediate as well as more indirect observations about politics. The big problem facing any such effort is well captured by John P. Diggins. Diggins' important study *The Bard of Savagery* encapsulates much of the intellectual history of equivocation and ambiguity in appraisals of Veblen's political ideas.[41] He gives substantial credit where credit is due and notes serious lacunae where they exist. But the end result is a painfully double-sided judgment.

Diggins applauds Veblen for insights into the hegemonic and disciplinary aspects of power, and for a theory of ideological control so acute that he merits consideration next to some of the most highly regarded political theorists of the twentieth century, including Antonio Gramsci and Michel Foucault.[42] Even more telling than his occasional comparisons of Veblen with Gramsci and Foucault, Diggins organizes his book around a juxtaposition of Veblen's ideas with those of the two giants of modern political sociology Karl Marx and Max Weber. These are authors whose major political works, along with those of Gramsci and Foucault, are of course widely taught, and whose influence in political science is accepted without question. They are authors in a canon of political thinking about power and social structure that has largely ignored Veblen. We can locate clues to this dismissal in the more negative dimensions of Diggins' assessment. For the same Diggins who conceives of Veblen on the highest intellectual plateau of political theorists also repeatedly criticizes him for lacking an appreciation of politics, political institutions, and immediate political developments.

By exploring briefly Diggins' own understanding of politics, we can better grasp both the scope of his indictment and the quality of his appreciation for Veblen's political importance. Diggins' interpretation has another advantage. It also furnishes the principles for a framework that can be used to understand how and why other theorists and scholars have evaluated Veblen's political ideas. Rick Tilman (1992) has considerably eased the possibility of such work with his study of Veblen criticism. Diggins supplements Tilman by framing what we might call a central political paradox of Veblen's work. He fully recognizes that Veblen offers penetrating insights into the human fascination with power. But he adds that this contribution is warped by a perplexing indifference to the daily tactical operations of that power in government.

To explain the paradox Diggins suggests that Veblen deals critically and originally with power at two levels. On the first plane, he examines the most intimate human relations of control, dominance, and exploit in what we might call their Foucaultian, social-psychological aspect, or the micro-social relations of emulation and exploit. On the second plane, Veblen turns his gaze toward the highest Gramscian levels of the total culture, or the macro-social politics of power and hegemonic ideology, with particular emphasis on the interrelationships of prevailing institutions and vested interests, and including the ways that popular ideas, cutting across institutional boundaries, buttress ruling class powers and curtail democratic possibilities.

Where Veblen fails, for Diggins, and we shall see this theme reappear in the comments of many other critics, is in not providing either an adequate account of, or even due recognition for the importance of, the interior processes of government. In short, Veblen pays virtually no attention to the hard-core politics of legislation, adjudication, and administration, or to the extragovernmental organs of political change: mass parties, interest groups, or social movements. He simply avoids the most familiar terrain of political science; he is a political thinker without benefit of political science.

With this distinction in mind, one might say there is a general tendency in the Veblen literature to insist that in concentrating on macro- and micropolitics, Veblen ignored the most essential feature of democratic politics itself—the mediating impact of the state on cultural and economic power, and with it, the potential for a positive democratic government to discipline and control economic and social power for popular ends. In this spirit, Diggins insightfully suggests that "Veblen's approach has much in common with the French Annales School; both perspectives suggest that to focus solely on politics, as in the older history, conceals the more immobile forces of the past, *la longue durée* of unchanging customs, or what Veblen called the survival of 'archaic traits.' As Fernand Braudel would insist a half-century after Veblen, political events could well obscure rather than reveal the actual causes of historical development, which are governed not by the momentary issues of the day but by the long-term persistence of *mentalité*."[43]

If Diggins is right, the challenge for political analysts of Veblen's work is to understand how he tended to treat political phenomena in two rather disparate ways. Veblen's most obvious and direct political relevance stems from his critique of the interest-driven ideological and social-psychological deployments of honorific power, which are the Gramscian and Foucaultian aspects of his work that lie closest to the surface of his writings. Stjepan Meštrović's recent emphasis on the importance of narcissism to Veblen's theory of emulation is very much in this tradition, for example.[44] These preoccupations form central and unifying themes in Veblen's work as a whole.

Conversely, when it comes to politics inside government, formal political institutions, political behavior, and the various means of collective action, Veblen's observations are at best episodic, fragmentary, and thin. At worst, such observations are missing in action. Still, it is important not to overlook the potential richness of observation in the scattering and disorder of Veblen's insights into formal and informal government. It takes some work to pull these observations into a form that makes generalization possible, but Veblen's point of view is consistent enough to support the drawing of generalizations.

While it is absolutely true, as Diggins insists, that Veblen avoided detailed empirical studies of the uses of power in government, this claim is also misleading. For in various works, especially the later war-inspired studies of *Imperial Germany, The Nature of Peace*, the essays collected as *Vested Interests and the Common Man*, as well as in *Absentee Ownership*, there is substantial evidence of Veblen's theoretical and empirical interest in the state, law, the institutionalized forces of war, capitalist democracy, and business power, as well as a host of pregnant observations about "the spirit of insubordination" and the character of quasi-anarchistic habits and institutions. Much of the critical Veblen literature has responded to various, usually isolated aspects of this political writing; but there has been a dearth of effort to unify these observations into a coherent view of Veblen as a political writer. The latter parts of this study aim to do just that. In the chapter to follow, however, we review in greater detail some of the main currents of Veblen criticism, looking especially for its political content and significance. However one wishes to judge the quality and limitations of Veblen's political writing, a reading of Veblen's critics helps to confirm the point that his readers have regularly situated its importance in relation to the dominant orthodoxies, problems, and debates of twentieth-century political thought.

3

THE ASSORTED POLITICS OF VEBLEN CRITICISM

Among writers who have important things to say about politics, Thorstein Veblen enjoys what may be charitably defined as an ambiguous status. Given his critical reception by thinkers who embraced political goals more confidently than he did, this situation is understandable. Most political writers connect their working notion of politics with values they believe it should serve. John Stuart Mill, for example, bound liberal democracy and personal autonomy, just as Karl Marx tied dialectical materialism to the ultimate triumph of communism. In contrast, Veblen's analysis of institutions conflicts with his most cherished social and political values. An unmistakable divide separates his preferences from his analysis. Veblen favored a postcapitalist economy geared to efficient production for basic human needs. He espoused a socially just, environmentally sustainable economy providing goods and services on a more or less equal, nonwasteful basis. As far as government is concerned, Veblen wanted to keep it simple, direct, industrious, and peaceful.

Veblen took these ideals seriously, but he did not think they would be realized, certainly not within "the calculable future." Though it would be too much to say that he was completely hopeless, Veblen was not optimistic. The main institutional drift of the twentieth century foretold continued predation, irresponsible power, and chronic warfare. Insurgent democracy might win battles, but the main drift favored oligarchy and war. He displayed a pretty fair sense of things to come. Patterns of oligarchy and militarism have resisted radical change. He saw no reason to believe that they harbored agents of progressive, much less revolutionary, change. All in all, Veblen saw the political future more clearly than Marx. But then unlike Marx, Veblen's aspirations and analysis were radically at odds.

Paradoxes like these suggest why Veblen has been spared a following among politically engaged intellectuals. Important writers who sympathize with his egalitarian values, or who endorse his view of the big trends, reject his pessimism. C. Wright Mills, Paul Sweezy, and John Kenneth Galbraith come to mind. Against the odds, they preserve options for hope; each finds ways to align his critique with his preferences. And their consistency certainly makes it easier for us to place their work in familiar categories. Mills looks to a more robust democratic public life; Sweezy sees a socialist future; and Galbraith celebrates welfare-state liberalism. What kind of a thinker, by contrast, is Veblen? Where does he fit? What promise does he offer? If it is gratifying to know that a thinker's approach fits a preexisting school of thought, or reaches toward some desirable end, it is frustrating to see our categories fail to categorize or our hopes go unfulfilled.

Veblen's oscillation between utopian hopes and dark conclusions is exasperating. We can't place his ideas in neat intellectual boxes.[1] There is at least one nice irony here though: Veblen, the frequent critic of taxonomy in science, defeats its application to his own work. But as he might quickly add, the virtue has its defect because it encourages accusations of confusion and fuzzy thinking. It also leads some readers to make strained attempts to place Veblen's work in categories that distort his elusive thought.

Consistency eases understanding and classification. But in Veblen's case, efforts to find it often come at the cost of grappling with the fullness of his outlook. It is also likely to be unfair to the structural integrity of his theory as a whole. As Veblen himself once noted, "Any given ground of distinction," including his own habit of separating analysis from preferences, "will seem insubstantial to any one who habitually apprehends the facts in question from a different point of view and values them for a different purpose," such as affirming the wisdom of familiar ideological judgments.[2] It is useful to remember this aspect of his sociology of knowledge as we review the ideas of some of Veblen's strongest ideological critics.

Conservative Complaints

A number of important conservative theorists, especially econo-mists, have taken Veblen's challenge to American institutions seriously. For a century, market champions have said that his work subverted the price system, liberal values, and the established order writ large. They have targeted their criticisms mainly at his economic thought, their work amounting to a defense of neoclassical theory. But conservatives have also seen good reason to challenge Veblen's political ideas. For such critics, Veblen's ideas have been too important to ignore.

That political sensitivity was perhaps most heightened in the case of Lev Dobriansky, whose formidable study *Veblenism: A New Critique* (1957) foreshadows contemporary neoconservative attacks on the moral relativism said to be inherent in evolutionary naturalism. Veblen's earliest conserva-tive critics, however, were mainly professional economists, including John Cummings, Irving Fisher, and Richard Taggart. Their point was to demon-strate how Veblen's attack on the economic calculus and moral psychology of the price system implied a potentially dangerous collectivist alternative to economic individualism. They understood that Veblen's critique of emulative consumption was tied to an alternative theory of impersonal, generic value. Though Veblen hardly developed this alternative, many conservatives took it seriously as a challenge to the justice and rationality claims of the existing commercial order. The fact that Veblen never saw fit to expound on his alternative value theory became a recurring charge among promarket critics, and not an unfair one either.

His silence on economic alternatives to market pricing only confirmed conservative belief that there was no economically rational alternative to the market mechanism. Absent a coherent substitute for market calcula-tion, Veblen's complaints sacrificed much of their force. In this respect, the main pattern of conservative criticism paralleled liberal charges that Veblen had no theory of corrective political reform as well as Marxist accusations that he had given up on revolutionary alternatives to capitalism. All such arguments add up to the common lament that Veblen is a critic without a cause, a man whose methodological claims as an evolutionary theorist do not insulate him from charges of political irresponsibility. Such arguments often go too far. Veblen did stand for specific substantive and progressive values, although, as we have seen, he did not project a politics on their behalf.

After Veblen's death, in the 1930s and beyond, the subtle conservatism of University of Chicago economist Frank Knight raised probing and problematic questions. Knight cut to the heart of what he regarded as the serious political pitfalls and weaknesses of Veblen's thinking. He saw danger in the policy consequences of Veblen's call for a more empirically and culturally sensitive economics. Veblen's demand for study of institutions, along with greater empirical concreteness in the scientific treatment of economic phenomena, he feared, implied a claim for the relevance of economic theory to public policy, a position favorable to national economic planning and regulation. This argument is solidly justified in the case of such other major institutionalists as John R. Commons and Wesley Mitchell. But it is less applicable to Veblen himself, given his many doubts about state rationality.[3] To reach his conclusion, Knight had to downplay the thrust of Veblen's critique of "pragmatic" inquiry, his sociological view of science, and his pronounced skepticism of government's ability to make reasonable policy in timely ways. Still, his discussion of Veblen illustrates important distinctions in each theorist's understanding of change.

Veblen's case for enhanced social rationality rested, said Knight, on a serious misunderstanding of the dualistic nature of social institutions and social change. Knight held that institutionalists elided or "slurred over the contrast between two kinds or meanings of institution, i.e., patterns of action moving in predestined grooves under the influence of relatively unconscious social forces, versus those embodying deliberate organization and control, such as the political organs of the state."[4] In an argument that echoed Friedrich von Hayek's more famous claims in *The Road to Serfdom* (1944), Knight insisted that mistaking such a profound qualitative difference in the forms of human action could lead to wrongheaded presumptions favoring planned direction of social and economic change, conceptions of "social engineering" that might culminate in a "superdictatorship, a government which would own as well as rule society at large."[5]

There is an irony here too, one not lost on Knight's fellow conservative Ernest Dewey. It lies in the fact that Veblen himself insisted on the very distinction that Knight drew. There is a crucial gulf, he regularly insisted, between the habitual or cumulative institutional dimensions of culture, which substantially limit the scope of possible changes, and conscious or deliberate policy change, which typically reflects these limitations. "Any established order of law and custom," wrote Veblen, "is always out of date, in some degree."[6] And when values and beliefs lag behind society's need to adapt, it is usually adaptation that suffers. Thus "short of social disintegration," Dewey rightly observed, Veblen's theory suggested that revolutionary change was unlikely. "The overthrow of a whole system of beliefs and values can come about only over a long period of time and piecemeal." Dewey thus concluded that Veblen's "biting satire and uninhibited criticism" notwithstanding, he was in fact "one of history's most sincere and sound apologists of the extrinsic value of the conservative's role in society."[7]

Veblen was undoubtedly impressed by the staying power of conservative belief, but he rarely praised it, tying his accounts of conservative institutions to doubts about chances for needed change. He was anything but a "sincere apologist" for the status quo. Cultural inertia, after all, strengthened "imbecile institutions." It made it only more probable that human beings would miscalculate the requirements of survival, especially in a "desperately precarious institutional situation."[8] Still, Dewey grasped better than Frank Knight the intimate relation between Veblen's pessimistic theory of social change and the improbability of a "soviet of technicians" bursting into power as a "superdictatorship." One might, as Marxists often do, legitimately complain that Veblen gave insufficient attention to revolutionary possibilities, or, as liberals do, criticize his undue pessimism about public policy. But to see his theory as a template for dictatorship not only fails to grasp Veblen's anarchist sympathies but also misapprehends the crucial link between his belief in the power of gradualism and his supreme doubts about chances for radical change.

The interpretive tension between Knight and Dewey also illustrates strains in conservative thought. Insofar as conservatives disagreed among themselves about whether individualistic or cultural factors are more precious to security for the status quo, Veblen could mean very different things to various kinds of conservative critics. This ambiguity only deepens with consideration of such other promarket interpreters as David Seckler and Lev Dobriansky.

Seckler claimed to have discovered a central paradox in Veblen's theory. This consisted of what he identified as Veblen's attempt to fuse a theory based on impersonal behaviorism with an embrace of liberal free will.[9] The behaviorist dimension, which Seckler believes dates from such later works as "The Place of Science in Modern Civilization" and *The Instinct of Workmanship*, is unmistakable in Veblen's emphasis on brute material causation in human culture, especially the cumulative impact of technology on social life. By contrast, Seckler insists that in earlier works, such as *The Theory of the Leisure Class* and "The Instinct of Workmanship and the Irksomeness of Labor," Veblen held humans to be purposive, willful, teleological agents. Crucial to Seckler's case is the assumption that what Veblen calls purposive behavior is, in fact, an attribution of "free will." But it is hardly clear that the two ideas refer to identical or even comparable phenomena.

When Veblen writes of a sense of purpose, he means that people act in relation to particular ends or goals; they are, as he often says, teleological agents. This concept does not necessarily entail the related but very different idea that either human purpose arises subjectively from the inner will of the individual, or it is a moral vindication of the choosing subject's autonomy. To the contrary, Veblen repeatedly explains how the heavy weight of culture and institutions condition the scope and range of human purpose. The individual's purposive mind, in Veblen, is a thoroughly social, cultural product. Personal choice always betrays or carries a tacit social residue. Indeed, in a series of passages quoted by Seckler, Veblen draws a distinction—not one that Seckler wishes to make—between the institutional economist, who is interested in the development of economic systems as historic totalities—Veblen's own chief interest—and the orthodox or neoclassical economist, who is preoccupied with the question of how individuals choose on utilitarian grounds, "under conditions that are presumed to be normal and invariable."[10]

Veblen's framework consistently situates the human fashioning of purpose, or choice, within cultural constraints and historical patterns. People take their ends "under given conditions." His chief theoretical interest lies in those conditions, how they came to be, and the forces working to conserve or to change them. Veblen has little theoretical interest in, and indeed is highly critical of, theories that describe the subjective or psychological aspects of individual economic calculation. If we want to equate purpose with freedom, this is a highly attenuated sense of freedom indeed.[11]

There is in fact, for Veblen, no question of "free will" in these cases. Even as his model recognizes that individuals may choose subjectively, it is within constraints not of their choosing. He recognizes that choices are not illusory. Individuals do indeed choose, but any robust idea of choice has to be aware of social contexts, habitual tendencies, and institutional patterns. The problem with Seckler's interpretation is that he obfuscates what Veblen wants to clarify: the relationship between human agency and the influence of society on the range of legitimate or appropriate alternatives among which human agents choose. Veblen's theory of emulative consumption, for example, encapsulates both subjective choice and a structure of market alternatives infused with social status aspirations. Seckler wants to enlarge the moral significance of that choice in ways incompatible with Veblen's theory of purposive action. Most telling, however, is that while a cultural conservative like Ernest Dewey claims Veblen as a closet traditionalist, Seckler attempts to capture at least a part of Veblen for inclusion among neoclassical libertarians, virtually a Hayekian in disguise!

If Seckler stretches Veblen to the limit of his individualism, and Ernest Dewey's treatment of Veblen as a closet conservative does not quite ring true, Lev Dobriansky's *Veblenism* offers a Roman Catholic, natural-law perspective on Veblen's materialism that deserves to be taken seriously.[12] Dobriansky rejects views of Veblen as either a traditionalist or an individualist. Dobriansky's is a through and perspicacious analysis of Veblen. It is, in fact, among the closest and most sharp-eyed critical readings to be found in the literature.

Dobriansky's main concerns are with Veblen's moral relativism, its roots in his evolutionary naturalism, and its negative implications for the legitimacy of Catholic as well as bourgeois values. Dobriansky writes with the disciplined fervor of a true believer in the ancient spiritual truths of divine law. His rejection of Veblen's historicism is comparable to Leo Strauss's critique of historicism in political theory, which runs along similar lines and has parallel implications.[13] In a considerably more sober and critical inspection of Veblen's theory of habit and institutions than Dewey's, Dobriansky believes these ideas signal Veblen's radical rebellion against the natural-law basis of conservatism. Veblen is guilty, in this view, of that same dangerous anti-intellectualism, the revolt against reason, to be found in such other late nineteenth-century writers as Nietzsche, Freud, Sorel, and Pareto.[14] At the same time, Dobriansky recognized that Veblen was anything but a nihilist; he understood how deeply moral values permeated Veblen's perspective. Dobriansky appreciated that Veblen advanced a definite system of values—altruism, craftsmanship, and community—which he used both to criticize existing arrangements and to point the direction toward a more humane order.

The error, and Dobriansky thought it was fatal, was that Veblen improperly derived these ethical norms from human instincts, from man's organic and material rather than spiritual being. This was an inadmissible maneuver, for it robbed ethical values of their transcendent moral, religious, and spiritual power. It failed to grasp the principle that the source of morals is not to be found in biology, or in anthropology, but only in a divinely ordained natural law. God, not evolution, can be the only secure foundation of human values. This error was profound, argued Dobriansky, because it left Veblen's values bereft of the truthfulness that can be imparted only by the absolute, eternal principles of the divine. The "very authenticity" of Veblen's values is thus "subject to fatal doubt." His "calculated attempt to substitute biologically oriented norms for the established principles of moral philosophy" was "a vain and hollow endeavor."[15]

In effect, Dobriansky powerfully linked familiar criticisms of Veblen's political quietism and ambivalence to a foundational critique of Veblen's evolutionary naturalism, insisting, very insightfully, that the equivocation or demurral of Veblen's political stance flows directly from his epistemological relativism. But Dobriansky insisted that the moral implications of this approach are far graver than the issue of doubts about mere institutional reform. Dobriansky's natural law critique, its confidence founded on unerring belief in God, mirrors equally strong critiques of Veblen that came from Marxists, such as Theodore Adorno and Paul Baran, who were as sure of their truth as Dobriansky was of his.

Within Dobriansky's Catholic framework, it is inconceivable that human values, such as altruism and truthfulness, might arise from anything but a supreme spiritual authority. Societies and groups face so many different situations that the imperatives of group survival must vary and change according to the immediate pressures that human beings confront. Universal moral norms cannot therefore be grounded in needs that change with humanity's shifting existential situation. Their source must be transcendent. Moral values cannot be based on a world in flux.

Veblen disagrees. The primordial underpinnings or conditions of human existence are not uniform, but they do not vary as much as Dobriansky thinks. Alternate forms of savagery may have taken root in different places, Veblen suggests. But as a unifying phase of human development, the crucial features of savagery—emergent human life in small groups of peaceful, sedentary, and poor beings—tended to yield more or less common instinctual and habitual consequences for our fragile and not very populous species.[16] Most important among these general patterns were surely concerns for the community's future (the parental bent), for the industry and workmanship essential to produce material life (the instinct of workmanship), and for a spiritual bearing (idle curiosity) that looked for coherent, meaningful answers to the mysteries of existence.[17]

Humans might, in response to different environmental pressures, devise alternate ways and means to support their perpetuation as a group. But whatever variety of institutions they fashioned rested on a common, generic inheritance of social sensibility, workmanship, and critical intelligence. This very slowly gathering evolutionary inheritance underpins what Veblen understood to be a diffusion of more or less common or generic ethical sensibilities across the range of savage cultures.[18] Barbaric culture developed out of savagery in radically particularistic, exclusionary, and bellicose ways, separating communities from one another. These divisions legitimated and authenticated the value of conflict and "the infliction of injury by force."[19] But barbarism never wholly supplanted the humane dispositions that evolved to help people survive the primitiveness of savagery.[20]

As William Dugger has argued, "Inherent to the process of evolutionary theory-building is the drive to make human beings a part of nature by de-mystifying our view of ourselves." This project implies first of all recognition of ourselves as members of a common human species, a sharing of features and needs far more fundamental than the invidious comparisons of competitive individuals and political communities.[21] As part of nature, human beings developed collective capacities to establish relations with nature as well as with other humans, evolving capabilities sufficient to support continuance of both the natural and human worlds. For Veblen such capacity is rooted first and foremost in instinctive tendencies toward craftsmanship, community, curiosity, dispositions toward work, social sensibility, and intelligent action, without which the species would surely perish. These dispositions must have appeared long before the now familiar conventions of western religious or political ritual.

The difference between Dobriansky and Veblen on this and related issues is great. It is really an unbridgeable ideological chasm, bounded on one side by a Catholic perspective on social relationships and ontology, and on the other by secular humanism. Yet for all the vast gulf that divides them, Dobriansky and Veblen share not only a common curiosity about the real bases of responsible communal living but a sense of the importance of the philosophical foundations of moral debate. Dobriansky repudiates the materialist foundation of Veblen's values, but he does not charge Veblen with lacking an ethic of solidarity or moral value. In contrast, Christopher Shannon's more contemporary and inflamed neoconservative attack on a series of conspicuous left critics of American society, including C. Wright Mills, Robert and Helen Lynd, Ruth Benedict, John Dewey, and Veblen, does charge them with launching a wholesale instrumental attack on moral value itself.[22]

For Shannon, writing at a time when the Catholic Church, a host of fundamentalist protestant denominations, and the Republican Party went on the political offensive against what Pope Benedict XVI calls an expanding "dictatorship of relativism," American leftists propose a purely instrumental version of social science.[23] Their positivist science "demands the suspension of all normative ordering principles as a prelude to the creation of value and meaning by autonomous human subjects." This error commits such thinkers to supporting a veritable "moral anarchy."[24] In contrast with Dobriansky's close reading of the Veblenian texts, however, Shannon fails to acknowledge the materialist basis of the generic, impersonal ethic that Veblen ascribes to the parental bent and instinct of workmanship. Veblen is ever critical of value judgments that approve the "relative advantage of one individual in comparison with another." In this respect, he opposes the very fluid, relational value model that Shannon finds so offensive. Veblen's notion of "economic conscience" and "the parental bent" look to common, universal foundations for social judgments. His ethic of altruism is rooted in human dispositions—or "instincts"—that span and transcend cultural boundaries. These Veblenian "instincts" serve precisely the ethical and normative purposes that Shannon claims do not exist for his radical thinkers. For Veblen, they answer "the question whether" the course of economic—and one might add political—action "serves directly to enhance human life on the whole—whether it furthers the life process taken impersonally."[25]

Now, one may fairly criticize Veblen for never delving fully or persuasively enough into the concept of impersonal generic value. It is entirely reasonable to complain that he rests far too much of the normative character of his theory on comments that cover barely five pages of *The Theory of the Leisure Class* and not many more in the first chapter of *The Instinct of Workmanship*. Veblen owed readers more thoughtful and substantive reflections on these serious matters. A disturbing intellectual lassitude or slackness marks Veblen's refusal to dig deeper into issues so important to social, moral, and political theory. Accusations of a kind of superficiality in Veblen's thought are not entirely or always unfair.

On the other hand, it should be obvious that anyone who embraces an impersonal standard for value is a long way from reducing value to its "creation . . . by autonomous human subjects." Claims to knowledge of "the life process taken impersonally," or to understanding of the needs of "the generically human," presuppose understandings of humanity's most unifying, invariant, organic character, what Marx called our "species being." Whatever the flaws in its specification and analysis, Veblen's reference to "the generically human" is worlds apart from the individual subjectivity and relativity denounced by Shannon. Veblen was surely relativist in his analysis of culture. But his belief in the generic interest of the species was not. Again, the point is not that Veblen adequately defended his generic standpoint—he did not. It is that his theory presupposed this standpoint as the moral basis of its critique. Dobriansky clearly understood this fundamental proposition; Shannon does not.

What stands out most perhaps in the various conservative readings of Veblen is how he serves as a foil for markedly different versions of conservatism. Reactions to Veblen illuminate contradictions between the individualist conservatism of a Seckler, who praises the "humanist" or purposeful tendency in Veblen, and the neoconservatism of a Dobriansky or Shannon, who find that same tendency most dangerous and repulsive. Furthermore, along with his emphasis on the eternal truths of Catholic doctrine, Dobriansky defended a positive mid-twentieth-century view of liberal government, an outlook confident in the state's capacity to regulate excesses of business power in the interest of justice and the common good. He believed that "modern democracies are sustained by sentiments, habits and convictions founded on personal rights, equitable law, and sound justice." In contrast, he felt, Veblen's despairing view of constitutional government badly underestimated the restraining hand of public opinion, grossly exaggerated the political power of business, and failed to grasp the benefits of patriotism.[26] At bottom, he suggested, Veblen attacked the democratic state on behalf of a naïve anarchistic individualism that simply did not appreciate the fact that "the political element," man's basic egoistic power drive, "is well nigh uneliminable."[27]

Although his argument is couched within a religious framework utterly incompatible with Veblen's materialist standpoint, Dobriansky identified crucial issues for any political assessment of Veblen. On the one hand, Veblen did explain the human enchantment with power as a fundamentally cultural matter. But the appeal of power is a cultural force whose habit-forming attraction within predatory institutions led him to treat it in ways that are comparable to those of realists, for whom "the political element is well nigh uneliminable." Such ideas play influential roles in Veblen's critique of the warfare state, "ostensible democracy," and patriotism. To be sure, his evolutionary viewpoint could not provide final answers to the question of power. But Veblen took the problem of power as seriously as any realist.

Finally, Dobriansksy is not wrong to conclude that the radical dimension of Veblen's critique of power, what we see as his realism, is indeed rooted in sympathy for radical, anarchistic values; not the individualistic anarchism of conservative libertarianism so much as the communal anarchism of a Kropotkin. But an appreciation of the relationship between anarchism and the critique of power is indeed a fundamental aspect of Veblen's political thought, and Dobriansky deserves credit for underscoring its importance. This is a theme that figures prominently in liberal critiques of Veblen too.

Liberal Disenchantment with Veblen

If conservatives charge that Veblen debased the major social and economic institutions of civil society, liberals are troubled by Veblen's unsparing view of politics, especially democratic politics. For many mid-twentieth-century liberals, Veblen's main weakness as a social scientist lay in failing to appreciate the democratic state's positive role in softening the edges of life in capitalist society. Considered today, what is striking about such claims is how much they assumed a degree of stability and permanence for FDR's progressive reforms, a capacity to survive that was seriously undermined by contemporary neoliberalism and neoconservatism. In this light, Veblen's respect for the resilience of conservative ideas looks appreciably more sensible today than it may have in the glory days of American liberalism half a century ago.

Whatever else one might wish to say about Veblen's liberal opponents, they surely represented the cream of the crop of twentieth-century American sociology: George Herbert Mead, Talcott Parsons, David Riesman, and Daniel Bell, among others. For these and a handful of lesser-known figures, Veblen's theory of change sorely underestimated government's ability to manage the problems of liberal capitalism. His liberal critics acknowledge that Veblenian ideas may have influenced some New Deal reformers, such notable figures as Henry Wallace and Rexford Tugwell, for instance.[28] But they argue that Veblen's basically negative attitude toward political institutions crippled his understanding of the beneficent potential of liberal democratic government, especially its capacity to apply sociological and economic expertise to political problems. For many of the major mid-twentieth-century liberals, in other words, the defense of a certain positive and instrumental view of social science and the apologetics of welfare state liberalism went hand in hand. And on this score his liberal critics were quite right: Veblen did dispute their optimism about the political uses of technical knowledge.

A guiding premise of liberal intellectuals in the past century—a tradition extending from Lester Ward and John Dewey through John Kenneth Galbraith and Daniel Patrick Moynihan—has been the belief that institutional development of social scientific knowledge in universities and research centers represented an intellectual foundation for increasingly sophisticated and effective intervention by public policy and planning in the management of social ills.[29] A rational and expansive state could, in cooperation with supportive private institutions, supervise economic and social processes with an eye to achieving decent liberal values: fairness, security, equality, responsible power, and community. American political culture reflected, after all, a strong pragmatic tradition of "empirical collectivism." Americans welcomed collective action, as long as it was widely deemed necessary and didn't extend beyond "minimal interference in the life of the community."[30]

Implicit in this view is belief in the possibility of rational insight into the emancipatory, enlightened, and functional uses of political and social power. Optimistic and enlightened reason promised major advances over the traditional bourgeois view of state power as an essentially repressive force in free societies. Politics did not have to be a zero-sum struggle of winners and losers. Enlightened power could support well-being for all. Naturally, this outlook carried significant policy implications. It also endorsed a large and creative policy role for intellectuals near the centers of power. As William Buxton has pointed out, Talcott Parsons was foremost among those thinkers who took issue with Veblen's idea of a limited social role for intellectuals.[31] Parsons claimed that the intellectual in advanced capitalist societies should give vibrant political life to the lessons of social theory. "By contributing to the cultural matrix, they could help insure the regulation of action, the continuation of the social system, and the generation of overall stability."[32] Parsons' attempt, for instance, to reconstitute and redirect the theory of social power was, in this sense, a technical expression of his deeper rationalist faith in social science and the civic mission of intellectuals. Rejecting familiar American obsessions with the dangers of power, Parsons wanted to "treat power as a *specific* mechanism operating to bring about changes in the action of other units, individual and collective, in the processes of social interaction." He identified this "mechanism" with the political "subsystem," which, with its broad "mandate of political support," and within constitutional limits, should do "what seems best."[33]

Not only may power serve social order, it can reasonably and responsibly supervise social and political change. In this sense, Parsons argued that among Veblen's greatest errors was thinking that power would likely be used more consistently to cripple the state's ability to ameliorate social and economic ills than it would be to relieve them. Veblen wrongly believed power to be "presumptively illegitimate; if people exercise considerable power, it must be because they have somehow usurped it where they had no right to it and . . . intended to use it to the detriment of others."[34] Parsons' view is in fact at odds with Veblen's positive assessments of collective or social power in the savage and handicraft eras as well as in northern European "pagan anarchy." But this point is less important at the moment than what it suggests about liberal dismay with Veblen's skepticism of reform.

Responding critically to Veblen's analysis of patriotism and the state in *The Nature of Peace*, George Herbert Mead, a colleague of Veblen's at the University of Chicago, made comparable arguments decades earlier. Like Parsons, Mead claimed that Veblen's excessively negative, repressive view of power and patriotism mistook how much these forces actually enhance and enrich the social order. In particular, Mead attributed much of Veblen's error to his underestimating how much the experience of conflict contributes to growth of individuals and to political progress. Conflict, for Mead, produced civic benefits, which Veblen simply did not consider. "Self-assertion in groups and individuals has led through rivalries, competitions, and finally cooperations to new types of individuals" and even to higher, grander forms of social union. In Mead's more robust appreciation of conflict, even war had positive functions: "at least one war in a generation was essential for the spiritual hygiene of the community."[35]

Veblen's critiques of the warfare state and business exploit signaled his failure to understand how political conflict leads to socially valuable adjustments among interests. Through sympathetic role-playing, Mead contended, including through rivalries of ambition and interest, human actors learn to appreciate and adjust to one another's needs, much as Adam Smith argued in *The Theory of Moral Sentiments*. In fact, Mead said, the organization of perspectives leading to integration and coordination of individuals' roles does not lessen freedom; it enriches and is essential to freedom. With other liberal sociologists, perhaps most notably David Riesman and Louis Schneider, Parsons and Mead indicted Veblen for not understanding how social and political differences associated with inequality and conflict actually worked to stabilize and improve American society. Veblen was disposed to see only the exploitative potential in power and conflict; he was blind to its pedagogic advantages for social cooperation and growth.

Echoing the Marxist pejorative that he was "petty bourgeois" in outlook, many liberals also reproached Veblen as a naïve libertarian or a politically immature anarchist, a kind of truculent individualist, someone incapable of adjusting himself to the political reality principle. Louis Schneider, in particular, associated Veblen with related utopian strains in Freud. Veblen's theory, like Freud's, was grounded in unrealistic, immature preferences for a society free of all social constraints, a community devoid of socialization and social structure. Veblen's theory aimed, as John Gambs also once suggested, at the complete extirpation of all relations of conflict and power.[36] Conversely, even as many liberals condemned Veblen for the political immaturity of his anarchism, some followed the critical line charted earlier by Frank Knight, who faulted Veblen's technocratic and authoritarian tendencies. In either case, critics found it exceedingly difficult to accept Veblen on his own chosen terms, which separated personal political preferences from cold analytical conclusions.

An important aspect of the budding authoritarian claim, one seconded by the Frankfurt School, is that Veblen's preoccupations with workmanship, adaptation, and instrumental rationality precluded his having a concept of what Karl Mannheim called substantive rationality.[37] That is, critics credit Veblen with understanding how human intelligence applies itself for purposes of increased mechanical efficiency. But he supposedly does not understand how reason might choose between alternative ends or values, especially when such ends conflict with one another, as they tend to in the real world of political economy. In this sense, the economists' criticism of Veblen for not explaining an alternative to the price system has its parallel in liberal criticism of Veblen for not facing up to the tragic choices facing political actors. In essence, Veblen lacks Max Weber's appreciation for an "ethic of responsibility" in political action.[38]

Daniel Bell's analysis of the Veblenian call for a "soviet of technicians" marries these charges, indicting Veblen for refusing to confront both the problem of power and that of choice. Having thoroughly attacked capitalist rule of the business system, Veblen seems only to offer a dangerous technocratic utopianism that gives no answers to imposing questions of power, direction, choice, and responsibility. Even more, insisted Bell, while it is true that Veblen's ideas were not themselves authoritarian, there were discomforting similarities between certain quasi-fascist aspects of the short-lived "technocracy" movement in America and "the qualities of inhuman scientism and formal rationalism" which bedevil Veblen's thought. Such claims mean that "in the end," as Theodore Adorno charged, Veblen's theory becomes "an attack on culture itself."[39] Bell and Louis Schneider were thus quite ready to proclaim their own "realism" and "antiutopianism," implying their own political maturity, while denying any sense of realism in the work of radicals, such as Veblen.

"Tough minded" intellectual posturing was a common trait of liberals in the late 1940s and 1950s, as it is today in liberal arguments favoring American empire as an indispensable condition of world order.[40] There is no room for utopia here, save for the curious suggestion in such notions as "the end of ideology" or, more recently, "the end of history," that U.S. corporate and state institutions define the achievable utopia, one that conforms to distinctly American values.[41] For this pattern of thinking, it is mandatory to subvert the critic's refusal to identify with the status quo, as if any hint of utopianism amounts to disqualification as a serious intellectual.[42]

Like many of his conservative critics, Veblen's liberal adversaries discovered the source of his utopianism in his biological metaphysics. Attacks on Veblen's instinct theory, along with its specific cultural association with primitive savagery, underpinned claims against his effort to disguise subjective thinking behind a mask of evolutionary theory. The result, for many readers, was a confused mixture of bad biology, utopianism, and political immaturity. Veblen could be analyzed and then dismissed, his theory serving only the cause of a futile, adolescent, apolitical naïveté. Expunge the utopian standpoint, exorcise the impossible dream of a more humane order, and it follows that existing society must be accepted as the immoveable framework of social scientific inquiry. Mature analysis begins with acceptance of power as it is.

An Apolitical Veblen?

Some of the major contours of Veblen's political significance should now be clear. They emerge unambiguously from the complaints of his diverse critics. Veblen stressed such themes as atavistic continuities in culture, the futility of religion, the irrationality and waste of the price system, the sabotage of production by absentee ownership, and the crippling of democracy by ideology and power. His conservative and liberal critics characteristically used Veblen as a foil for their defense of prevailing institutions. Conservatives, of course, warmed to a state that protects and supports free markets while encouraging a greater public role for religious institutions. Liberals, meanwhile, desired a contrary balance of state roles, urging more state regulation of markets while keeping religion and government apart.

Advocates of each position readily concede the other's presence as a legitimate partner in intellectual debate. Much of conventional democratic politics concerns their agreement to struggle over the proper boundaries of relations between market, state, culture, and religion. Indeed, the forces of science and secularism have aroused a more than trifling religious countermovement to vindicate traditional values. And this movement has successfully associated itself with the U.S. political party least diffident about its ties to American business. Consequently, the intensity of conflict has grown over issues that are, from Veblenian perspectives, bound to reinforce laggard institutions and shopworn patterns of thought.

Veblen never denied the formal democratic legitimacy of debates that echoed popular beliefs and habits of mind, however skewed such opinions might be by ideology and mystification. But beyond their contribution to reinforcing the status quo, these familiar debates held little interest for him. As far as he was concerned, conventional political disputes offered opposing arguments for mildly different versions of a maladroit and archaic political order. Although important as ongoing barriers to what he considered the demands of intelligent adaptation and change, their substance consisted of appeals to imponderables, the outcome of which only inhibited intelligent adaptation to the brute facts of material and technological life.

As John Diggins rightly stressed, this is why Veblen saw little value in studies of the internal conflicts of ordinary politics. Instead, he probed the foundations of business society. His conclusion was clear: there was no good reason to expect that the democratic state would fairly supervise the business order or uphold a socially just moral order, except in the conservative terms that business, the state, and organized religion were prepared to concede. There is, in short, hardly anything in Veblen's theory to appease the advocates of markets, defenders of religion, or proponents of state-led reforms. In essence, he opposed the central organizing institutions of American society. The ire of his mainstream critics is thus unsurprising, except for the fact that many of the bones picked with the nominally apolitical Veblen are very political bones indeed.

Radical Questions

That many left-wing intellectuals have welcomed Veblen's work is equally unsurprising. Still, radicals have proffered criticisms as bitter as any to be found on the right. But there are obvious differences. Where conventional writers concentrate on Veblen's sabotage of orthodoxy, radical critics seem most aggrieved by his explanations of history and human nature, especially the implications that follow for skepticism about the potential of subversive politics. Not much lower on the radical complaint list is Veblen's apparent turn to engineers as a force of social change. But above all, the agonizing problem that Veblen poses for the left is that while he shares its progressive values, his theory of history displays minimal faith in mass political action. The problem is not only that he assigned a potentially major political role to technical elites but that he rarely, if ever, displays hope that the working class—or "underlying population"—will struggle to improve its life through either democratic engagement or insurgency.

Veblen took democracy seriously, but he had grave doubts about its progressive promise. Probably more than any other feature of his work, his pronounced skepticism of radical politics explains Veblen's comparatively low stature in the pantheon of American radicals. For all of their historic divisions, after all, most people on the left are democratic optimists at heart. They believe in a beneficent future brought about by popular action. Progressives have thus had a hard time coming to terms with Veblen's curious blend of radicalism and realism. But Veblen's skepticism, his radical realism, is much more than a matter of temperament. It stems directly from his cultural theory. Prevailing institutions, he regularly insisted, possess an uncanny ability to retard the rationalization and secularization of consciousness, without which there is little chance for progressive political change.

History, institutions, and consciousness empower the habits of mind of the predatory past and present. These entrenched attitudes stand in the way of a more liberated future. Nor is it that a better tomorrow is precluded only by facts of history or conventionalized human nature. Human beings are smart enough to set up more-reasonable social and economic arrangements. The problem is that reason is not the ruling factor in social life that radicals wish it to be. There is simply no warrant for expecting to find in the historical process an inner logic likely to change the complicated and persistently conservative cultural dynamics of political thinking and behavior. Reason, such as it is, remains embedded in traditions and cultures of unreason.

If anything, Veblen's agnosticism about the future places heavy burdens on radicals to develop a progressive politics that can weaken the conservative grip. And they must do this while struggling to bring about a more humane society, one whose outlines they cannot really specify in advance. A crucial implication of Veblen's political skepticism, then, is to demand of those committed to social change that they work harder to identify and develop the forces of political progress from within their own situation and experience, and not to rely on abstract theoretical templates. If Veblen has any message for political activists, it is that they must search popular experience and the material, cultural situation at hand for clues to strategy and tactics. They should not look to general theories of social change. But the fact that Veblen has virtually nothing to say about strategies of ideological transformation, and that he sticks stubbornly to a focus on impediments to change, understandably heightens the frustration level of activists. Moreover, beyond his critique of teleology, Veblen further aggravates the frustration of left readers by insisting that earlier epochs of human experience really did achieve a primitive version of community, craftsmanship, and creative thought. But this savage achievement was very, very long ago.

Here then is the terribly painful ambivalence of Veblen's radical meaning. His theory claims that humanity is capable of so much more civility and reason than predatory culture permits. But it equally insists that we must never underestimate the repressive power of imbecilic institutions. Indeed, all conventional things being unequal, the forces of unreason and cultural destruction are probably more likely to win out than those of reason and sanity. In essence, then, Veblen's difficulty for the left is that he promises a better society with one hand and withdraws it with the other. Conservative and liberal orthodoxy cannot abide Veblen's radicalism; radicals abhor his realism. The master theorist of chronic dissatisfaction offers a theory that no revolutionary can ever find more than dissatisfying. Veblen's agonizing political ambiguity and equivocation exasperate the best radical minds that have read him. Consider the observations of critical theorists Theodore J. Adorno and Herbert Marcuse.

In his formidable essay on Veblen, Adorno perfectly captured the essence of radical disquiet with this most stubborn and equivocal of American critics. In language that eloquently evokes Veblen's genuinely tragic sensibility, Adorno observed that "His sad glance disavows his progressive philosophy."[43] Adorno offers penetrating criticisms of Veblen, for example, his reluctance to envision how art may protest against the "drabness of industrial rationality," or his failure to take the critique of sports far enough to envision its authoritarian and fascist implications. But perhaps the most consequential and revealing of Adorno's challenges concerns what looms as a fundamental ideological limitation of Veblen's Darwinian theory of change and adaptation. Such a theory, he argues, committed Veblen to capture by the status quo, by whatever is real, practical, and immediate in the social situation. That is, for Adorno, Veblen's radicalism was limited less by his appraisal of the power of conservative habits than by his commitment to the idea that change happens through adaptation, rather than through revolution.

To embrace adaptation as the crucial human experience of change precluded imagination of transformational changes beyond the logic of existing arrangements. Veblen's theory of change, in other words, represents a limitation of thought that ultimately exhausts the ideological and political potential of his critique. Indeed, it is this limitation that explains how Veblen can yank away the promise of liberation even as he makes the case for its necessity. Here is the source of Veblen's "unduly pessimistic and latently conservative" outlook, the very quality that Ernest Dewey cheerfully embraced as Veblen's unintended gift to conservatism.

Though hardly the most optimistic thinker himself, Adorno held that Veblen's error went beyond the mere sentiment of pessimism. His mistake reflected a deep and dangerous contraction of political thought. Darwinism led Veblen to be absorbed by the instrumental premises of existing society. Compressing reason into conformity with its own limitations, Darwinian adaptation theory precludes more sweeping projects. It thrusts empirical, technical considerations into the central preoccupation of the mind so that mind loses the critical competence to imagine something qualitatively better than what currently exists. "The less human beings think of reality in qualitative terms," Max Horkheimer once observed, "the more susceptible reality becomes to manipulation."[44]

Veblen did indeed view things just the other way, offering objections of his own to the sort of abstraction advanced by critical theory. As with his relation to Dobriansky, the gulf with Adorno runs wide and deep. As Veblen saw it, the embrace of abstract thought, as in critical theory, leads precisely in the wrong historical direction: backwards. The more that human beings incline toward intangible, abstract thinking, the more prone they become to atavistic abstractions, the very spiritual beliefs that buttress ruling class power. Habits of abstraction, he claimed, encourage reification, belief in illusory concepts that form religious and political foundations for quasi-barbaric institutions. Instead, Veblen believed, albeit with careful qualifications, that technical rationality harbored potential but by no means inevitable political benefits. Especially when facing brute, material pressures, the mind's adaptable, instrumental quality might gradually loosen the hold of outmoded or irrelevant spiritual ideas. This corrosive effect on atavistic abstraction might do much to weaken or undermine ruling class capacities to engineer consent. Ultimately, workers and consumers might actually begin to see their material interests in straightforward tangible terms.[45] In effect, for Veblen, the more politics remains abstract and elusive, the less it is likely to support adaptable, innovative, progressive mind and action. This relatively hopeful position on working class consciousness reflected Veblen's assessment in 1904, when he published *The Theory of Business Enterprise*. Later works suggest a growing pessimism however.

In the years surrounding World War I, as Veblen focused on such political institutions as the state, war, and patriotism, he tended to moderate, if not abandon, the view he expressed in *The Theory of Business Enterprise* that adaptation could be reduced to purely technical encounters between instrumental rationality and the material world.[46] Increasingly, in the later overtly political works, we see how culture, social habits of mind, and ideology unavoidably influence and contaminate the various modes of technical adaptation. For all their exposure to cold science and material reality, even engineers could not escape this social influence. Even the engineers drifted to the right.[47] The mature Veblen truly despaired of chances for imminent structural change. Exploitation, in Veblen's work, begins and develops conjointly with processes of ideological abstraction, reification, and imputation. In this sense, Veblen insists on the importance of ideology as much as the critical theorists, a fact that helps explain recent tendencies in the literature to associate Veblen with Gramsci.[48]

The Machine Process and Technical Rationality

In contrast with Adorno, Herbert Marcuse credited Veblen with offering novel critical understandings of the rationalizing effects of the machine process. For Marcuse, Veblen revealed how human adaptation and thinking now increasingly oriented and limited themselves to the cold, implacable logic of technical rationality and the industrial system. The problem was, as Marcuse explained, that such rationalization constituted mammoth new historical opportunities for the repressive forces of domination and unreason to co-opt and exploit technical thinking for their own purposes. Insofar as the powerful could claim that technical rationality itself demanded human adjustment and conformity to a mechanistically imposed reality principle, security for the status quo was confirmed by the empirical, impersonal imperatives of the machine process itself. In effect, the venerable and explicitly social principles of bourgeois ideology resting on natural rights, market rationality, the religion of work, and entrepreneurial creativity—the whole structure of the older style of class legitimation—was becoming radically desocialized. Capitalism's appropriation of technology rendered ideology objective, impersonal, a matter of functional rationality itself. Business's celebration of the machine system converted technological rationality into a new order of opaque mystifications of power. Now, "By virtue of the way it has organized its technological base," Marcuse warned, "contemporary society tends to be totalitarian."[49]

Hegel's cunning of history had indeed played a terrifying joke on Veblen's last best hope for rationality. Instead of spurring an emancipation of reason, the machine process incorporated and subordinated reason. Now it concealed from, rather than revealed to, popular consciousness the power of the vested interests.

At the same time, Marcuse also probed a significant weakness in Veblen's analysis: the tendency to confuse technical and critical rationality. For in Veblen's work, it is true, there was often no real division between technological and critical truth-values. As with his concept of "economic conscience," Veblen often compressed the two together so closely that no real qualitative distinctions were possible. On the other hand, Veblen argued that "idle curiosity" drives intelligence to seek knowledge for its own sake. With its valuation of knowledge for itself, idle curiosity is indifferent to considerations of adaptation. Thus it leaves open possibilities for the growth of noninstrumental critical capacities distinct from technical reason.[50] It is this very principle that underlies Veblen's critique of the pragmatic bent in orthodox and Marxian social science that we noted earlier, and that he associates with the critical alienation of those skeptical intellectuals, who, like Hume, are less than "gifted with a facile acceptance of the group inheritance."[51]

Furthermore, Veblen not only was mindful of the novel ideological dynamic that Marcuse later identified;[52] in ways foreign to Marcuse and critical theory, Veblen also detected human penchants to experience "revulsion against the inhumanly dispassionate sweep of the scientific quest, as well as against the ruthless fabric of technological processes."[53] In effect, Veblen's theory of spiritual holdovers left analytical space for antitechnical spiritual movements to emerge against the business organization of technical rationality. It also showed a possible reversion by business to traditional entrepreneurial rationales for capitalism, or worse, the authoritarian use of technological rationality for distinctively barbaric ends. Moreover, whereas Marcuse's theory of technical rationality is at odds with the buoyantly procapitalist, triumphantly neoliberal resurgence of recent years, not to mention resurgent religious fundamentalism, Veblen's theory of change, while not predicting such developments, understands their sources in the enduring power of archaism.

The Timid Revolutionary?

Beyond the critical theory school, many other Marxist and radical authors have commented on Veblen's relation to Marxism, socialism, and the politics of social change. Sympathetic critics such as John Hobson, Paul Sweezy, Arthur Davis, and Douglas Dowd, for example, praise Veblen for rich contributions to our knowledge of the interplay of economic and political power, the state in capitalist society, and the uses of patriotism as an instrument of class rule.[54] At the same time, many Marxists have accused Veblen of being a tentative, passive radical, even a timid one, whose work, whatever its other merits, requires the supplement of a more generous and emboldened theory of social change and political advocacy. They point to Veblen as a theorist who resists revolution and whose radical indictments lack the conviction necessary to inspire social change.

Veblen's want of revolutionary ardor is, for many leftists, partly attributable to the Dorfman-inspired image of him as the lonely iconoclast. Veblen is the eccentric social scientist whose provincial, petty bourgeois Minnesota farm background supposedly accounts for his politically naïve attraction to populist, anarchist, or radical liberal rather than socialist leanings. Paul Baran, for example—echoing an interpretation that runs from Dorfman through Adorno and Riesman, and that continues to influence as balanced a contemporary critic as Dorothy Ross—claimed that Veblen was an angry ascetic, who "resembles an embittered shopkeeper irate about his burden of taxation . . . decrying each and every kind of government spending."[55] Baran's Veblen becomes a kind of patron saint of the Tea Party!

Other Marxian critics see a more sophisticated critique emanating from Veblen, but one still marred by a case of advanced bourgeois liberalism or by a transitional location between the demise of capitalism and the rise of socialism.[56] Veblen is thus said to be a "nostalgic socialist," whose lack of a revolutionary political theory "obliged" him "to remain immured within the present," with no "clear-cut view of the future."[57] At the same time, some left critics, partly following Daniel Bell's lead but then diverging from it, have seen in Veblen's ideas an altogether too clear and disturbing vision, what Bernard Rosenberg called "the total rationalization" of society.[58] For him, Veblen wisely foresaw the emerging outlines of technocratic or bureaucratic collectivism, against which it is Marx who stands accused of utopian thinking. However, far from applauding Veblen's insight into rationalization, Rosenberg criticizes Veblen for having erred in the same way as Freud: each hoping to realize a "total rationalization" of social life and "to extirpate unreason altogether."[59] Still, relying heavily on *The Engineers and the Price System* and the analysis of administrative rationalization in *The Higher Learning*, Rosenberg concluded, "We must credit Veblen with realizing that the next step" beyond capitalism "would not be Marx's classless society, but still another class society, with its bureaucrats on top as the new men of power."[60]

Rosenberg's interpretation of Veblen as a theorist of bureaucratic power stands out in the literature for perceiving how Veblen's ideas about social change must not be confused or conflated with his political preferences. With a handful of other scholars, such as Hodder, Patsouras, and Tilman, Rosenberg maintains a dutiful separation between Veblen's anarchistic sympathies and his more dispassionate and nonteleological sense of the direction of social change.[61] This is a sense of direction that included not only fears of administrative rationalization under business control but also worries about chances for a distinctively militaristic authoritarianism rooted in the state-centric conditions of modern imperialism . . . or as we have recently learned, in responses to global terrorism.

Others on the left beside Rosenberg share the view, also found in such conservatives as Knight and Dobriansksy, that Veblen embraced technocracy and the rule of a new techno-bureaucratic class. Here we see once more the inordinate influence of *The Engineers and the Price System* in shaping political criticism of Veblen. Among the most interesting and provocative treatments along these lines is Donald Stabile's *Prophets of Order* (1984).

Capitalism, Technology, and Exploit

Like other left critics—Brian Lloyd (1997) is another, whose work we shall discuss below—Stabile accuses Veblen of an excessively limited version of radicalism. As a result, Veblen's legacy has been to poison the progressive potential of American socialism, encouraging critics to put more stock in the role of technical elites than in the potential for popular action. Indeed, for Stabile, Veblen was an influential ideological counterforce to rebellion from below, someone whose effect was to popularize technocratic and elitist theories of progressive change. Veblen muted traditional class politics in favor of a "new class" theory of political leadership by engineers. As "chief ideologue" for this new class of managers, Veblen's main political contribution to American socialism was to curtail possibilities for radicalizing working class consciousness.

Stabile is prepared to grant Veblen's "intellectual accomplishment" in "recognizing the persistence of anachronistic ideas even under the duress of economic deprivation." But he interprets this contribution as a Pyrrhic victory. According to Stabile, Veblen's ability to see the holding power of archaic ideas made it necessary for him to identify a new elite capable of leading revolution from above. Stabile described this supposed imperative as "the logical necessity of prescribing a social force that conceivably implanted a new and more worthy consciousness among members of society."[62] This agent, of course, was the engineer.

It is not clear, though, why Stabile believes that a turn to the engineers, or a quest for a politically effective force of any kind, was a "logical necessity" of Veblen's theory. Veblen repeatedly criticized teleological theories, after all. It is the "logical necessity" of a *telos* that compels theorists to identify the political agents who will make their dreams come true.[63] Besides, Veblen computed the chances of an engineers' takeover as less than slim.[64]

Stabile incorrectly imputes to Veblen a teleological need to produce an analysis favorable to his view of progress. In truth, Veblen cared much more about the dire prospects of war and economic crisis than he did about locating effective agents of political change. In any event, within Veblen's idea of social change possibilities always remain contingent and constrained. It is hard, therefore, to understand why Stabile finds within Veblen's theory a "logical necessity" to nominate a leading political force. Veblen probably made a less than savvy political decision when he wrote *The Engineers and the Price System*, but it was hardly a "logical necessity." In fact, it is the very absence of such a felt necessity toward political advocacy that makes many radicals understandably impatient with Veblen's hesitance.

On the other hand, Stabile does make a number of valuable observations about shortcomings in Veblen's understanding of the capitalist labor process, specifically the ways that capital manipulates technology to cheapen the value of labor. In conjunction with such arguments, he criticizes Veblen for failing to understand that alienation arises not only from the grip of outmoded ideas and beliefs but, as Marx suggested, from the deadening character of industrial work itself. Veblen, according to this argument, was so impressed by the liberating effects of technology and science that he did not see clearly enough how capitalists use technology to cripple the meaning and value of labor. There is much truth to this claim. Marcuse pointed the way toward it years earlier, in fact, and Harry Braverman's later research did much to substantiate it.[65]

At the same time, Stabile's presentation of Veblen's theory of alienation falls short of the understanding to be found in John Diggins' closer reading.[66] A brief look at the limits of Stabile's interpretation is a useful precursor to arguments we shall make in the next chapter on the political foundations of Veblen's theory of power. Much of that interpretation rests on Stabile's problematic treatment of the sources and character of predation in Veblen's work. As this subject forms a major theme of the present study, and specifically the next chapter, we will only outline the issue here. Suffice it to say that an understanding of Veblen's theory of the nature and origins of predatory power has to be a crucial concern for any serious interpretation of his political ideas. Stabile traverses this issue in a remarkably off-handed way. He notes simply that "On Veblen's terms the only sure way for predation to enter a peaceful society is through the operation of the instinct of idle curiosity. *At some point in pre-history some idle day-dreamer probably startled himself with the sudden insight of the predator's perennial question, why should I work if I can compel someone else to work for me.*"[67]

First, nowhere does Veblen argue, or even suggest, that predation entered history "suddenly," nor does he ever suggest that it is a product of "idle curiosity." Predation is the most instrumental of human dispositions. Hence if it has a place anywhere in Veblen's instinct theory, it belongs with the instinct of workmanship, "whose functional content is serviceability for the ends of life, whatever these ends may be."[68] In contrast, "idle curiosity," Veblen's instinctive basis for science, is utterly indifferent to purpose or utility. Its pleasure or delight comes from explanation for its own sake, the gratification that flows from knowing and understanding as ends in themselves. Technology is pragmatic; science is not.

To understand this basic distinction is already to see how the theory itself posits the problematic character of rule by engineers. Instrumental action, any purposive action inspired by the instinct of workmanship, is vulnerable to "contamination" by predominant cultural and political interests. An inquiry into the empowerment of the engineers would thus have to take up the question of the interests and values they might be expected to serve, a question of politics and power that, according to Veblen's understanding of the contingent ends of workmanship, is anything but predetermined by technical rationality. We need look no further than the preface to *The Instinct of Workmanship* to find a crucial methodological observation that explains how Veblen treats the double-sided relations of technology and culture. There he insists that claims to the importance of technology as "fundamental and definitive" in shaping social life must simultaneously—and dialectically—consider "the degree to which . . . other conventions of any given civilization in their turn react on the state of the industrial arts."[69]

Though Veblen does not explore corporate capitalist contamination of the labor-machine relationship, his theory of instrumental rationality is entirely open to such inquiry. But the problem of rule by engineers is further complicated by the historical habits of prowess, predation, and power that are so much a part of recent human experience. It is on this score that the question of the origins of predation and power demands closer scrutiny than Stabile gave it.

Roots of Predation and Power, and Waste

Veblen's explanations of the beginnings of predation, which are not always consistent and are always tentative, can be found in several important and related texts, notably *The Theory of the Leisure Class* and two important essays published a year earlier, in 1898, "The Beginnings of Ownership" and "The Instinct of Workmanship and the Irksomeness of Labor."[70] In these works, Veblen traces the origins of predation in subtle, slowly developing processes of cumulative change. He describes how primitive peoples gradually assumed the habit of imputing human features to refractory aspects of their environment. These imputations slowly gave shape to attitudes that identified conflict and mastery with appropriate strategies for confronting the unknown. Savages learned how to tame the dangers they confronted if they approached such threats with the assumption that unfamiliar forces are governed by familiar, humanlike qualities of will and purpose. As early humans projected their own willfulness onto mysterious or alien forces, they discovered new strategic possibilities for collective control and security. Assimilate the unknown to the known, and it might be controlled with predatory force and fraud.

Where they proved effective, such habits of mind gradually became customary. As they did, the altered patterns of belief worked slowly back on current understandings, feeding an increasingly more vigorous sense of individual formidability and prowess with respect to mastery of external phenomena: first nature and the spiritual mysteries of the environment; later women as the first human slaves, trophies of male power.[71] Veblen clearly identified evolution of power with a projection and perversion of humanity's teleological, purposive character. As humans infused their own sense of willfulness, purpose, and prowess into explanations of external resistance to their goals, they started to value the successful domination or conquest of oppositional wills. Exhibitions of power as a personal quality became honorable in their own right. Predation evolved, for Veblen, out of a deepening human enchantment with the capacity to exercise personal mastery over other things and people. Slowly, only after a long period of gestation and development, patterns of social approval and personal gratification meshed into habits of legitimacy and dignity that surround the possession and use of power.

Power's root, for Veblen, lies in complex, opaque evolutionary processes of reification and projection. Human abilities for effective action, which everywhere flourish and depend on communal supports, resources, knowledge, and technology, come to be interpreted culturally, politically, and narcissistically as the unique, formidable powers of individuals.[72] It is this cultural and ideological transmutation of collective powers into individual powers, this reification and enchantment of the individual as a unique agent who possessed remarkable inner endowments, which Veblen locates behind the development of predation.

This distinctively anthropological view of power must be considered in any evaluation of the "soviet of technicians" thesis. Recent debates about *The Engineers and the Price System* have focused on whether aspects of Veblen's identitification of the engineers as an agent of social change stem from earlier aspects of his work.[73] The more challenging political question, however, is how an assessment of the engineers thesis might be conditioned by an appreciation of Veblen's theory of power. This important issue has not been the focus of political studies of Veblen, however. Ben Smith well captured the problem when he observed, "The greatest failure in the interpretation of Veblenian political thought arises primarily as a result of the failure adequately to codify the conceptual components of [his] general relational scheme."[74] A familiar problem in the Veblen literature is critics' tendency to isolate individual elements from their broader theoretical context, and especially to devalue or to overlook the theory's interconnected foundations.

We have already seen how Veblen's sense of the limitations of political action is shaped by his theories of culture, institutions, and adaptation. This does not mean that critics like John Diggins are wrong to criticize Veblen's tendency to ignore social movements, class struggles, and political conflicts. For a theorist who not only took political power seriously, but who also sympathized with the aspirations of working people, Veblen's indifference to issues of mass political organization and mobilization is as maddening as it is disappointing. Veblen did a poor job of relating his assessments of the agonies of working people's lives to an understanding of how their critical sensibilities might be aroused. But then political arousal was just the kind of pragmatic step that Veblen believed he should not take. Diggins, as we saw earlier, attributes such indifference to an outlook that Veblen shares with the French Annales historians. The idea here is that history has too often been written with a "focus solely on politics," concealing "the more immobile forces of the past, *la longue durée* of unchanging customs, or what Veblen called the survival of 'archaic traits.' "[75]

Veblen did indeed complain that the role of political conflict and aggressiveness has been overstated in history, but inasmuch as exploit and predation constitute central themes of his own work, such comments are not very persuasive rejoinders to complaints about indifference to concrete political developments. Some Marxists have argued therefore that a main problem with Veblen's political analysis is a concentration on ideological superstructures at the expense of interest in how exploitation gives rise to conflicts.[76] A closely related complaint is that avoidance of immediate political struggles inured him to the potentially progressive implications of religion and patriotism, factors that can buttress the courage and solidarity of oppositional forces.[77]

But there is a big difference between legitimate charges that Veblen paid too little attention to tangible political battles and far more debatable accusations of political indifference. One finds even in the most knowing of Veblen's critics, such as Diggins, claims that "Veblen wrote almost nothing about politics and political institutions."[78] In fact, it would be fair to say that the central thrust of Veblen's whole theory is an ongoing study of contrasts between human productiveness and wasteful, abusive fetishism of power.

On the other hand, a more interesting and revealing criticism is that Veblen's analysis of exploit suffers from a diffuseness that fails adequately to understand its changing historical content, including its potential transcendence through the dialectics of revolution. Veblen's opposition to teleology and his criticisms of the Marxian dialectic explain a good part of this criticism, which often amounts more to an apology for Marx than to a strong case for rejecting evolutionary naturalism. Critics such as Paul Baran and Arthur Davis offer sound objections to Veblen's tendency to reduce history to the qualitative divide between savagery and barbarism, thus failing to develop sufficiently nuanced accounts of exploitation in its various historical guises and transformations. Veblen's imprecise account of the transition from feudalism to capitalism exemplifies this weakness. But the more basic trouble, as Marxists see it, is that Veblen tends to stress waste over exploitation as the primary human injury of irrational social arrangements.

In the following chapter we will begin our account of Veblen's politics with a look at what he understands by "exploit" and how it is governed by considerations of power as much as the lure of benefit from another's labor; indeed, the themes of power and economic exploitation as well as waste are inextricably interconnected in Veblen's version of the critique of political economy. But because Marxist critics make so much of the distinction between waste and exploit, it may be useful to preview this central connection.

From *The Theory of the Leisure Class* forward, Veblen argues that waste is harmful because it constitutes an economically unnecessary sacrifice of resources that might otherwise benefit the community. This sacrifice is made on behalf of ruling class interests in celebrations, rituals, and monuments that memorialize power, habits of conspicuous display which underlying populations learn to respect and even to mimic. A host of pressing organic human needs that might otherwise be met with some technical ease are frustrated by a siphoning of resources to meet the qualitative needs of rulers to impress others with their grandeur. In order to produce, justify, and honorifically display the invidious value of their unequal status and strength, ruling classes divert social labor and resources into ever more extravagant trappings of privilege. This interminable conversion of work and output into symbol and ceremony appeases the chronically anxious political psychology of ruling classes, for whom there will never be enough to display their intangible superiority over underlying populations.

The animating spirit of Veblen's position on the relation between waste and exploit was perhaps most directly stated by Herbert Marcuse, when he proclaimed that "the only needs that have an unqualified claim for satisfaction are the vital ones—nourishment, clothing, lodging at the attainable level of culture." Thus the crucial question, which obtrudes everywhere in Veblen's critique of existing society as well as in Marcuse's, is "How can these resources be used for the optimal development and satisfaction of individual needs and faculties with a minimum of toil and misery?"[79] Veblen's embrace of the value of "fullness of life" means nothing if not the spread of opportunities for members of the species to live a robust, fulfilling life consistent with humanity's technological capacity. Waste expresses a social power that reserves to itself, through a variety of historical institutions, including ostensibly democratic ones, the authority to establish "what may be safely done or left undone in society."[80] Most of what is legitimately "left undone," Veblen predicts, will be things necessary for the common good.

Waste is thus not distinct from exploitation. It is a key mechanism and expression of exploitation, which is the systematic subordination of the unqualified needs of human beings to live decently in order to support the highly qualified needs of ruling groups to dominate, in large part, through living conspicuously indulgent lives. There is, in short, for Veblen, no waste without exploit and no waste without a power structure of institutions that operates at the expense of "the life process taken impersonally." Marxists are surely right to demand careful examination of exploitation in any critical political theory worthy of the name. Indeed, it is precisely because his theory so piercingly analyzes the exploitative character of market and democratic institutions that defenders of these institutions take Veblen's work sufficiently seriously to tackle its claims.

Revolution, Theory, and Society

One of the harshest left-wing critiques of Veblen is also one of the most recent, a sign perhaps of the growing frustration among radicals at the recent triumph of conservatism. Brian Lloyd's *Left Out* prominently includes Veblen along with John Dewey and William James as major influences in vain efforts to wed American pragmatism to Marxian revolutionary theory, efforts that, he contends, had disastrous implications for the American left.[81] Like Stabile, Lloyd accuses Veblen of substantial intellectual responsibility for the fecklessness of American socialist politics.

But Lloyd's indictment is much less temperate than Stabile's. By robbing Marxism of its theoretical power to indict capitalism at its roots, Veblen's pragmatism helped to torpedo chances for an American variant of Leninist-style revolution.

Revealingly, Lloyd does not examine the concrete politics of working class struggle that others, including Stabile, indicted Veblen for ignoring. He concentrates on the purely theoretical errors of "positivism." Lloyd defends his preoccupation with intellectuals with a remarkable but not inaccurate observation that movements of the left in America and elsewhere have "functioned primarily as an intellectual tradition." For Lloyd, this pattern doesn't so much address radicalism's narrow political base and its limited appeal to the masses as it registers the fact that workers become revolutionary "only after making themselves the agents of a worldview that equips them to direct its course. Such mastery requires a kind of knowledge produced during most periods—our own for sure—by people not directly involved in the production of goods."[82]

Radical theory, as Lloyd presents it, requires privileged separation from tangible work. Activist intellectuals must abandon factory work for the theoretician's study. Perhaps they are the leisure class of revolution. In any event, for Lloyd, intellect becomes the site of the most intense and consequential forms of class struggle.[83] Thus his target is the main philosophical error of pragmatism, the politically debilitating effects of a positivism that can seek modification only of what is. In this sense, Lloyd reproduces arguments advanced earlier by Adorno. But he adds to Adorno's accusation of Veblen's instrumentalism new arguments against Veblen's presumed positivism and his attitude toward science, positions worth closer review.

Lloyd's point is that Veblen's positivistic notion of science led to a flawed hypothesis: exposure to the machine process would liberate worker consciousness from capture by atavistic belief. Unable honestly to confront the error of this thesis and the deeper problem of his wrongheaded positivism, Veblen slyly avoided the issue by introducing into his theory, in devious ways, an altogether nonpositivistic, hermeneutic cultural analysis of social behavior. As his hermeneutics explored the many avenues of social mediation of experience, specifically the ideological influence of prevailing canons of belief, Veblen effectively jettisoned the postulate of a direct one-to-one relationship between empirical fact and social thought.

This idea, of course, formed the core of his early prediction of machine-driven radicalization. The resulting contradiction between Veblen's avowed science and undeclared hermeneutics, argues Lloyd, accounts both for his great success as a satirist and for his poverty as a radical theorist.[84] This is an important claim but also a highly problematic one.

Veblen's understanding of science is not always precisely or lucidly expressed, and there is ample room for debate on this subject.[85] But it is reasonably clear, from a variety of statements in his methodological essays as well as from formulations found in such books as *The Instinct of Workmanship* and *The Higher Learning*, that Veblen approached science, including his own version of social science, as a highly self-conscious sociologist of knowledge. Even as he described the essence of the modern scientific outlook as an increasingly impersonal, matter-of-fact disposition to study ongoing processes of colorless change, he also never failed to remind us that this is only the *current* view of science. Other views of science prevailed in the past; different ones will emerge in the future. Clearly, science, no less than society, is enveloped by ongoing processes of change, reflecting the principle—the relativist cultural principle, it might be stressed—that "Science and the scientific point of view will vary characteristically in response to those variations in the prevalent habits of thought which constitute the sequence of cultural development. The current science and the current scientific point of view, the knowledge sought and the manner of seeking it, are a product of cultural growth."[86]

At any given moment, science, its methods, and its problems are products of cultural development; they are embedded within predominant cultural schemes and institutions. The view here is a consistent expression of the caveat noted earlier, that technological and material forces are themselves subject to counterinfluence by "other conventions" of culture. This position hardly conforms to a hard-edged, or even to a softer, positivism that claims to understand science as governed by direct, unmediated relationships between knower and known, subject and object. If science, a realm of the most self-disciplined intellectual workers, is a culturally mediated phenomenon, thoroughly enmeshed in society, industrial labor is no less exposed to the cultural mediation of experience. The industrial and mechanical workers who most directly undergo the rationalizing effects of technological processes are also products of cultural factors and powers.

They too are prey to conservative habits in their interpretations of experience, a point that Veblen never tires of making whenever he toils in the
related fields of political analysis and radical hopes. At bottom, Lloyd fails
to see that science and hermeneutics are not separate analytical maneuvers in Veblen, with the hermeneutics designed discreetly to save a flawed
positivistic political analysis.

Hermeneutics is inherent in Veblen's attempt to understand science
as a cultural product. Science is a part of the social evolutionary process,
embodying forms of knowledge that reflect the inescapable and evolving
influence of social institutions and social powers. Even economics is an
evolutionary science, or it should be, claimed Veblen. Not only in the sense
that it should study economic activity as an evolutionary process, but in the
sense that the discipline itself must change and evolve. Political science is
hardly less exempt from its cultural situation. That the evolutionary factor
has not sufficiently influenced either of these major social sciences is itself,
for Veblen, a question of the sociology of knowledge that helps to situate his
confrontation with social scientific orthodoxy and with the problem of power.

The present chapter has suggested how a look at an array of Veblen
critics from diverse ideological perspectives exposes the many political
issues implicated in his work. Questions of appropriate relations between
market and state; the very nature of the state itself; the political implications of technology; the relationship of culture and ideology; understandings of class, social change, and the possibilities of reform and revolution;
the limits and scope of human purpose and freedom—all these and other
essential political matters have been considerations more or less central to
discussions of Veblen's work.

This literature suggests something of the range and depth of the
Veblenian challenge to the presumed certainties of familiar ideological
standpoints. Veblen offers a multidimensional structure of critical social
thought, an unsparing criticism of power, war, and capitalism. This critique
is underpinned by an evolutionary naturalism that reflects the influence
not only of Darwinian science but of liberal values, a heady respect for the
power of old ideas, and a fierce insistence on putting the claims of power
to the test of incisive critical analysis.

4

THE POLITICS OF POWER AND PREDATION

Among Thorstein Veblen's most influential essays, one posed the question, "Why is economics not an evolutionary science?"[1] Veblen, of course, believed that economics should be "an evolutionary science." He struggled to make the discipline sensitive to the influence of social change on economic life. This was not an easy job. Orthodox economics resists the idea of institutional or cultural change. Most conventional economists take markets to be natural, ahistorical institutions, after all. Moreover, markets supposedly operate independently of cultural values, as long as those values support free markets. Markets reflect eternal and universal principles. Rational self-interest and exchange work anywhere. All they require is freedom for competition. Let government protect economic liberty and free markets will take care of the rest. The rules of supply and demand bring universal beneficence. Orthodox economics shows why society and state are wise to let markets follow their natural inclination toward a happy equilibrium for all concerned.

Veblen's institutionalist standpoint could not be more different. His version of economics emphasizes the interaction of social change, history, culture, and institutions. He looks at how different conditions of culture, power, and technology can alter the character and functioning of economic institutions even as those institutions manifest strong inertial tendencies. Where orthodoxy sees change as an unwelcome disturbance of natural tendencies toward equilibrium, Veblen proposes that change is the essence of social and economic life. Veblen's theory is all about the forces that provoke and retard change; orthodoxy generally ignores this problem.

In Veblen's real world of economic institutions, beneficial outcomes are likely, especially for those enjoying concentrated social power. For the less well endowed, not so much. As Veblen encapsulated the key relationship, business and government institutions regularly contaminate and distort—or "exploit"—the community's production of needed goods, its "industry." Industrial output bends toward the interests and preferences of power, not the common good.

Industry and exploit reflect fundamentally different patterns and norms of human action. But they are hardly separable. Industry and exploit—"the coercive utilization of man by man"—intersect one another throughout the political economy. They represent different sides of a more or less continuous human experience of material and cultural life. Industry is about people making useful things for the community in increasingly efficient ways. Exploit is about the ambitions of the powerful, particularly their quest for the prestige that flows from successful mastery of others. Society, through its institutions and arrangements of power, coordinates the different aims and values of industry and exploit, but only the latter's aims are socially privileged and culturally esteemed. In essence, prevailing institutions of power reconcile and adjust the workings of industry and the pressures of social change to serve the interests of exploit. Habits of industry and exploit mingle and collect throughout the social and economic structure, and government has a lot to do with their mutual development. But Veblen never lets us forget that interests in exploit and industry are very different. An economic theory that pretends to be only about industry, and that fails to grapple with the evolution of exploit, masks the darker, ugly half of human experience. Veblen's work is a constant reminder that the right hand must be called to account for the activities of the left.[2] A pretense to science is no excuse.

Veblen's essays and books delve deeply into the economic and social relationships of exploit and industry. But in the Veblen canon, there is no equally well-drawn critique of political science.[3] His theoretical perspective justifies an interrogation along comparable lines. It is also reasonable to ask, Why is political science not an evolutionary science? Indeed, as Russell

Bartley suggests, an even more pertinent question concerns the issue of why political economy as a discipline was dismembered into reductionist fields of economics, political science, and sociology.[4]

A Veblenian answer might run along the following lines. Much of conventional western political science rests on normative assumptions about human behavior drawn, as in the case of orthodox economics, from various individualistic strains of modern liberalism. Political science as we know it in the United States constituted itself with assumptions about what a supposedly normal, liberal democratic order looks like. Liberal democracy is what happens when individual citizens motivate themselves to concert and execute their political goals within a system of legally regulated institutions subject to their control.

Understandings of the larger course of global political modernization follow suit. Their foundation is a set of marketlike assumptions about the natural course of human self-interest. Consequently, political development is governed by a sequence of historical moves veering toward some semblance of the forms and procedures of western liberal democracies. And those democracies are likewise the product of a calculation of individual interests akin to those governing the market. Lift the artificial encumbrance of repressive or authoritarian rule anywhere in the world, and liberal democracy will naturally flourish along with the free, voluntary institutions of civil society. As President George W. Bush proclaimed, "these principles are right and true for all people everywhere. No nation owns these aspirations, and no nation is exempt from them."[5] So the president thought as he applied "coercive democracy" to Iraq. Intervention within markets is bad; intervention to create markets and civil society is more acceptable. Indeed, it is liberating. Overall, the appropriate division of labor among liberal institutions is nicely reflected in the structure of the social sciences. The state's main function is to protect self-regulating markets and the freely formed voluntary institutions of civil society. Political science, economics, and sociology reflect the approved ideological divisions and linkages between government, economy, and society.

In a very different way, Marxist theories of the capitalist state take class relations rather than individuals as their starting point. For all their differences with liberalism, though, Marxist theories resemble liberal political science in their embrace of a preordained order to history. Marxism, like liberal pluralism, is teleological. Liberalism invokes the utilitarian *telos* of the greatest good for the greatest number. Marxism's teleology is one of historical materialism, class struggle, and the determined route to working class emancipation. Liberal and Marxist political theorists, convinced of the truth of their starting points, arrive at conclusions about the state that tend to reflect their assumptions. They steer their modes of analysis toward a kind of self-closure. It is the same tendency that Veblen criticized in orthodox economics. The logic of that critique is no less apt for much of political science.

In fact, Veblen did take occasional methodological swipes at political science and jurisprudence, accusing them of being essentially ceremonial disciplines. But with the partial exception of his idea of the monarchical origins of the modern state system, Veblen never carefully studied, that is, in a detailed empirical way, the evolution of political institutions. *Imperial Germany and the Industrial Revolution* comes closest to being such a study, but Veblen's main focus there was on the tragic consequences of cultural lag between Prussia's militarism and its rapidly modernizing economy. On this score John Diggins is right to say that Veblen failed to take the conventional politics of government seriously enough.

Searching for the Political

Few scholars would debate the point that there is little overt political science in Veblen's writings. He would hardly disagree. On the other hand, Veblen never gave politics a complete pass in his critique of institutions. To the contrary, he sprinkled many unkind words about governments and politics throughout his writings. The following observation is fairly typical of Veblen: "All is fair in war and politics. It is a game of force and fraud. There is said to be honor among thieves, but one does not look for such a thing among statesmen."[6] But much more is involved in such bitter rebukes than a mere distaste for politics and politicians. Veblen condemned conventional politics because he believed that it was similar to other futile, conflict-based, nonproductive, predatory institutions: competitive sports, warfare, organized crime, and the system of business enterprise, for example. All these activities share a singular dedication to mutual defeat, waste, aggressive habits, and valuation of mastery. They are all part of a distinctively aggressive, conflict-centered, predatory scheme of thought and action. At bottom, they add up to a design for "exploit"— "the coercive utilization of man by man."[7] Veblen conceived of exploit and conflict as elements in a common configuration of human habit. Binding them together is an evolutionary bent, originating in barbaric cultures, toward making invidious judgmental comparisons among individuals and groups. Whether in business, sports, politics, entertainment, or even crime, the individuals and groups able to display mastery or superiority over others win the plaudits and esteem of the community and the lion's share of its material rewards. We like to pride ourselves on being civilized, Veblen suggests, but, in truth, we value conquest and triumph as much as any archaic barbarian culture. Politics grows here. It thrives in the context of the value we assign to exploit. Amidst institutions of exploit, tests of power are inevitable; conflict is to be expected, and with it, politics. These are precisely hallmarks of what classic political realism has regularly identified as distinctively political phenomena.

"All political structures use force," observed Max Weber. In the face of this coercive reality, "All politics is a struggle for power," adds Hans Morgenthau.[8] This omnipresence of force and power helps to explain why, in the words of a distinguished American political scientist, "At the root of all politics is the universal language of conflict."[9] Nietzsche's (1968) "will to power," an idea of fundamental significance for Weber and Morgenthau, creates an unbreakable human circle of domination and resistance, politics and conflict.[10]

Realism naturalizes and normalizes connections between power, conflict, politics, and human nature. In treating these phenomena as essential features of the species, realism defines their grip on human institutions as an eternal human problem. It is just this normalization of conflict that distinguishes the genus of "exploit" in Veblen. Realism makes power an inexpugnable feature of human existence. Veblen treats it as a particular, culturally shaped motivation or habit, the most conspicuous interest of barbaric cultures, the point of view that guides and shapes "the predatory phase of culture . . . when the fight has become the accredited spiritual attitude for the members of the group."[11] We will explore Veblen's specific theory of the evolution of power later in this chapter. Here we want to stress its historicity.

Only when exploitative institutions emerge from the late stages of savagery, argues Veblen, does conflict truly begin to furnish the framework for a competitive, belligerent life. With the evolution of predatory habits, people lose the savage's sense of industrial cooperation and peace. Instead, they begin to understand their life and experience as a series of competitive trials and struggles with other human beings and nature, its primary challenges and limitations governed by forces of ambition, conflict, and power. Once relations and inequities of power become decisive, the normative, desired, emulated character becomes the narcissistic, aggressive personality.[12] Only in the face of these cultural values and changes does the habitually "bellicose frame of mind—a prevalent habit of judging facts and events from the standpoint of the fight"—fully take hold.[13] With this evolution of exploit, the various *political* institutions of exploit begin to share the common feature of favoring and rewarding "coercive utilization of man by man."

Increasingly habituated to struggle within their own species as well as with others, humans come to doubt and question their common humanity. Competition clashes with community. Still, Veblen insists, we don't completely abandon a lingering sense of shared human interests and needs. Through it all, a stubborn human spirit persists. Suppressed perhaps but not suffocated, the instincts of workmanship and parental bent continue to function as its most powerful instinctive sources.[14] In the age of savagery, before barbarism made exploit seem natural, habits of industriousness and communal sensibility blended into the practicalities of everyday life. With the coming of barbarism they retreated to a seemingly unattainable moral realm, their practical significance muted by what seemed to be iron facts of power and exploit. Political communities separated themselves from one another. They accentuated their partisan solidarities and introduced ideological camouflage to mask the cynical and exploitative interests of their rulers. It is in just these respects that the political—a preoccupation with power, struggle, and conquest—appears for Veblen in any form of human activity whose main features consist of an emulative contest for mastery: war, sports, judicial combat, the sharp elbows of business competition, and, of course, struggles for power in and among states. The political in Veblen, as it stems from exploit and conflict, is a sphere of separateness, alienation, and competition. Its inherent tendencies favor war and mutual defeat, not peace and cooperation, and the forging of enmity, not the solidarity of the species.

The state is one, but by no means the only, predatory institution to emerge in human culture. Hence an adequate study of the political will encompass analysis of bellicosity and power-motivated habits wherever they emerge. Evolutionary study of the political will thus come to mean a historical study of changes in the forms, direction, and purposes of "the coercive utilization of man by man."

Coercive Utilization

To identify politics with the competitive, predatory, and coercive features of human behavior is of course hardly shocking or original. The idea that humans are naturally aggressive and lust after power is virtually emblematic of western culture. "It is held," Veblen writes, that "men are inclined to fight, not to work—that the end of action in the normal case is damage and not repair."[15] At the same time, Veblen reminds us, human beings are purposive, goal-oriented creatures; they do not act randomly or without intelligent reason, and they are not naturally sadistic. Evolution and function running together, the appeal of aggressiveness must therefore be serviceable or useful to certain human ends. People seek power over others for rational reasons, although perhaps not exclusively for rational reasons. Coercive use of others has significant economic implications, of course, as Marx showed. But Veblen wants us to see how exploit has been just as deeply engaged in cultural processes. Leading groups in many cultures enlist systems of honor, status, and prestige to infuse coercive success with spiritual and moral dignity. As Veblen stresses, the dignity and honor and social esteem, closely associated with rank and class, that people derive from exhibitions of power are typically a main motive for power seeking.

In this sense, claims to status and class honor are effectively claims to power. Dignity derives from reputations for unusual competence in the uses of power, just as the "concept of dignity, worth or honor, as applied either to persons or to conduct, is of first-rate consequence in the development of classes and class distinctions."[16] The fusion of honor, dignity, class, and power virtually defines the social structures of predatory civilization. Triumphant generals, victorious athletes, clever lawyers, daring business executives, and masterful politicians enjoy enhanced status not available to ordinary workers. The symbols of their mastery are many and various, none perhaps more expressive of these governing habits of mind than the "trophy wife." "The coercive utilization of man by man" may have well begun, after all, with the coercive utilization of woman by man.[17]

But whatever the specific evolutionary start of exploit, and the variant combinations of intimidation and guile in which it appears, when leading groups make claims to honorific power they stand for a social organization that esteems and rewards domination. Their elaborate rituals and regalia highlight and legitimize those claims. In effect, they institute *political* systems. And the thrust of it all is toward an unmistakable celebration of abilities to compel others toward action and purpose not of their own choosing.

Many of these ideas, as we have said, overlap with realist traditions in political thought. As Hans Morgenthau explained in a classic essay, Jean-Jacques Rousseau made a profound error when he said that man is born free yet finds himself everywhere in chains. Man is born in chains, observed Morgenthau, and condemned to live in them. The deeper tragedy is that he seeks to escape those chains not to become free, but to establish mastery over others. The inevitability of politics lies in the nature of human aspirations to dominate and control other human beings. These motivations affirm both the inescapability of power and the eternal conflict over its possession and use. "Man's aspiration for power," he insisted, is "not an accident of history . . . a temporary deviation from a normal state of freedom; it is an all-permeating fact which is of the very essence of human existence."[18]

In one form or another, Morgenthau's idea pervades western political thought. We can find it in Plato's Thrasymachus, in the works of St. Augustine, Machiavelli, Spinoza, Hobbes, the American framers, and Nietzsche. Veblen's analysis of the power implications of exploit follows this trail, but only as it evolved through epochs of barbaric feudalism and quasi-peaceable capitalism. Only in this qualified but still-revealing sense does Veblen's account dovetail with realism. Veblen, like the realists, posits power and its associated prestige to be decisive motivations for competition. However, and this distinction is crucial to our qualified analogy, Veblen radically differs with realism on the fundamental issue of the origins of power. His evolutionary method excludes all views of power, exploit, and conflict that make these things "the very essence of human existence."

Veblen refuses to take power lust or humanity's supposedly combative, aggressive nature for granted. He does not accept that such features are endemic to human nature. He objects to any theory of a natural drive toward power, and to any theory that marks human nature and power as essential qualities, fixed and eternal.

Above all, Veblen wants to understand, from within anthropological and hermeneutic perspectives, how and why humans learned to court reputations for power, and how and why they were attracted by its special lure in the course of their evolution as a species. This is not a question of Morgenthau's reference to a historical accident but an inquiry into the social evolution of humanity's enchantment with power. Veblen tried, in other words, to explain "why man, unlike the rest of the animal kingdom, was not content to confine himself to what life objectively requires."[19] In short, Veblen wanted to account for how power obtained its human mystique, why it is that we human beings make a fetish of power. He engages this analysis comparatively, drawing contrasts with forms of action and value that, from his evolutionary viewpoint, must have preceded the development of exploit into a full-blown cultural practice and norm. Right from the beginning, with his basic evolutionary distinction between industry and exploit, Veblen puts the nature of power into doubt. He makes it a relative rather than an absolute or essential human concept. He carefully situates power within a theory of exploit that describes its halting separation from industry. He treats power as a distinctively personalized, egoistic phenomenon that, within the confines of a specific barbaric social order, estranges itself from the value of impersonal work.

In a sense, the deepest difference between Veblen and most realists is that his evolutionary perspective treats all human phenomena from the viewpoint of the species and its life process, considered generically. Phenomena of power grow, however unwittingly at first, out of this material, economic life process. In contrast, for example, the great German realist thinker Friedrich Meinecke offers a radically different judgment of power's derivation. For him, we cannot locate the origins of humanity's quest for power in "the mere satisfaction of bare physical needs." The industrial domain of "mere technique . . . belongs to the realm of physical nature." As Meinecke adds, "That which is merely useful and necessary can never lead beyond the static technique of animals and animal communities."[20]

This industrial or, as Morgenthau described him, scientific or technological man, can tell us nothing about "political man."

Veblen refuses to draw such a sharp distinction between the industrial and the political. Instead, he posits an ongoing set of successive comparisons between two tightly related but increasingly distinctive phenomena. There is, first of all, the life process and the generic needs and capacities of the species—all those organic activities of labor and technique that most immediately function to reproduce human existence—the material realms that Meinecke and Morgenthau specifically identify with nature, industry, and science. Then there is the evolutionary fact of humanity in its gradually differentiated cultural development as a collection of disparate groups—the realists' domain of politics. For Veblen, each community will possess its own particularized version of the life process, human needs, and institutional capacities. Most will sooner or later reorganize themselves on the basis of power relations that dominate and direct industry. But power is never immune from industrial influence; technological change necessarily affects the conditions of power. Invention, as Veblen liked to say, "is the mother of necessity."[21]

For Veblen, then, power relations do not represent an analytically discrete, much less nobler human realm than the economic. Power develops out of human experience and is shaped by pressures, skills, techniques, and habits learned in the course of humanity's material or "animal" life. Veblen is dealing with what he conceives as a subtle and mutually reinforcing web of human developments, a network of closely knit industrial activity and hermeneutic experience. His view refutes familiar separations of disciplines and fields of knowledge, economics and politics, natural science and social science.

At bottom, Veblen simply is not convinced by the orthodox realist claim that there is an unfathomable mystery to human desires for power. His method—indeed his normative standpoint on the illuminating possibility of reason—urges him against such arguments as Meinecke's that humanity's "higher and lower abilities, the element of mind and the element of physical nature, can be in Man at one and the same time both causally connected and yet essentially separate," a fact that expresses "the dark mystery of life."[22] If vital elements of mind become attracted and habituated to power, this attraction cannot be left to "the dark mystery of life."

Power is too important a feature of social life to accept that some unbridge-able line of obscurity bars our comprehension of it. For Veblen, there has to be a rational explanation for our fascination with power. He believes that it can be uncovered by grappling with certain hermeneutic processes characteristic of the human mind.

Instincts, Economic Conscience, and Work

Following a Kantean lead, Veblen argues that the mind projects itself—or rather applies features of knowing that it experiences within itself—to explain its relation to the mysteries it encounters outside.[23] We can find the sources of humanity's enchantment with power, Veblen suggests, by understanding how such imputation unfolds and how it subsequently helps to remold habits and institutions. To follow this evolution, it is necessary to say a little more about Veblen's theory of the instincts and their contribution to human survival.

Psychological factors, what Veblen calls instincts, influence us through the medium of social institutions and environmental forces. But their basis is generic; they are properties of the species. Reflecting a strong Darwinian emphasis on survival, Veblen believed that most of these psychological factors evolved through natural selection.[24] The durable and self-reinforcing effects of human experience give increasingly greater weight to culture, habit, and environment in the evolving human makeup. But the basic instinctual factors in human psychology have lasting significance. These factors include instincts of workmanship, which encourage us toward useful, effective work; a parental bent that stimulates our concerns for the future well-being of children, community, and species; and an "idle curiosity," which presses us to search for conceptual, theoretical understanding of the world and its phenomena. Idle curiosity also brings the uniquely intellectual gratification of acquiring knowledge as a value in itself.

Veblen deploys his arrangement of instincts both to understand and to evaluate human behavior. His psychology is descriptive as well as normative. Insofar as the instincts support the life process, they have an empirical aspect. They explain how and why humans choose ends that maintain life. And the life in question here is more than individual life, it is social life, species life. Above all, Veblen's theory of the instincts ascribes value to the flourishing of human life in its most collective, generically human sense.

The fundamental or primary instincts enable the species to live, for it is only through collective, social efforts that individuals can have any biological chance. At the same time, the psychic trait that stimulates useful work, the "instinct of workmanship," also has firm moral implications. Beyond encouraging industry, the instinct of workmanship also gives us a generic, impersonal standpoint for considerations of economic judgment. It entails a certain moral, critical outlook on economic life.

Workmanship conceives of production in relation to skill and efficiency, to be sure. The larger biological or metabolic point of industrial skill is its contribution to satisfaction of the species' material needs. In this sense, workmanship expresses more than an industrious self. As a matter of implicit "economic conscience," it motivates us to evaluate and compare the products of labor in terms of their relative serviceability to social needs. It is this "economic conscience" that leads people in so many different cultures to abhor waste. It also can inspire us to consider the worth of economic activity "apart from any specific personal or group advantage."[25] Governed by the instinct of workmanship, "economic conscience" gives us a "test" that many of us regularly, if implicitly, use to judge and criticize wasteful patterns of production and distribution. It prompts us to ask, Does our use of resources serve "directly to enhance human life on the whole?" Do our economic choices and priorities further "the life process taken impersonally?" In a host of ways, we ask such questions all the time. When we throw back our heads in annoyance at some egregious example of government excess, or mock our neighbor's vulgar display of consumption, or lament the existence of global poverty in the face of planetary abundance, or anticipate the costs of global warming, we speak the language of economic conscience.

Veblen's point is not that "economic conscience" dominates our sense of economic life. He knows perfectly well how profoundly market institutions have encouraged us to value personalized happiness above shared need. But even the market's highly biased image of utility speaks to capital's need to find a broader social rationale for itself than mere self-interest. And even though most of us accept capitalist criteria in our economic judgments, many people still grouse about its ingrained patterns of inequality, impoverishment, waste, and injustice. These complaints speak to what Veblen suggests is our innate sensitivity to the impact of our economic action on something larger than ourselves. Even as business society has taught us to make economic choices in terms of self-interest and self-advancement, economic conscience spurs us to a nagging moral awareness of the impact our choices have on the lives and fates of others. Altruism, philanthropy, international debt forgiveness and efforts to aid remote disaster victims, and the global green movement all suggest the presence of Veblen's "economic conscience."

Economic conscience is moral and evaluative. It is also industrial, mundane, matter-of-fact, material, and profoundly social, without being, in the slightest realist sense, political. Economic conscience is not a phenomenon of power. It is the moral dimension of material life. At a fundamental level, Veblen suggests, humans can live without exploitative power. Without economic conscience, the species would perish. Nor does Veblen intend his observations about economic conscience to be taken as metaphysical speculation. He presents them as hypotheses anchored to an empirical conception of evolution and human behavior. Put squarely, for Veblen, most of the human species, for most of the time it has occupied the planet, has been busy at work. Labor is what people do directly to enhance their chances of survival. And hardworking people have an especially keen eye for waste, because it usually comes out of their economic pocket.

There is no surprise in the fact that most ordinary people, in whatever civilization, spend the preponderance of their time and energy "at work to turn things to human use."[26] They live, act, work, and feel in small productive worlds of work, clan, and village. The experience of community for most people tends to be lived and felt through more or less intimate circles and a small milieu of shared industry and workmanship. But the cumulative effects of intimate association with work and community extend beyond the pleasures of family and the parental bent. Without necessarily intending it in any conscious way, ordinary working people, in their everyday activity, enhance the life process generally. The life process is after all the work necessary to keep our metabolism going.

In contrast with the life of the workaday household and job, the drama of power politics, the intensity of political conflict, and the will to exploit are aspects of experience that if not quite alien to daily life, are for most human beings secondary and distant. Murray Edelman's observation that

"Politics is for most of us a passing parade of abstract symbols" reflects the Veblenian point that ordinary life enmeshes itself mainly in workaday industrial concerns. It unfolds close to home, in an "immediate world in which people make and do things that have directly observable consequences," not at a distance, the way power politics does. Where the absentee drama of political, military, and athletic exploit "exhausts men's energies in passionate attachments to abstract and remote symbols," life for most members of the species draws on the instincts of workmanship and parental bent to get by in the village, neighborhood, or city, with ample gratifications stemming from "planned manipulation of the environment."[27]

In light of the disproportionately small amount of time and effort devoted to predation, by a disproportionately small percentage of the human species, Veblen's evolutionary framework offers little choice but to reject a priori judgments about "political man." No doubt, "coercive utilization" of the other is an impressive feature of the human story. And habits of exploit tremendously influence the development of human productive energies and partisan human loyalties. But it is the development or growth—the *evolution*—of exploitative institutions and habits which demand explanation. The need to work is self-evident. Grasping for power is not. Power may dominate industry, but as most of humanity spends its time working to produce things rather than fighting for power, realist claims for the naturalness of power lose their force. However important aggression is to the human experience, and Veblen thinks it is very important indeed, we should be very leery of identifying it with something pervasively and generically human—until, that is, humans begin to slowly remake themselves, turning themselves into creatures of the habits of power.

In sum, acute differences separate realists' assumptions about human nature from Veblen's evolutionary approach. Still, certain commonalities are striking. Veblen's study of human institutions, especially in the post-savage epochs of barbarism and quasi-peaceable industry, shares the realists' concentrated focus on power and its workings, celebration, and human cost. There is in Veblen, as with the realists, great sensitivity to power, and especially to the psychic, political, and economic toll exacted by chronic dissatisfaction in its use. Both views carry an air of the tragic. For both Veblen and the realists, those who possess whatever passes for a given society's instruments and rewards of power seem chronically anxious, uncertain, unsure, disquieted. They are driven by insecurities, ever intent on confirming their strength and prowess with further extensions of their use. Frustration drives power even as power yields more frustration. Insecurity abounds. Even for the most celebrated among the powerful, sufficiency of power and honor seems elusive. There is never enough power. As a human motive, power seems inhabited by a ceaseless, restless pressure to guarantee its claims, vouchsafe its status, affirm its possession, and justify its necessity. The chronic dissatisfactions of power form no small part of what Morgenthau called "the all-permeating fact" of power, an energizing force of supreme importance in the dynamic of politics.

Animism and Power

The opening of The *Theory of the Leisure Class* offers a view of power that parallels realist thought. Veblen's point is to unravel the origins of "the leisure class," whose dual distinction is its ability to avoid industrial work and to be honored for doing so. However much the leisure class may have changed since it first appeared, Veblen's evolutionary method presumes that traces of its origin still bubble about in modern societies. For example, the leading groups in today's societies do many things; one thing they rarely do is physical labor. But then "All that has gone before was not lost," Veblen liked to say, and "many things were carried over."[28] So "before we can even begin to talk about overcoming" relations of power and alienation, "we need to discover where such phenomena came from in early archaic society. It was this task," as John Diggins notes, that "constituted the anthropological imperative" of Veblen's theory.[29]

Gently pruning away many layers of cultural accumulation, searching carefully back in time, Veblen reached an epoch of the "lower barbarism," where "we no longer find the leisure class in fully developed form."[30] Here, Veblen suggests, leisure and other classes seem indistinct. Social divisions are at best murky, unsettled, and vague. This is a propitious place to think about and to hypothesize—and that is all that Veblen does—the factors that probably influenced the earliest formation of social classes.

Strikingly, Veblen does not think that the leisure class began with violence, or with some kind of forcible expropriation of the many by the few. The deepest root of class division lies elsewhere, in forms of intellect and thought, of meaning and understanding, of interpretation and perception. The tendency toward class division, he supposes, started in people's efforts to understand and explain their encounters with Meinecke's "dark mystery of life." To be able to survive in it, early people needed to understand their enchanted, opaque world. Exploit and the first classes owe much of their start to a certain immature and confused development of humanity's reaching effort to know and to understand that world. The original basis of class lies in a certain way of thinking about humanity's relation to a poorly understood world.

Instincts of workmanship and idle curiosity, Veblen suggests, motivated human beings to better explain and use their world. One way they did this was to distinguish external phenomena according to their perceived sense of spirit or vitality. Some aspects of the environment seemed to be very different from human experience, as if it were made of inert, lifeless stuff. These sorts of external things lacked vibrancy or inner force. They had none of people's lively sense of will, intent, or purpose. These phenomena seemed oddly separate and apart from immediate human experience. Absent a will of their own, this brute stuff yielded sooner or later to intelligent human skill and tools. Our instinct of workmanship increasingly proved their equal.[31]

Action aimed at inert material was more or less one-sided and instrumental, the productive activity of human labor. Controlled force and intellect could turn lifeless matter into useful goods. Uneventful, quiet industry produced beneficial economic results. Perhaps savages believed that it was the absence of human spirit in such things that accounted for their conformity with human purpose. In any event, human abilities to work effectively with these relatively benign materials generally led to harmonious and productive relationships with the environment. Human industry, cooperation, nature, and peace went together. Labor was necessary, difficult surely, but not yet irksome. To the contrary, human industry moved in a world of compliant, adaptable materials.

Other features of the environment seemed rather less tractable or compliant. These did not submit so readily to human ends; they resisted human willfulness. To gain control and effective use of the resistant forces, people faced a difficult question: what caused such resistance, what was behind it? With Veblen's account of this interrogation, we encounter propositions that become fundamental to his political thought.

In essence, Veblen attempts to reconstruct the mental process early people used to understand basic questions of cause and effect as they tried to unravel the puzzle of the unyielding forces in their environment. His short answer is, they looked inside themselves to understand what was inexplicable outside. Without intending it, they nonetheless set humanity down a progressive but tragic path toward exploit, invention, and predation.

Human life is practical and active—action everywhere insinuates itself into human thought and feeling. "Man's life is activity, and as he acts, so he thinks and feels."[32] If human life is activity, its keynote is the sense of purpose that drives action. Humans are inherently prone to think and feel in goal-oriented, teleological terms. Therefore, wherever early humans found lively obstruction in the outer world, it would make sense to them to imagine that it possessed an equally inspired, humanlike willfulness. As early humans met frustration, they probably construed its sources "in the only terms that are ready to hand—the terms immediately given in his consciousness of his own actions."[33] When humans faced resistance to their ends, inner experience of their own activity—"the only terms that are ready to hand"—likely suggested that they were dealing with phenomena more or less like themselves. In essence, Veblen guesses that primitive people interpreted refractory phenomena in mimetic ways, as "animate" mirrors of their own willfulness. Something like the same spiritual forces that humans felt inside themselves seemed to inhabit the animate forces that opposed them. As such things act, so do *they* think and feel. Unlike the inert stuff, animate phenomena reflected defiant, purposive abilities that people sensed within themselves.

In a sense, Veblen observes, primitive peoples explained the mysteries of resistance by an imputation that suggested how animate phenomena are less alien but potentially more disturbing to humans than inert things. This defiant animate presence created occasions for clashes of will. Here are the first stirrings of a primal power struggle. In direct contrast with Meinecke's view—that "the striving for power is an aboriginal human impulse, which blindly snatches at everything around until it comes up against some external barriers"—Veblen holds that "aboriginal" humans probably had no interest in conquest until the appearance of "external barriers" stimulated that interest.[34] Power does not meet its limit in barriers, according to Veblen; barriers only stimulate desires for more power.

This difference in perspective has momentous consequences. It profoundly informs Veblen's anarchism, including his doubt that power holders will recognize prudential limits to their power, or that such limits can be built into reliable systems of checks and balances. Veblen suggests the motivation of power is not untamed desire, people "blindly snatching at everything around." It is the gratification that comes from breaching barriers and surpassing limits. To expect that power holders will temper their dispositions with prudence, or that they will readily defer to external checks, is excessively optimistic, even utopian. It misses the basic thrust of power to overreach. In this respect, Veblen, the anarchist sympathizer, is perhaps more realist than the realists.

At the same time, we can see how ancient animistic and anthropomorphic tendencies of mind illuminate Veblen's theory of human alienation. As humans mistake their relation with aspects of nature, they begin to misperceive their relation to society.[35] Resistance becomes understood as an invitation to use intelligence to master the other. Experience of conflict persuaded human intelligence gradually to set itself the question of how to discipline, control, and "exploit" the energy and will of obtrusive forces. The agent's animating purpose became a matter of "exploit . . . the conversion to his own ends of energies previously directed to some other end by another agent."[36] Contrary to Adorno, who claimed that Veblen opposed the waste produced by capitalism rather than its exploitation, the critique of exploit literally precedes the critique of waste in Veblen's analysis; moreover, exploit is the social and evolutionary precondition of waste.[37] Waste, after all, is largely what the leisure class does to glorify its claims to power. Far from being secondary, the analysis of exploit is fundamental to Veblen's whole theoretical assault on predation, capitalism, and politics. Exploit is the process by which an agent in a social relationship aims to capture, control, and displace for his own purposes another's ability to direct her own energies to her own ends.[38] Profoundly political implications follow.

As pursuers of dominance, exploiters seek and intend to violate another's organic spontaneity; the latter's self-generated purpose is to be denied for one's own.[39] Exploit signifies the struggle of a human will to defeat another animate being's self-generated ends. Exploit is literally predation against another's purposefulness and intentionality. It is the act of turning another's independent life force away from its goals to serve the exploiter's interests. In this sense, exploit radically attacks and subverts the very purposefulness that Veblen identifies with the human trait most essential to survival. Tragically, exploit both affirms and denies the other's powers of spontaneity and independence from hierarchical control. It is also a supremely political act, for it aims to realize Morgenthau's sense of mastery. The human experience of exploit is domination. Of course, for Veblen, humans' earliest experience of such power was inspired by opaque relationships with animate nature, not with other human beings, but that changed soon enough, when male warriors first took female captives as slaves to signify their exploitative prowess.[40] The key point is that primitive and illusory relationships with the animate world gave slow birth to new mental abilities, to strategic thought, to force and fraud as techniques of dominance, to control and exploit. These would become for predatory culture the skills worthy of the highest honor, praise, and dignity.

As a classic instance of cumulative causation, Veblen tells us that the experience, habits, and rewards of exploit imperceptibly built on themselves. Gradually, successful exploit laid foundations for what would evolve into an unmistakably different experience than people found in industrial activity. This is the anthropological root of increasingly wide invidious distinctions between industry and exploit. It is also the beginning of industry's submission to exploit. Industry, after all, dealt with lifeless, spiritless materials, objects with no notable capacity to offend human purpose. Industry lacked drama and intensity. Of course, whatever industry lacked in these experiences it more than made up for in its productivity. But the fact remained that industry could not arouse much emotional tension or psychic strain. It lacked the excitement stimulated by sharp encounters of clashing wills. Industry was matter-of-fact, dispassionate, and cool. Industry was sober. It inspired none of the acute nervous stimulation created by the hovering about of occult forces, magical spirits, and willful challenge.[41] Exploit possessed all of these aspects of drama and intensity. It sparked human interest and drew human praise.[42]

Exploit placed experience in theatrical, tension-ridden, political contexts. It suited the creation of audience and applause. Because it put humans face to face with something like themselves, Veblen suggests that acts of exploit seemed to touch human beings in especially stimulating ways, to enliven their consciousness in intimately human ways. Because we can put ourselves in its place and sympathize with that obstructive other, we can imagine its purposefulness, anticipate its strategies, and act to defeat them. In observing and honoring exploit, we recognize something aggressive at work in ourselves that we are willing to project against others who are like ourselves. The target of exploit is an opponent, a rival. But that rival is a curiously familiar enemy; he is a replica of the aggressor, and shares the most distinctive features of the aggressor's purposive humanity. The exploited other is one whose identity with the predatory self is the very condition of exploitation. Veblen proposes that his dialectic of exploitative sympathy best explains why humans evolved from conquerors of nature to become masters of their own species.

Perhaps, then, if he is right, it was not really alienation, a feeling of strangeness—or difference and enmity—that favored the evolution of power and politics. Instead, it may well have been a kind of implicit, imputed sense of false familiarity and recognition, a certain sympathetic miscomprehension of the spirit of obtrusive things that led the way to the political and to our embrace of it. If this is so, politics has its roots in very ancient and profound misunderstandings of how the world works, a sort of anthropological wrong turn with momentous significance. For it was belief in the stimulating presence and obstinate recalcitrance of animate phenomena that inspired human proficiency to aim at improved techniques of "coercive utilization." Better tools made exploit more efficient. But it was not technological change that defined the beginnings of barbarism. "The substantial difference between the peaceable and the predatory phase of culture is a spiritual difference, not a mechanical one."[43]

Primitive forms of sympathy and projection spawned a new spirit of combative engagement that also inspired passions of estrangement and alienation. This peculiar dialectic explains, for Veblen, how humans could enter, despite their economic conscience, into conflict-ridden relationships with each other, how they could turn their mysterious world into a political domain of intrigue, strategy, deception, and gamesmanship.

As humans act, so do they think and feel. In activity of predation and exploit, primitive peoples acted, thought, and felt as if they were dealing with phenomena most like themselves; they thought, acted, and felt as members of a singular but divided community of others, a kind of proto-political community of warring communities. In short, Veblen suggests, as they began slowly to inhabit relations and activities of exploit, and as such habits began slowly to inhabit them, humans began a long historical acquaintance with their emerging political, predatory selves. In all this, Veblen clearly distinguishes between what we might call the material or objective conditions for the full-blown development of predatory culture, and the alteration in the human spirit that led to humanity's enduring interest in the personal qualities associated with power.

Materially, the onset of predatory culture required sufficient economic and technical means to produce a wealth surplus, "a margin worth fighting for." Tools, technology, and especially weapons must have developed "to make man a formidable animal."[44] But material progress by itself did not change peaceable savagery into warlike barbarism. "The substantial difference" in the emergence of a new human order was again "a spiritual difference," a difference in the way that humans interpreted and calibrated value among themselves. It was a difference in the personal qualities, talents, and skills they came to admire and to emulate.

Gradually, the community came to value and honor skills of exploit over the diligence people showed in producing useful goods. Perhaps grudgingly, people learned to associate honorific acts with impressive "assertion of the strong hand." With this, "the predatory phase of culture is attained." In Veblen's words, "Under this common-sense barbarian appreciation of worth or honor, the taking of life—the killing of formidable competitors, whether brute or human—is honorable in the highest degree. And this high office of slaughter, as an expression of the slayer's prepotence, casts a glamour of worth over every act of slaughter and over all the tools and accessories of the act. Arms are honorable, and the use of them, even in seeking the life of the meanest creatures of the fields, becomes a honorific employment."[45]

As far as Veblen is concerned, the combative human personality that realism erroneously presumed to be natural only now changed into a "human nature" fit for the fight. Indeed, now that "the predatory attitude has become the habitual and accredited spiritual attitude for the members of the group, when the fight has become the dominant note in the current theory of life (and) the common-sense appreciation of men and things has come to be an appreciation with a view to combat," we can see how uniquely personal and spiritual claims to power—Max Weber's concept of charisma, for example—are rooted in very ancient predatory understandings.[46]

As Weber explains, the most telling aspect of charismatic leadership is the followers' imputation of "supernatural, superhuman, or at least exceptional powers or qualities" to the charismatic leader. "It is recognition on the part of those subject to authority which is decisive for the validity of charisma." Charisma, he warns, must not be understood sociologically as intrinsic to the leader's being or person. Imputation, action, and results are crucial to the political relation of charismatic authority, and they exist in the eyes of its beholders. "If proof and success elude the leader . . . if he appears deserted by his god or his magical or heroic powers, above all, if his leadership fails to benefit his followers, it is likely that his charismatic authority will disappear."[47]

What Weber called charisma appears in Veblen as an ideology of "the strong hand," in its most perfected, most personalized and spiritualized form. In effect, Veblen gives us an anthropological account of how predatory culture leads to social, political, and psychological conditions that underpin possibilities for charisma. The followers, or, in Veblen's terms, "the underlying population," slowly learn to identify with virtues of power and to embrace and honor them. It is this popular identification that enables the appeal of charisma.

The evolution of exploit, with its various versions of predatory legitimation, including the charismatic, increasingly absorbed human relations in institutions and networks of power, emulation, prestige, and wasteful display. Thus it is Veblen's focus on the power, or *political*, aspects of economic life that underpins his critique of business enterprise as the master predatory institution of the twentieth century. Absentee ownership, after all, is but a contemporary expression for much older patterns of exploit. It is the way contemporary rulers do what rulers have long done: establish a "legitimate channel by which the community's surplus product [is] drained off and consumed, to the greater spiritual comfort of all parties concerned."[48]

The matter of the community's "spiritual comfort" is no small thing. For sustaining exploit, nothing is more convenient or important than an ideology to afford the exploited "spiritual comfort" with the going order. The adoration and mystification of power contributes one part of that ideology; no doubt, for Veblen, the most vital part. But beyond enchant-ment of strength for its own sake, Veblen sees a politically useful comple-ment in the idea of the "irksomeness of labor." This ancient notion imputes to ordinary people a deep-seated, indeed a natural, aversion to labor. Labor, after all, is intrinsically burdensome and loathsome. It is a harsh, repulsive, and undignified necessity, whose biological imperative must be imposed on workers. To perform this political task is the lot of rulers and managers. Veblen's critique of this idea is a defining, crucial aspect of his analysis of power. It is also a major clue to his analysis of savage political forms, what might be termed Veblen's quasi-anarchistic bent. To repudiate the idea of the "irksomeness of labor" after all is to open the possibility that ordinary people are capable of making their own way without absentee direction.

5

SAVAGERY AND ITS ANARCHISTIC LEGACIES

Industry and Anarchy

Peaceable, quasi-anarchistic institutions flourish, suggested Veblen, when circumstances allow people relatively easily to follow their instinctive bents toward workmanship, curiosity, and altruism. Such conditions probably exist to some extent in all social orders, so everything depends on just how freely savage habits can develop without major contamination or distortion by predatory institutions. Savagery will have its best chances, therefore, in communities that distribute control of resources, tools, and technical knowledge widely and directly among the population. Veblen believed that left alone, without political direction from on high, people tend to work, unobtrusively, with and for one another. They routinely perform daily tasks necessary to keep their community going. The apologetics of power notwithstanding, ordinary people do not need to be reminded or commanded to work in order to live.

By far the most important corollary of these conditions concerns the character or quality of social control itself. As more or less voluntary collaborations of small, peaceful, industrial populations, savage communities have minimal governments at best, with very little in the way of formal political authority. They rely mainly on noncoercive, implicit social controls to achieve order. Legal and economic coercion are in abeyance. Such communities do regulate behavior. No less than other communities, industrious communities have to keep recalcitrant members in line. But their small scale and cultural support for labor allow generally peaceable habits to flourish. Because most people orient themselves to mundane work, with a spiritual life that celebrates production and fertility, they can use more or less informal arrangements and norms to preserve order and accomplish needed work. In other words, they provide order through collective and individual patterns of self-government, guided by informal but vivid pressures for conformity.

The Theory of the Leisure Class offers the best-known Veblenian sketch of savagery, with its most conspicuous feature the absence of class hierarchy and exploit. In humanity's earliest days the mystique of power and the force of ambition are largely absent, although he acknowledges that "some fighting" probably occurred, probably on account of "sexual competition." But a "bellicose frame of mind" did not yet provide the organizing framework of social life.[1] Instead, savage communities comprised "small groups," with simple, nonviolent, and roughly egalitarian social structures. Ordinarily they were sedentary, peaceful, and poor: "individual ownership is not a dominant feature of their economic system."[2] Above all, savage communities were industrial in outlook. Their members valued work as the primary social responsibility. In effect, labor formed the population's common and reciprocal bond, their universal obligation. If, as Veblen insisted, every coherent form of culture has a "certain characteristic tone or bias," the "bias" that "runs through the whole" of savagery obligated everyone to do his or her share to enhance the well-being and fullness of life of the group as a whole.[3] In other words, when human beings lived in communities that relaxed pressures of ambition and aspiration for invidious honor, people busied themselves with useful work. Peace could prevail without politics. But humanity's spiritual and intellectual endowments also helped. Governed by instinctive proclivities to work, and by the parental bent's orientation to care for children and the future, savage communities valued industry over conflict. And their idle curiosity led them to work up schemes of myth, ritual, and belief that assimilated spiritual values to productive ones.[4] In this sense, Veblen's notion of savagery shows he could imagine possibilities for a kind of harmonious coexistence of industrial and religious values. In all these ways, savagery was a cultural and spiritual configuration suited to the biological and social perpetuation of the human organism.

The organic basis of human life, after all, is work, which is why most members of the species, according to Veblen, "have almost everywhere, in their daily life, been at work to turn things to human account."[5] But the character and social meaning of work have, of course, changed historically—in economic, technical, and political terms. For Veblen, the most radical change by far was a fundamental transvaluation of the social and ideological meaning of work itself. Under the impetus of barbaric culture, when exploit and predation came into their own, industrial work—"effort that goes to create a new thing"—lost much of its status, indeed its very dignity. In effect, leisure classes presided over a thoroughgoing shift in the discourse, and the ideological value, of labor. People once regarded work as a perfectly reasonable and necessary feature of life; with barbarism they came to see it as obnoxious, a human burden, onerous, irksome, and undignified. Labor became an activity to be shunned, not embraced. Only then, Veblen suggests, did the desire for power realize its perfected rationale.

Irksome Labor as Rationale of Power

Under barbaric conditions, as exploit and predation became honorific, the new ruling strata gradually detached dignity from felt human needs to work. They reoriented or redeployed the meanings of good repute away from labor toward yearnings for freedom from work. In essence, they achieved something truly remarkable. They inaugurated a spread of cultural values that set human beings *against* the dictates of the life process, against nature and the necessities of survival. For by celebrating and honoring their own class exemption from work, they also established the value of immunity from direct contact with nature as a productive force. Honor flowed toward those most able to extricate themselves from—and to command from a distance—the industrial life process, those able to shelter and estrange themselves from its compelling bio-economic force.

Only with this evolution and its resulting transvaluation of habits and values, Veblen argues, does the most essential consequence of power become economic exploit, the ability to make others work for one's keep, to reap where one does not sow, to convert others' energies to production of one's own life process. Once this species-altering evolution occurs, self-organization of work becomes conceptually and ideologically impossible.

A whole new set of negative cultural values stands between the call of the life process and standards of social honor. Organic connections between work and life suffer an irreparable rupture. Now, in effect, predatory society separates and estranges what nature once united, the values of life and the imperatives of work. Work will now be mediated and contradicted by novel understandings of human nature, conceptions that turn the valuation of life process on its head. These ideological changes made power seem more natural and imperative than work.

Once predatory class structures establish themselves, cultural common sense favors the seemingly obvious idea that work is onerous and repulsive. People learn that "man instinctively revolts at effort that goes to supply the means of life."[6] Left alone, according to the now legitimate barbaric view, people will strive to avoid work. All things being equal, people will try to escape biological imperatives to labor. This gradually prevailing common sense became a truism.[7] But it is one that on examination confronts us with an existential contradiction: "men desire above all things to get the goods produced by labor and to avoid the labor by which things are produced."[8] This contradiction leads inexorably, under the sway of barbarism, to claims for the necessity and worth of power. For if people shun work while valuing its product, exploit looms as the obvious solution: take what others make. As barbarism makes work seem inherently irksome, the community develops needs for a system of power to enforce duties to labor. It rewards whoever has the power to make others do what is necessary. Barbarism enforces a new social order that confers prestige and status upon those able to lay claim to what others make.

Veblen points out that if such claims were true, one of two pernicious outcomes must follow, at least at the beginning. Either the labor-averse could not survive, or they must be led to exploit others' industry. Suicide by dint of indolence, or a lawless culture of rapine, power, and theft—for primitive communities, these are the irrational and unjust choices facing work-averse, power-hungry people. Of course, there *is* a third option: barbaric society can legitimize rapine, seizure, and theft through spiritual and political means. That is precisely the path Veblen sees leading from savagery to barbarism.

According to this perverse but entirely legitimate barbarian logic, where people left to themselves must choose between death or theft, it stands to reason that some humans must compel others to work. Power's claim is that it makes us abide by requirements of the life process that we would otherwise prefer to ignore. Political institutions arise ostensibly to insure that men and women do their work. Driven by their indolent and foolish nature to avoid doing what is necessary, such people need the lash and force of other men, and their powerful institutions, to realize their natural needs. Hierarchy becomes necessary to complement and complete nature's weakly felt imperatives.

The laborious necessity of the life process, far from being natural and spontaneous in its imperative, must be culturally imposed by agencies of power. The barbarian rationalizes this power by insisting that most humans will act purposefully against their own interest. Power justifies itself because it does the economically necessary thing: it reunites nature, work, and man. The division of labor and the coercion of labor fuse. Power and force become indispensable conditions of socially necessary work. This is the basic political economic expression of the exploit whose anthropological and psychological motivations we examined earlier. Traces of this argument about the natural irksomeness of human labor can be found in the whole literature of western political theory, running the gamut from Plato to Hobbes all the way to such contemporary critics of the welfare state as Edward Banfield, Charles Murray, and Lawrence Mead.[9]

Veblen's *political* theory is a systematic assault on the premise of onerous labor. It is a sustained attack on the ideology of irksome labor and the coercive power imperatives to which it leads. Of course, if it were true that humans naturally tend to evade work, "then the trail of the Edenic serpent should be plain to all men."[10] The most grievous original sin would be indolence. But if so, humans would then truly stand alone in the animal kingdom: the only species whose members are so congenitally irrational as to be incapable of spontaneously understanding and satisfying the terms of their own survival. For in no other species can we find examples of a similar "aversion" to life-sustaining action. From an evolutionary standpoint, insists Veblen, such a premise is absurd. There is simply "no chance for survival of a species gifted with such an aversion to the furtherance of its own life process."[11]

In light of his critique of "irksome labor," anarchistic savagery looks profoundly more reasonable and biologically sensible. Its benign correlation between workmanship and freedom from coercion conforms to what Veblen thinks nature and human biology demand of us—that we work in order to live. This pattern is absolutely fundamental to Veblen's political thought. Where communities widely value work, individuals will readily or instinctively move toward their work. As a result, the main ideological, cultural props for coercive power lose their force.[12] In these conditions, which Veblen sees replicated in forms as diverse as primitive agrarian matriarchies, Scandinavian pagan anarchy, and the handicraft era in England, coercive power weakens and recedes. Such cases suggest that when major institutions inveigh less against labor's indignity, when people can more easily express their instinctive, spontaneous inclinations toward work, freedom grows and peace prevails.

Maternal Anarchy

It is unfortunate that many readers draw their impressions of his concept of savagery exclusively from *The Theory of the Leisure Class*. Other Veblen texts furnish more-vivid and nuanced accounts of savagery. These descriptions frequently convey more detail and observation and, especially in the case of pagan anarchy, are more sensitive to the mix and blend of savagery's varied institutions. *The Instinct of Workmanship*, for example, offers a surer, more-detailed source for grasping Veblen's conception of the savage. Whereas he gave a preliminary, indeed, one might even say, a cursory, look at savage economics in *Leisure Class*, the later work delivers more-sustained and elaborate reflections. He imbues it there much more noticeably with considerations of gender and ecology, and the relevant politics more than hint at anarchy. Especially by contemporary standards of green and feminist politics, the whole discussion is steeped in political meaning.

In *The Instinct of Workmanship*, Veblen presents savage institutions as noticeably more gendered, as distinctively matriarchal. Women's sympathetic and magical nurturance of plants and animals, he argues, underlies their special role and influence, materially and spiritually. Here primitive savagery connotes something like a communal, feminist ecology, one based on cooperative, noncoercive relations of production. The relevant chapter, which Veblen calls "Contamination of Instincts in Primitive Technology," offers an intriguing tension. First Veblen paints a convivial portrait of maternal industry. But he couples this image with a salient observation that cuts in a less positive direction. Primarily agricultural, savage matriarchy rested on kindly human relations with an animate and giving nature. This harmony nicely sustained the community's relation with benevolent nature, but it also inhibited or curtailed further technological development. This is because, according to Veblen, the development of sympathetic, spiritual connections with fertile animals and plants did not call for much skill in the way of tool making. There was no large economic barrier that invited the growth of technical prowess or power. The impersonal outlook required for mechanical invention did not flourish here. Other benign economic skills proved to be more valuable in this environment.

Agricultural industry represented a qualitatively different enterprise than mechanical invention. Led by women, early agriculture denoted impressive technical skills in its own right, a level of economic sophistication that developed more rapidly than progress in brute mechanics. And while its harmonious blend of feminine guidance, animistic magic, and ecological cooperation could take humans only so far in a mechanical sense, the cultural, political, and ecological institutions of matriarchal savagery were remarkably civilized. The model illustrates impressive institutional balance: ecology, industry, peace, and female leadership blend smoothly to further goals of collective well-being and fullness of life, at least within the constraint of limited mechanical knowledge. But then the prevailing culture was not yet much contaminated by predation, male domination, emulation, and war, the great stimuli of technology.

"What men" and women "can do easily is what they do habitually," said Veblen.[13] And from readings of the available research into primitive cultures, he concluded that early human intelligence, which is to say substantially female intelligence, found it easiest to work with nature rather than to challenge it to a fight. Women discovered that being helpful to the livelihood of plants and animals, the "wordless others" in the neighborhood, was peculiarly conducive to communal good. Experience taught that caring, nurturing relationships with plants and animals, ministrations comparable to those of human mothers for their children, brought valuable returns in production. Putting themselves in the place of wordless others in order better to understand the possibilities of their "joint life," female farmers developed a kind of anarchistic maternal ecology, one which stood them well in economic terms. Sympathetic animism favored reciprocity, cooperation, and productivity.

It must have seemed reasonable to early women farmers, Veblen speculates, that when dealt with benignly, the speechless neighbors that formed the immediate locale of plant and animal life would repay the kindly efforts of their human helpers.[14] Increase, fertility, and affection flowed best in two directions. Where hunters prowl the land in search of prey to kill, farmers till the land and nurture its fields and plants to promote fecundity and growth. Early agriculture is about mutuality; hunting is about domination.

Kropotkin described a similar kind of ecological reciprocity; he called it the system of "mutual aid." As it thrived in nature, so did mutual aid serve human beings as a reasonable principle of cooperative self-government.[15] Matriarchal savagery showed that, given appropriate conditions, humans could fashion ways to live and work together without hurting each other, or nature. They had it within themselves to "live and let live." And in this savage ecological context, "live and let live" did not mean the mutual indifference characteristic of liberal laissez-faire. Here it implies obligations of mutual support and sustenance within and between species: humans, plants, and animals laboring to support the life process of the whole. "Live and let live" here suggests something of what we would today consider the fundamental principal of ecological balance. In the savage context, it implies symbiotic reciprocity of giving and receiving, complementary connections through which both human speakers and wordless others reproduce their lives. Live and let live here means mutual aid and cooperation, not self-help. In this animistic symmetry of women and nature, plants and animals gave willingly of their energies, suggests Veblen, because their ends and purposes meshed with those of their nurturers. The shared end in view is livelihood, and there need be no competition about that goal. The difference with Veblen's concept of exploit is clear. With exploit, the predator turns the others' energies away from self-directed purposes; he converts them to his own. Resistance and struggle ensue. Politics emerges. In savage agriculture, the farmer's ends of living and growth support and reinforce the prolonged fertility of soil and animals. The latter are indispensable to the farmer's own good, even as the farmer nourishes fertility among the wordless others. There is no question here of a radical shifting or displacement of ends. Ends converge and reinforce each other. Relationships take the form of reciprocity and fluidity; recalcitrance and resistance have no place.

Russell Bartley and Sylvia Yoneda write eloquently of this central aspect of Veblen's thought, linking it "to that of his contemporaries John Muir and John Burroughs, as well as to the views of later figures like poet/paleontologist Loren Eiseley, conservationist Aldo Leopold, Norwegian ecophilosopher Arne Naess, and entomologist Edward Wilson—renegade voices of humility who return the human species to its proper condition of oneness with other life forms within a delicately balanced, finely woven ecological web."[16] In striking ways, Veblen's writing on the female centricity of savagery also anticipates aspects of contemporary ecofeminism. Like many of today's ecofeminists, he argues for "the intrinsic worth of . . . species, the intelligence of all life," and perhaps most especially, in an anarchistic sense, "the self-organizational capacity of beings."[17] Ecofeminism not only celebrates womanhood, after all. It proposes the idea of "a unique female closeness to, and alliance with, nature and the earth."[18]

For Veblen's savage females, as for contemporary ecofeminists, nature works spontaneously according to its own fertile logic. This is a logic "often wiser" than that of men, a logic that naturally fecund women are more inclined than their mates to grasp sympathetically. Understood in these animistic terms, nature and women bond in relationships of special symbiotic compatibility. Nature, it seems, responds to the living example of careful nurture, because nurture flows with spontaneous and understandable energies of organic life. Nature is, in a sense, the partner of humans, but not their student. Agriculture and husbandry are matters of "imitative propriety." Involved here is a kind of noninvidious emulation or mimesis in which pedagogic mastery or command has no place. In Veblen's words, "these subtler ways of influencing events are especially to the point in all contact with these non-human sentient beings, since they are speechless and must therefore in the main be led by living example rather than precept and expostulation." "All that is worthwhile, humanly speaking," flows from "motherhood," Veblen once observed.[19] This warmly voiced maternalism, a chief expression of the parental bent, offers provocative clues to Veblen's understanding and appreciation of savage institutions and to his broader political outlook.

Insofar as savage cultures exhibited noncoercive, collaborative governance, we can see, however dimly, the outlines of a prepredatory concept of politics in Veblen, one removed from unbalanced equations of politics and power. Notably, for this model, Veblen does not accentuate differences between guidance and leadership. The kind of maternal example that he describes for the relation of farmers and plants suggests just the kind of nurturing leadership that may be most suitable to quasi-anarchistic schemes. This is precisely leadership by example, sympathetic guidance that unfolds in the day-to-day activity of agricultural work. In effect, cooperative relations with nature blend into cooperative human relationships. They become a model for social organization: natural forces and human institutions pulling in common directions of collaborative self-governance. As the life process and organic work come naturally to each, force is superfluous. Moreover, because women seem imbued with magical powers of creativity and productiveness, the legitimacy of their role is intrinsic to their immediate economic function. Women's guidance signals intrinsic spiritual and material value, their "work-womanship."[20] At even deeper levels, the community's valuation of motherhood also reflects free play and mutual reinforcement of parental and industrious attitudes.[21] There is nothing here of the predatory debasement of labor.

Veblen self-consciously drew his portrait of maternal anarchy in contrast with Hobbes's image of human conflict in "the state of nature." He also took on the prevalent biological view of his own time, which held that "evolution had conferred selective advantage upon groups who were naturally pugnacious, internally cohesive, and who practiced genocide against competitors."[22] Against Hobbes's view of individuals as anxious fighting men, Veblen answered, as we have seen, that culture and institutions cannot be explained by individual psychological dispositions, or reduced to them. Individuals everywhere live amid institutions, and they tend to follow ingrained habits of institutional action and thought. This reality makes it difficult at best to isolate human motives and behavior from the influence of prevailing social biases and understandings. This, of course, is the main Veblenian criticism of hedonistic theories.[23]

As for the militant biology of his own day, Veblen read the growing anthropological record as lacking support for the natural violence hypothesis. Available studies showed little evidence of weapon-rich primitive cultures. Archeological digs suggested that savage communities earned their keep with simple technologies and hard work. Thus they probably avoided constant bickering with their neighbors, especially where the latter lacked wealth sufficient in size and portability to make raids worthwhile. This is not to say that fighting and conflicts were unknown in savagery. Nasty differences might arise on any number of matters; savages were human beings, after all, with "quite as many . . . economic failings as virtues."[24] Furthermore, savage communities often existed in isolation from one another, sometimes in a state of "estrangement." In these respects, savages were not necessarily "at one with their instinctual nature."[25] Clearly, processes of mystification and alienation were already gestating in savage life.

But the key issue is not whether savages ever became aggressive or fought with one another. The main question is whether canons of conflict influenced the main bias or tone of savage culture. The issue is whether proclivities to conflict were vital elements in that "degree of solidarity . . . mutual support and reinforcement among the several lines of habitual activity" that comprised their scheme of life.[26] It is on this score that Veblen believed the anthropological evidence was wanting. In essence, savage political economy does not appear to have depended on or to have valued violence. The most one might say is that predation, to the extent it existed, was culturally subordinate to cooperation. Just as, in the opposite sense for today's pecuniary culture, we tend to rank cooperative values and achievements below competitive ones in esteem and reward.[27] Again, some primitive communities may have made war on others. But the more belligerent savages inclined to the economic extremes. Either they were exceptionally productive, so that, as work pressures receded, power motives could ascend, or they were exceptionally poor, and disposed by their own material failure to project responsibility for economic defeat onto neighbors they saw as "alien and unnaturally cruel."[28]

One additional point is worth noting about Veblen's matriarchal savagery thesis. And that concerns Veblen's strong emphasis on the intimate association of economic and spiritual factors. There are revealing implications here for Veblen's concept of human nature as well as for his idea of the inseparability of economic and cultural phenomena. That people do not live by bread alone, he was fully prepared to admit; nor are human values simply determined by economic interests. Fullness of life was a robust concept, and its implications enclosed more than a full belly. Even the value of usefulness has about it a "quasi-aesthetic sense."[29]

The larger point, Veblen suggests, is that people are inclined to look to ulterior or ultimate values to impart spiritual significance to their everyday activity. They aspire to place some intangible, symbolic significance on their works, including virtues and values that reach beyond temporal and material worlds.[30] Humans make their economic life in response to a wide range of sensibilities and purposes. There are bountiful opportunities for predatory mystification and ideological manipulation in the longings of the human spirit, a point central to Veblen's critique of politics.[31] This is the profound historical defect of humanity's spiritual bent. Yet Veblen clearly opposed tendencies in western thought to distinguish between reason and passion, the material and the spiritual, nature and culture, tangible and immaterial phenomena. Our "spiritual nature" encourages us to inosculate, or blend, the material, spiritual, and aesthetic aspects of activity. Veblen's references in *The Theory of the Leisure Class* to "fullness of life" speak to the power of humanity's spiritual and aesthetic sensibilities and their relationship to generic well-being. His critique of pecuniary culture is in crucial ways a critique from precisely this point of view. It demonstrates how the market aborts potential fullness of human living, everywhere reducing qualitative values, including aesthetic and spiritual values, to monetary terms. John Diggings hit the point squarely when he wrote that "The ultimate problem" of what we might call Veblen's political economics "is not production . . . not how goods come to be made but how they take on meaning," or value.[32] These meanings will vary with the length and breadth of cultural diversity and historical developments, including variations and complications of instinctive contamination, environmental pressure, and human institutions, all of which together influence "the spiritual nature of the race."[33]

All told, we have a view of savagery here that is both complex and mediated in character, something a good deal short of utopia. With one qualification, "it would be more accurate," Edgell says, "to note that he provided a balanced account of this era."[34] The qualification concerns gender, and it touches on several delicate issues.

First, Veblen is curiously silent on the place of men in matriarchal savagery. Within agricultural communities, whose economic fate rested in the kindly hands of women, what did men do? Did they make such tools as the women needed; did they clean, cook, build, and repair shelters, help in the fields, or teach the young? Were honorific differences in dignity and status attached to matriarchy? Or did savage men manifest essentially the same benign and sympathetic features as women? And then there is that term "essentially." Even as he anticipates aspects of today's ecofeminism, Veblen is, with ecofeminists, vulnerable to the charge of "essentializing" women. His rhapsodic account of maternal savagery may go too far. It smacks of reducing women to qualities associated with childbirth and parenting. The obvious problem is that, perversely, identification of women with unique talents for nurturance and family responsibility can legitimate their exclusion from power.[35] We might press this argument even harder.

Some might interpret Veblen's celebration of maternal animism to indicate that he believed women are less likely to succeed in industrial and technical fields, which demand colder, impersonal, nonanimistic dispositions. Veblen did say that matriarchal agriculture lagged in mechanical progress, after all. Harvard University's recent president was hardly rebuked by women scientists, among other groups, for even stating the hypothesis that women may be less fit than men for scientific work. Indeed, the controversy ultimately cost Lawrence Summers his job.[36]

It is easier to imagine a Veblenian response, albeit an imperfect one, to the second charge than the first. Silence on the role of men in matriarchal savagery is simply inexplicable. We have a right to expect Veblen to say something about the men. Indeed, we would probably have a clearer idea of Veblen's notion of generic human nature if we could see how he understood the male savage in matriarchal society. Veblen's failure to examine or to theorize about the male role in maternal social orders bespeaks a major weakness in his concept. But it also reflects Veblen's characteristic reluctance to explore the full dimensions of a crucial idea. However, the omission may also shed light on Veblen's difficulty in conceptualizing the role and character of men outside predatory contexts. This feature of his work reinforces our suspicions of essentialism in Veblen's handling of gender.

The issue of gender essentialism is indeed provocative. Throughout his work Veblen argued that women are, if anything, disproportionately "endowed with . . . the instinct of workmanship." They are, he insists, especially prone to think ill of futile effort and wasteful expenditure.[37] Only in the face of enormous cultural pressure from predatory men and institutions did women, specifically leisure class women, become vicarious consumers in a social stage-play designed to gratify male sensibilities.

The social power and conditioning needed to establish gender inequality not only robbed women of the fullness of their potential contribution to economic life but also violated their deepest and most humane potential to enhance the community's life. The fact that men have so thoroughly barred women from developing their potential for creative work suggests that females have borne the heaviest brunt of civilization. The deprivation in Veblenian terms has been staggering, for "The impulse is perhaps stronger upon the woman than upon the man to live her own life in her own way and to enter the industrial process of the community at something nearer than the second remove."[38]

Consistent with his view, Veblen heard the rallying calls of contemporary feminism as "Work" and "Emancipation," principles integrated precisely by their common subversion of male power and the social disparagement of labor.[39] In an evolutionary sense, Veblen seems to suggest, the master-less woman actually appears earlier than her male counterpart. In the face of innumerable fighting cultures, however, it has taken her millennia just to get to the point of even broaching the question of her emancipation, including rights to work with the whole complement of her intellectual faculties. The implications for Veblen's sense of women's technical capacity should be evident. If maternal animism was useful to early agriculture, this serviceability signals the benefit of that habit only within limited circumstances. The claim says nothing about the inadequacy of women to perform advanced technological work. Veblen's sense of women's unusual endowment of "workmanship" points just the other way. That "she must unfold her life activity in response to the direct, unmediated stimuli of the economic environment with which she is in contact" makes her fitness for technical and scientific work axiomatic.[40]

Still, the issue of essentialism remains. It is not empirically or logically clear whether, or why, women would have been unusually gifted in an industrial sense. And then, does it follow that men have equally dispropor-tionate tendencies toward sportsmanship and aggression? Again, Veblen's painful silence on men's role in savage matriarchy only adds to the puzzle. What is more certain is that Veblen does understand men to take the lead in pagan anarchy and the handicraft era, later quasi-savage forms that share the high valuation placed on work by matriarchal savagery, but that also show the heavy trace of established barbaric traits.

Pagan Anarchy

Veblen's interest in what he called "the pagan anarchy" stemmed from his inquiry into the case of German authoritarianism. An application of his genetic method, chapter 2 of *Imperial Germany and the Industrial Revolution* considers "the remote ancestry of the North Europeans," beginning with "the earlier neolithic stone age," the earliest period for which "certain evidence" exists.[41] This material, enriched by an unusually long "supplementary note," furnishes abundant detail on Veblen's view of prefeudal economic, cultural, and political life among the Baltic peoples. It is important to remember, though, that his main point in this study is to explain the peculiar pattern of German industrial modernization: the late coming of feudalism to Northern Europe, its thrashing of pagan anarchy, and the long endurance of feudal institutions and predatory habits in Germany, especially Prussia. For Veblen, the vigor of barbaric institutions explained both the lateness of German industrialization and, once begun, its aggressive leadership by the state.

Germany's militaristic authoritarianism was, of course, a major factor in the first world war, but the whole pattern of authoritarian modernization under state leadership intrigued Veblen intellectually because it challenged his theoretical expectations. British industrialization confirmed his expected links between technical rationalization, secularization, liberty, limited government, and peace. German industrialization reflected the imperatives and leadership of a warfare state. Britain became a quasi-peaceable nation, with a constrained, relatively democratic state; German development only enhanced Prussian militarism. Clearly, there is no single logic of modernization or capitalist development. In England, weakened feudal institutions encouraged the spread of workmanship, handicraft industry, masterless men, and a revival of quasi-savage norms of peace. Just as Veblen would expect, as aristocratic power ebbed, workmanship thrived, and democracy and capitalism developed slowly and organically. In Germany, feudal institutions held on. There was no comparable relapse away from domination. Predatory elites repressed pagan workmanship and creativity. Exploit prevailed and industry stagnated, until German warlords used state power to mobilize private economic forces for belligerent ends.[42]

Indeed, Veblen was impressed by the compatibility of some features of German culture with the imperatives of scientific and industrial development. He noticed the presence of certain liberal elements in German society, the substantial role of women in the workforce, for example. He also recognized that German authoritarianism was itself politically limited or curtailed in some ways: its ruling class had to make definite compromises with popular interests. Moreover, the Prussian ruling class did not completely destroy the old pagan industrial habits. German politics was one-sided to be sure, but not wholly so. German politics and society had nuances and contradictions that Veblen did not ignore.

Most important for our purposes, the fact that the German state propelled national industrialization stimulated Veblen for the first time in his scholarly life to take a fresh look at the subject of political institutions. As he considered political influences in economic modernization, Veblen worked from the perspective of his familiar intellectual habit of considering modern developments in light of savage origins and institutions, but with this difference. As his organizing intellectual preoccupations converged on explanations of evolving forms of the state, his point-of-view in respect to savagery also became more politically focused. He returned to descriptions of savagery, but in ways that sharpened his analysis of its diverse forms, habits, and institutions, as well as their problematic survival and evolution.

Several issues are at stake here. First, in *Imperial Germany* Veblen begins to offer a subtler, more finely grained interpretation of savage politics. As his point of view shifted toward specific understandings of dynastic states and the conditions of twentieth-century warfare, perhaps Veblen felt compelled to clarify political distinctions between savagery and barbarism. In other words, we can read this later, more explicit discussion of savage politics as an effort to render more acute the implications of the modern state, industrialization, and mass politics, especially for values of peace, democracy, and responsibility.

Second, with *Imperial Germany*, Veblen takes the study of savage politics out of the realm of "prehistory." Now he begins more often to stress contrasts between prefeudal and feudal experience as a decisive factor in political evolution. In other words, Veblen writes less of "prehistory" and more about prefeudal political forms. His overarching point is that quasi-savage political forms lingered in the interstices of the fragmented and disorganized post-Roman world, while barbarism was associated with the growth of feudalism.

His concept of pagan anarchy draws from admittedly fragmentary evidence of Stone Age Baltic communities, along with later expressions of that once-prevalent culture in prefeudal northern European villages. Veblen also draws considerably from Scandinavian and Danish materials to portray a distinctively mixed, hybrid, and polyglot culture. Its technical basis and social ethos suggested "a relatively advanced savagery," while its unequal social relations hinted at a "relatively low stage of barbarism."[43]

Third, throughout his later works, Veblen adapted or modified his original notion of savagery, adding political meaning to the concept as the cultures he dealt with became more overtly political. If the savage reappears, it is only in an evolved and altered form, mediated by barbaric experience and context. Values and institutions that he once identified with prepolitical savagery Veblen now connected much more explicitly with anarchistic and democratic political arrangements, with institutions that surface in precapitalist as well as capitalist societies. The very category of "pagan anarchism" indicates a sharper political focus, just as ideas like "the masterless man" and "natural rights" attest to the politically liberal character of "the handicraft era." In this respect, Theodore Adorno is only partly right to say that Veblen always desired "resurrection of the most ancient" habits.[44] Veblen's later discussions of quasi-savage institutions point to their contemporary relevance, especially as elements of savagery assumed more explicitly democratic expression. But he never claimed such developments were part of a definitive movement back to noncoercive habits of savagery. Such an ahistorical, anachronistic stance is completely alien to Veblen.

Finally, it is notable that as Veblen turned to more recent forms of savagery, the roles of both technology and men loom large. Veblen never abandoned his feminist dispositions, but he was now dealing with savage forms after the onset of barbarism. Male dominance, the logic of the fight, and technical progress were definitive features of social life. Men took center stage as the main historical actors in politics, led by "the masterless man" of the early modern era, and the political framework of their action owes much to the technical foundation of their world.

In addition to gender, the most striking differences between maternal savagery and pagan anarchy lie in their material and cultural biases. Pagan anarchy anticipates main features of the handicraft era. For one thing, it embraces political habits and institutions whose scope and character fall in line with the workaday habits and small scale of a community that uses simple manual tools. Agriculture remains predominant, but now the emphasis moves away from animist imputation as an economic value to greater reliance on impersonal tools and inert materials, such as stone and wood. From economic and technical standpoints, the community draws its keep from a petty industrial form of production. Limited scale, reliance on manual labor, and close personal contacts afford the material basis for a loosely regulated, quasi-anarchistic industrial community.

As we have seen before, Veblen claimed that work with hand tools and inert material stimulates, although it does not directly cause, impersonal outlooks and skeptical sensibilities. This tendency is the persistent theme of Veblen's reflection on pagan anarchy. As the culture leans on industry, animistic and anthropomorphic tendencies are attenuated. They do not disappear by any means. Spiritual life goes on. But men are keener now to adapt tools more impersonally to the composition of their materials. Patterns of matter-of-fact industrial insight take firmer hold. Their object is less an animistic spirit than the cold hard features of inanimate material. Consciousness follows this lead: it too becomes somewhat colder and harder, more materialistic.[45]

Small technical scale underpins an intimate and comparatively loose circle of tools and socioeconomic relations. Individuals can place their own peculiar stamps on the life and activity of their community. With technological simplicity and face-to-face economic relations prevailing, "the substantial fact" of anarchic community becomes "the personal force and temper of the human individual."[46] Within such arrangements, the individual as craftsman begins to have a substantial meaning for himself and for the community. He is not an instrument of others, because he directly owns and uses small instruments. Working by hand insures "personal contact through the senses."[47] Even before the masterless man appears, Veblen's pagan anarchists carve new niches for individual creativity, filling out and enriching life's prospects. And definite political implications once again follow.

Communities founded on simple hand tools limit social distance, enhancing opportunities for responsible social relations.[48] It is easier in close quarters for individuals to judge others' intentions with the tangible evidence of "their hands" rather than with what, in more distant relationships, turns out to be the illusory evidence of "their eyes."[49] Elites, of course, can hold mass unrest at bay with the aid of fabricated images and slogans. Veblen agreed with the classical republicans on this point.[50] But he splits from them on the relative importance of political and technical scale. Classical republicans always held that small geographic scale is crucial for the intimate civic virtues of popular government to flourish. To be genuine civic communities, republics must be no larger than city-states. In contrast Veblen argued that the size of political units is not enough to promote civic action. Nor does small scale have to inhibit absentee power or exploit.[51]

In the language of political science, Veblen identified political scale as a dependent variable and technological scale as the independent one. As Franz Neumann summarized the basic generalization, "The higher the state of technological development, the greater the concentration of political power."[52] We can count Veblen among that group of modern social theorists, including Saint Simon, Weber, and Michels, who insisted that organizational principles given by technology influenced the scale and power of political institutions. To what extent, though, might unequal social relations modify the anarchic implications of small tools? This is an important question, to which Veblen gives a surprising answer.

Though Veblen found evidence of substantial social stratification in the Baltic anarchies, these inequalities lasted a long time within the anarchistic scheme before gradually giving way to feudalism. Here we can see the brunt of Veblen's thesis: stability of small-scale industrial patterns reinforced anarchistic habits and institutions, despite the existence of social and economic inequality. Veblen's discussion of prefeudal Baltic community is a highly qualified description of a mixed social form, a collection of seemingly unlike and oddly fitting institutions that enjoyed real staying power. Though free and roughly equal farmers provided most of the agricultural labor, the community expected all able-bodied men and women to work. And it included slaves and semi-free farmers as well as a gentry class that owned greater estates. There were even traces of kingship. Social relationships were thus notably differentiated, though probably not by tribe or clan. And while ties of kinship probably resembled those of modern European families, Veblen admits that it is difficult to know the exact significance of prevailing social distinctions. The place and function of pagan monarchy is especially mysterious.

Later, in the Viking era, Veblen suggests that pagan kingship followed the centralizing patterns typical of late feudal Europe. But before that, it appears to have been "an indispensable factor in the social fabric" but of "slighter material consequence." In other words, the early kings were probably ceremonial leaders. The office may originally have been "loosely elective," subject to a "tolerant consent" by "popular choice," though it apparently evolved in ways that narrowed the scope of popular choice to members of the royal family. These early kings may have also enjoyed priestly or quasi-priestly functions, adding some kind of religious sanction or legitimation, for example, to the convening of popular assemblies. But the crown possessed "little in the way of legislative authority and no police power" beyond its own personal resources and lands, which it enjoyed under rules of tenure comparable to those of freeholders. "Perhaps," Veblen concludes, "the only semblance of political or civil power that can confidently be imputed to him—apart from cases of forceful personality—is his presumptive leadership in times of war, defensive or offensive."[53] In short, the early pagan monarchy, somewhat like the present British version, coexisted with institutions of popular self-governance. Its war functions aside, the crown seemed more a symbolic than a materially powerful political institution. And it was close enough to the free class of working farmers to prevent its becoming an autonomous executive body.

Much the same is true for religion. A pagan cult bound members of the community in some kind of joint faith, including "traces of coercion" in religious obligation, but the church, such as it was, featured "no appreciable hierarchical organization and no great degree of coercive organization." Indeed, the relatively loose and informal character of religious institutions paralleled the fluid patterns of civic life and local self-government in general. Each reflected a "conventionally systemized anarchy regulated by common sense." It was all in all a pretty loose-fitting regime of local self-government. Most of the effective social control flowed not from government as such but from mutual surveillance and self-regulation by neighbors, who were bound by consensus on appropriate ways of thinking and acting. Steady close contact, Veblen says, invited "a certain (effective) solidarity of neighborhood sentiment on all matters touching the conditions of life of the group."[54]

Sharing close spatial, social, and economic contacts and a common language, the inhabitants of pagan anarchistic communities evolved "an effectually homogeneous culture." Out of the common norms and habits of such a culture emerged spontaneous, self-generated, and direct forms of social power. Responsibility was not a specialized legal function whose imperatives were directed by impersonal law. Responsibility grew, as it did in matriarchal savagery, out of the consensus, the immediacy and directness of social relations, and a social structure based on small-scale technology. Control emanated from implicit understandings of appropriate action but also from the compelling force of social consensus to keep people living and working in approved directions. These rudimentary and mainly informal controls provided the functional equivalent of "a legal system" that prescribed any number of "specific and even minute, provisions of law covering all conjectures likely to arise in such a society."[55]

At the same time, for all its informality, pagan anarchy was considerably less communal than primitive savagery. Peasants and farmers living near the Baltic coast lived quasi-separate or distinct lives. Subtle forces of individuation operated, and gender changes probably had a lot to do with this shift. Pagan anarchy, after all, is a postpredatory institution, reflecting a "relatively low" but noticeably barbaric stage; men have already assumed cultural predominance, and the idea of the fight increasingly shaped local canons of conduct. It may be slight by comparison with today's institutions, but pagan life incurred a somewhat more coercive tone than that of earlier savagery.[56]

Watchful neighbors offered useful reminders of rules, expectations, and boundaries, much as in Richard Sennett's model of urban self-regulation.[57] Given such cues, Veblen suggests that interests in privacy and self-regulation reflected sensible libertarian adjustments toward a policy of "live and let live," although here the phrase has much more libertarian resonance than the ecological significance it enjoyed in matriarchal savagery. Indeed, it is just in this context of fragile balance between communal and private dispositions that Veblen introduces for the first time the crucial notion of a "spirit of insubordination."

Veblen had never mentioned this insolent spirit before, and he provides no self-consciously theoretical or methodological explanation for its appearance here. This cantankerous new political factor emerges as a kind of sui generis political influence in culture. Its sources are painfully vague and inchoate. Once again, Veblen introduces a potentially rich and important political idea, but without conceptual rigor. We can only speculate that a focus on pagan politics may have led Veblen to reflect on the root sources of opposition to dynastic and other forms of irresponsible power. Closer study of the state, especially an authoritarian state, may have suggested to him a need to theorize about progressive possibilities in political conflict that earlier he could set aside. As forces of resistance often accompany the acquiescent tendencies of mass politics, even in dynastic states, the politics of opposition needs explaining. To fill in this important conceptual blank, we can suggest—but no more than that—the following kind of Veblenian argument.

People accustomed to a loose-fitting anarchistic form of life might well be unhappy with some pressures to conform to certain social norms. Self-directed labor is, after all, conducive to feelings of freedom. It is reasonably clear, for example, that Veblen does not regard insubordination as an instinct; he introduces it as part of the culturally evolved habit pattern of pagan anarchy. It seems therefore to be more a spiritual expression of the independence inherent in peasant handicraft, reflecting habits of self-dependence, self-guidance, and autonomy in everyday work life. As Veblen put it, "the spirit of insubordination" is "the vital spirit" of the system of "local self-government," the animating impulse behind the libertarian sense of "live and let live."[58] That Veblen believed humans have a "spiritual" dimension is, of course, a point we have already established; we have also seen that he understood women to possess an especially keen "impulse . . . to live life in her own way." It seems reasonable to assume that Veblen believed men have similar dispositions, and especially so after the canons of conflict are solidly established. It is not difficult to see how strong feelings of self-protectiveness might develop as an "appropriate sentiment" in connection with the primacy of pagan workmanship.[59] According to this logic, an insubordinate spirit perhaps gathered its strength from people's workaday experience of autonomy, a specific form of their second nature that developed in relation to the material and cultural context of pagan life, "the material surroundings . . . state of the industrial arts . . . and neighborhood management by common sense" through which men and women now earned their living. Such an argument makes sense in Veblenian terms. But, again, he does not advance it explicitly.

Strengthening this view of the spirit of insubordination is the fact that community members seemed prepared to tolerate considerable individual eccentricity and idiosyncrasy among their neighbors. Social control was, therefore, not only compatible with a measure of independence and resistance, but it may have actually encouraged assertions of difference—insubordination—a readiness to defy what some, perhaps eccentric, individuals might regard as unreasonable bids to limit socially inconsequential personal behavior. As Veblen put it, "individual idiosyncrasy runs free so long as its bearing on the common good is indifferent."[60]

For Veblen, the pagan anarchist's standard of communal necessity is the same as it was in maternal savagery: service to the community's material needs.[61] Presumably, pagan anarchists felt that they were entitled to sanction or punish acts taken against the community's economic good. Or as Weber wrote, in rural communities, "neighborhood is brotherhood," but only "in an unpathetic, primarily economic sense."[62] So, when untoward behavior threatened collective material interests, Veblen indicates that offending individuals fell "under the corrective intervention of common sense as soon as it swells to such excess as to stir the neighborhood into action."[63] The applicable force here is communal or public opinion, not separate institutions of legalized coercion and police power. "It is characteristic of this archaic system of justice that no public authority and no legally concerted action ordinarily is called in to redress grievances." The community exacts its own "reprisal" against offenders, its "right" to do so inherent in its character as Weber's "economic brotherhood."[64] The resulting repression is targeted, informal, democratic, and powerful.

Against such reprisals, offenders seemed to have little recourse, though Veblen is characteristically vague about informal limits to collective control or to individual insubordination. He offers no suggestions concerning what may have been the appropriate benchmarks, guidelines, or limits of control, though he adds that regulation was not completely informal. There was a somewhat more formalized political power too. Much of that institutionalized political power, he says, was vested in a "popular assembly" of free farmers, including perhaps, he suggests, some of the women. Mainly a "deliberative body," the assembly probably exercised legislative, executive, and judicial powers. Perhaps it also served as a court of appeals, but it is impossible to say for sure. The crucial point is that relationships between the strong assembly and weak monarchy precluded the existence of a separate organ of executive power. There was no state apart from the community.

Neither body—assembly or king—had a "police power" that existed apart from "established conventions" and norms. There was neither a "conception of a 'king's peace,' outside the king's farmyard, nor any idea of a 'public peace' to be enforced by public authority of any kind, outside the precincts of the popular assembly."[65] Pagan anarchy was a form of direct "democratic government, the executive power of which is in abeyance," or, in other words, an "anarchy qualified by the common sense of a deliberative assembly that exerts no coercive control."[66] So, protopolitical democratic institutions existed in pagan anarchy, but they were subordinate to normative regulation by collective "common sense."

Given the inevitable strains and conflicts that arise in social relationships, Veblen's assurance that the assembly exerted "no coercive control" is unconvincing. For one thing, the very fact that slavery existed implies a use of physical force about whose organization and administration he is silent. Moreover, repressive power can very effectively be expressed through normative consensus.[67] Those who violate communal norms and become targets of public condemnation know all too well the coercive effects of public stigmatism. It is still a matter of keeping the recalcitrant in line. Public dishonor and loss of respect in small communities can have more than mildly unpleasant punitive effects. Long before Foucault taught us about the acute economic efficiency of knowledge/power, liberals like Madison, Mill, and Tocqueville warned of the spiritual harms arising from conformist pressures. Indeed, Plato did too, in *The Apology*.

Even more to the point, in her analysis of the social politics of late nineteenth-century German villages, the most direct inheritors of Veblen's anarchistic traditions, historian Margaret Anderson charted the highly repressive consequences of neighborly surveillance. Penalties for nonconformity abounded, including not only ostracism but loss of shelter and employment too. Studies of such small German communities in the Nazi era yield even more cause for concern when it comes to repression of the individual. "Conformity," after all, "may be as powerful a force as authority."[68]

As Veblen is the keenest of writers when it comes to appreciating the psychic effects of lost esteem, it is both surprising and troubling that he avoided the coercive implications of obedience to "common sense." When he discussed the social force of anarchistic arrangements, his usual skepticism of the politics of esteem failed him. Perhaps this is but another indication of Veblen's anarchistic sympathies. It is still a serious weakness in his political thought.

The Politics of Handicraft

Political writers have not paid much attention to Veblen's ideas about pagan anarchy or the spirit of insubordination. Maybe that is because Veblen tucked most of his argument away in a lengthy footnote at the end of *Imperial Germany*. Yet for Veblen himself these ideas were of more than antiquarian interest. Later generations of northern Europeans, he suggests, remain strongly wedded to pagan anarchy's felicitous blend of community and freedom, work and civic life. Europeans have, after all, "been restlessly casting back for some workable compromise that would permit their ideal of 'local self-government' by neighborly common sense to live somehow in the shadow of that large-scale coercive rule that killed it."[69] Consider, for example, the current state of popular opposition to the European Union's central administration in Brussels.[70]

In contrast to pagan anarchy, Veblen's concept of the "era of handicraft" has been subject to far more analysis, though the prevailing tendency among scholars is to stress its role in Veblen's economic theory of capitalist development. The economic focus is reasonable but too limited. Considered in light of Veblen's remarks on earlier anarchistic forms, the "era of handicraft" has specific political importance as part of what he treats as a discontinuous but hardy tradition of local self-government. Furthermore, aided by the concept of a "spirit of insubordination," the politics of the handicraft era helps to clarify Veblen's understanding of liberalism and capitalist democracy. It also affords us a decided urban contrast with one of Veblen's ripest images, the rip-roaring speculation of the American country town.

Veblen's treatment of "the handicraft era" resembles his discussion of pagan anarchy in several respects, just as it does such related anarchistic concepts as maternal savagery and indeed savagery writ large. Like its "cogeners," "the handicraft era" points to a revival of cultural biases favorable to "peace and industry, in which direct and detailed manual work assumes a leading place."[71] In essence, material changes and technical improvements associated with the late medieval era—changes that were accentuated by new increments of wealth, population, trade, and peace—gradually undermined the coercive rule of feudalism. These changed economic conditions also gave vent to considerable political opposition and insubordination. Roughly extending from the fourteenth or fifteenth through the eighteenth century in Europe, a period covering the decline of feudalism, the rise of the nation-state, and the emergence of industrial capitalism, the handicraft era shaped western culture generally, but especially its political and legal ideas down to the current day. Indeed it is the resilient but increasingly misplaced currency of those ideas which, as much as any other factor, make understanding of this period an indispensable element of Veblen's critique of "ostensible democracy."

The master ideas of the handicraft era became the master ideas of liberal democracy, but they also stayed around to become ideological props of mature capitalism and its system of absentee ownership. But once upon a time, for Veblen, these ideas were not so misplaced; they provided more or less accurate representations of the material, philosophic, and civil life of their time. It is in these terms of relevance and material adequacy that we should understand the politics of the handicraft era.

To appreciate this new era of liberalizing urban politics, we have to understand how it reflected a very specific and unique combination of individual and collective forces. That is, in his explanation of these emerging petty industrial institutions, we see Veblen attempting, perhaps more transparently than anywhere else, to balance in a politically meaningful way the formative effects of cumulative material circumstances and human agency. And he tries to achieve this balance on both individual and collective levels. Most important, now the free human being really begins to take center stage in cultural development. For in the handicraft era, one striking fact stands out above all others. It begins with nothing less than deliberate acts of self-emancipation: the self-liberation of feudal peasants from the grip of irresponsible authority.

"The point should be kept in mind," Veblen emphasizes, that "the beginnings" of the handicraft era did not just unfold in impersonal or brute mechanical ways. Those beginnings were "made" subjectively by "masterless men," that is, by men who freed themselves by acts of deliberate insubordination. Rebels by flight, they abandoned "the arbitrary power of the landed interest" for an illicit life on the move.[72] Evoking the infamous language of the U.S. Supreme Court's Dred Scott decision, Veblen speaks of these masterless men as akin to runaway slaves, as beings who, in conventional terms of repute, "possessed no ratable human value and no rights which honest folks were bound to respect." In contemporary class terms, Veblen suggests, they might best be thought of as forerunners of the Industrial Workers of the World, or Wobblies: drifters and hobos, recalcitrant vagabonds, the rootless unemployed, who, shortly after Veblen's own death, Woody Guthrie would memorialize in songs of Depression-era wayfaring men.[73]

Cumulative historical forces created material conditions for the handicraft era, but rebellious people created the new era of freedom by their action. Insubordinate through and through, and empowered by a "tenacious assertion" of liberty, these rebels were anything but aimless.[74] Their purpose was clear: to work; to build with their own hands and tools a robust life of serviceable labor; to earn their own keep in their own industrious way; and to own, use, and dispose of their property as they wished. These were aspirations generously supported by the economic conditions of their time, but they were above all human aspirations to live and let live.

These "masterless men" enlivened a vigorous and radical new individualism. Liberal philosophers, such as John Locke, vindicated their claims to political emancipation, "honest industry," "natural rights," and a novel system of civil government based on impersonal law.[75] Locke may have erred in universalizing and naturalizing the experience of a particular group and the epoch of their ascendancy. But he did so, Veblen suggests, with a keen feel for the reigning historical motives of industry, property, freedom, and self-government.

And government was very important indeed to these masterless men. For while they freed themselves through flight, they did not wander the back roads or evade civilization; they did not form "primitive hordes"; nor were they like Hobbes's fearful and insecure men.[76] They drifted purposefully toward urban life, back to the possibility of self-governing community. And they came in such numbers, and with such substantial economic effect, that soon they assumed political control of handicraft or industrial towns. The politics they fashioned was both roughly democratic and class based. Propelled by their rebellious movement and material effect, these industrious wanderers "made good in time their claim to stand as a class apart, a class of ungraded free men among whom self-help and individual workmanlike efficiency were the accepted grounds of repute and livelihood."[77]

Veblen does not closely analyze the specific features of this new urban class politics. But he does identify it as a specifically "class tradition of initiative and democratic autonomy." Handicraft towns engendered a local class politics that empowered a new urban leadership that functioned through craft guilds and city councils, and that bound itself together "with a jealous eye to the common material interests at home and a stiff defense to the outside."[78] So, even as they struggled to liberate themselves from rural aristocracy, the "masterless men" advanced their civic cause with the aid of "that trained sense of partisan solidarity which the factional struggles of feudalism and the devout intolerance of the Church had already ground into the moral tissues of Christendom." These partisan legacies would have even more telling consequences for the emergent nation-state.[79] But there is a more urgent point here.

Veblen stresses how the handicraft era's urban liberalism promoted belief in the harmony of private claims and class power. For masterless men of the city, collective political power to shape municipal government in the interest of private property was the civic heart of a new individualistic economic order. In effect, the business functions of local government were ideologically settled *before* the nation-state became indelibly capitalist. The power of this nascent business class, derived in large part through its control of municipal government, endowed the workmanship and livelihood ethos of masterless men with shared ideological meaning; its diffusion supported, legitimated, and helped to consolidate their bid for urban political power.

Handicraft urbanism meant that the masterless men, as self-employed, self-directed workers and property owners, were indeed a body of substantial citizens, archetypical possessors of the economic means of democratic citizenship. But while this substantial citizenship was a category whose de facto content would gradually slip away, emptied by the evolving force of imperial states and absentee ownership, for men of the handicraft era, especially in England, local citizenship was not illusory. Democracy was no trick, no swindle; the idea of democratic citizenship was a central part of the social power to organize the communal life of a new historical epoch, a power based on the hardening economic realities of private property and self-organized labor.

Veblen's account of the coming of "the handicraft era" offers an inviting portrait of ascendant, buoyant liberalism. The liberal influence on his thinking is probably more transparent here than anywhere else in his thought. But there is also much to be criticized in Veblen's images of the masterless man and handicraft era.

Perhaps most important, the role of class violence, the aristocracy's coercive dispossession of the feudal peasantry, is a chief historical factor in the breakup of feudalism, yet Veblen says little or nothing about it. Most of those "masterless men" and still-mastered women who wandered into cities and towns did not go voluntarily. They were torn from the land by aristocratic expropriation and enclosure. Marx explained the bloodiness and violence of this process more accurately, and with a much fiercer sense of outrage than Veblen showed.[80] Moreover, once urbanized, the ex-serfs did not always enjoy abundant opportunities to work. Unemployment and impoverishment was often their unhappy lot. Without property in tools, they became the reluctant employees and servants of others, the human instruments of the "masterless men," who owned the tools and controlled the commerce and credit of the commercial towns. Indeed, as Karen Orren has shown, feudal habits derived from England continued to shape legal relations between capital and labor well into the nineteenth century in America: "The law of master and servant . . . persisted into the era of capitalism."[81] In ways more consistent with Veblen's larger argument about the lingering effects of illiberal habits in liberal society, Orren's work effectively undercuts some of the power of Veblen's claims about "masterless men." In the face of these conditions, well-established predatory arguments about the need to make men work would gain renewed life: Parson Malthus was soon to come.

To be sure, Veblen does recognize that natural rights claims of ownership included rights to lend capital, to hire the labor of others, as well as to sell one's labor for a wage. Indeed, it was through these "two lines of credit and hired labor . . . that absentee ownership" began "to dominate the organization of industry and . . . (take) over the usufruct of the community's workmanship."[82] Even more pertinently, Veblen scorned capital's later pauperization of the English working class—a class of human beings "undersized, anemic, shriveled and wry-grown."[83] But evidence of the earlier historic realities of class violence and mass unemployment support those critics of liberalism who see in the "era of handicraft" more of an emphasis on possession than industry, on acquisition over workmanship, and on class struggle more than private insubordination.[84]

Conclusion

Overall, this look at Veblen's idea of savagery and its quasi-anarchistic legacy supports a mixed judgment of its intellectual strengths. There are serious deficiencies here. These include the vague anthropological detail of savage forms, especially the missing role of men in matriarchal savagery; the lack of discussion of the roots of insubordination; and the notable omission on injustices incurred in the growth of urban capitalism. The celebration of masterless men is particularly open to charges of excess, bordering as it does "on the fulsome."[85] As an economic historian of the relationship between workmanship and anarchy, Veblen is uneven at best. Still, given tendencies to ignore his political observations, our analysis suggests that Veblen's political insights into savagery have been underrated.

Most central is the way the concept illuminates basic Veblenian contentions about relations between work and community, which, when immediate and spontaneous, permit social controls to develop in relatively noncoercive ways. To the extent that conditions in later cultures allow workmanship and industry to thrive, power claims lose some of their force. Human beings who can follow their spontaneous, organic sense of the life process, Veblen suggests, require little in the way of external coercion.

In this way, we can see how, for Veblen, the moral legitimacy and economic rationality of democratic institutions arise out of the immediacy and directness of economic activities and relations. In such circumstances, politics does not have much "to bluster and give off fumes about."[86] Only when social institutions empower an economic minority to free itself from the life process does it become politically necessary to enforce the imperative to work on the economic majority. Only then does ideology have to enforce cultural conceptions of work as irksome and power as imperative.

Only then, Veblen suggests, do human beings truly remove themselves from the animal kingdom, becoming the only species irrational enough to insist on imposing the life process as an institutional rather than an organic necessity.

Clearly, for Veblen, liberals did not discover a new order of nature; the rights which they claimed to intuit were "at best" evocative of "a partial return to a 'state of nature' in the sense of a state of peace and industry rather than return to the unsophisticated beginnings of a new society."[87] Far from highlighting the intellectual superiority of the West to earlier savage phases of civilization, Veblen suggests that liberal democrats are really unconscious inheritors of the traditions of uncoerced savagery. Moreover, the political system they invented, however much it leaned away from irresponsible and coercive authority, was not immune to contamination by forces of irresponsible predation and exploit, forces comparable to the ones that undid earlier epochs of workmanship and quasi-anarchistic democracy. And so, like their pagan anarchistic brethren of the Baltic north, today's liberal inheritors of savage traditions restlessly search "for some workable compromise that would permit their ideal of 'local self-government' by neighborly common sense to live somehow in the shadow of that large-scale coercive principle that killed it."[88]

6

ILLIBERAL HABITS, WAR, AND
STATE FORMATION

The handicraft era sparked truly remarkable political changes. It furnished technological and economic foundations for self-governing cities in Western Europe. Liberal expectations and democratic hopes sprouted. Indeed, long after the machine process, large-scale corporate enterprise, and central-ized states changed capitalism, handicraft habits endure. But their legacy was not all positive. Europeans experienced the handicraft era at different times, in different ways. In some places—Prussia, for example—feudal institutions held on long after England nurtured petty industry.[1] Among variant societies developing at different tempos, chances for mutual envy and rivalry multiplied. Dynastic interests added fuel to a competitive mix, as they continued to rule much of the continent until early in the twentieth century. Thus the toll of European warfare, if anything, increased even as democracy spread. Charles Tilly describes the awful trend: "Since 1900 . . . the world has seen 237 new wars—civil and international—whose battles have killed at least 1,000 persons per year; through the year 2000, the grim numbers extrapolate to about 275 wars and 115 million deaths in battle. Civilian deaths could easily equal that total. The bloody nineteenth century brought only 205 such wars and 8 million dead, the warlike eighteenth century a mere 68 wars with 4 million killed . . . From 1480 to 1800, a significant new international conflict started somewhere every two years, from 1800 to 1944 every one or two years, since World War II every fourteen months or so."[2]

Clearly, handicraft habits did not pacify states. Indeed, much of Veblen's interest in the state stemmed from apprehensions that despite, and in some respects because of, diffusion of liberal democratic governments, warlike tendencies remained strong. Imperial interests of corporate capital offered one reason. Coupling expansionist business interests and illiberal political habits augured poorly for peace. Together they promised to undermine the pacifying effects of handicraft-era habits. Under their sway, Veblen feared, liberalism's masterless man would learn to embrace the military man. Above all, he stressed the state's own intrinsic penchant for war. Like Robert O'Connell, Veblen believed that "the essence of war" is "military and political, not capitalistic."[3] His view is unmistakable: the nation-state is in origin and character "an enterprise in intimidation," an engine of war making.[4]

Governments have crucial domestic responsibilities, of course. But their orientation is often outward, toward rivals and competitors in the sphere of what is politely called international relations. Accordingly, Veblen considers the state most seriously as an international actor.[5] In the global realm, business surveillance of state action remains important, but it is more attenuated, weaker. Once caught up in international relations, state leaders tend to act for their own political reasons. The motive of action often shifts "from business advantage to dynastic ascendancy and courtly honor."[6] Power and prestige become more salient than profits. Business enterprise may reign supreme in domestic politics, but "the national honor is beyond price."[7] In this sense, although not many writers have thought of him in this way, Veblen is actually in the tradition of political thinkers who urge removal of "boundaries between the national and the international, the political and the economic."[8]

This chapter will focus on Veblen's assessment of liberalism's illiberal habits and their influence in shaping emerging modern states and their politics. We offer a model of these habits, specifically predation, class, and mystification. Then we move on to suggest connections between Veblen's ideas about the state and the related work of other theorists who link state formation with violence and war. We then turn to Veblen's evolutionary, historical analysis of state formation in the handicraft era.

The Politics of War

Characteristically, Veblen looked to the past to explain popular deference and loyalty to militant state authority. Steven Edgell aptly terms

Veblen's approach "the theory of the historical and judicial authenticity of obsolete ideas."[9] It explains much about Veblen's critique of resurgent, illiberal, and aggressive tendencies in liberalism. Militant and illiberal tendencies keenly expressed themselves in early modern states. Long before that they dominated the archaic history of predatory power and war, when clans and tribes organized political aggression. As James Galbraith notes, "The normal function of the clan, tribe, family unit or company is not to enrich the owner or master at the expense of the underlings, but to enrich him at the expense of surrounding clans."[10] Once barbarism takes hold, Veblen sees more internal predation than Galbraith, but he agrees that the earliest forms of predation aimed outward.

Illiberal habits and institutions preceded liberal democracy, but then, in many subtle and not-so-subtle ways, carried over to it. In so doing, they betrayed democracy's liberal promise. Precapitalist, preliberal forms of political and social domination encouraged habits too strong to uproot. Their staying power explains Veblen's dour assessment of political prospects in modern democracies, particularly the frequent war-induced reluctance of citizens to hold their leaders accountable. In particular the residual grip of such habits on popular thought helps to explain why seemingly enlightened populations might willingly defer to militant chief executives, tolerate violations of civil liberties, or accept cold, hard arguments for torture, at least for a while anyway.[11] Three closely fused habits are especially important in this context: predation, class rule, and mystification. Each reflects illiberal practices and habits that haunt the modern, indeed the postmodern, political world. Each favors decrepit habits of irresponsible power in modern guise. Though each is closely interconnected with the others, for purposes of clarification and emphasis we treat them sequentially.[12] These elements describe much of the cultural content that, in various ways, war chieftains still invoke for belligerent national purposes. Within the modern state "all that has gone before was not lost . . . Many things were carried over."[13]

Predation

Commentators on Veblen have said, sometimes critically, that his analysis of power in capitalist society centers primarily and perhaps too heavily on ideology.[14] Veblen's version of capitalism seems to these writers less violent and coercive than Marx's. Certainly his apparent indifference to the violence of enclosure during the handicraft era suggests as much, although Veblen's repeated condemnations of forcible predation make us skeptical of this view. Still, for purposes of the present argument, let us assume that Veblen does see capitalism as a comparatively peaceable organization of power, one whose principal muscle consists of ruling-class control of ideas. To the extent this claim is accurate, its importance lies in comparison with what came *before* liberal capitalism.

Veblen wants us to measure the workings of quasi-peaceable capitalism against the standard of systems of power that antedate the business system. In precapitalist predatory systems, rulers generally used or threatened direct physical force to exploit others. They used coercion to seize the fruits of others' labor. Though Veblen notes exceptions—the Icelandic Republic, for example, or pagan anarchism, and even to some extent the handicraft era—the precapitalist systems he discusses are conspicuously brutal and parasitic.[15] Though not lacking in belief systems or legitimation, the "strong hand" of traditional barbaric rulers enjoyed freer sway with subalterns, especially aliens and strangers. Thus Veblen regularly stresses links between internal domination and opportunities to subjugate outsiders. Predation, it seems, is most aggressive and effective against foreigners when it takes the forms of war and conquest. It has a distinctively international aspect. Predatory exploit of those politically perceived as outsiders, Veblen suggests, is a main factor in the growth of irresponsible political power.

For Veblen, conditions of political, sectarian, and racial animosity favor a kind of moral provincialism, a predatory moral relativism. Thus people are often prepared to victimize and abuse members of alien races and ethnic groups in ways that they would find reprehensible among members of their own community. The record of immigration politics in the United States is replete with examples.[16] Yet, for all the importance of this idea, liberal theory has been relatively mute on the ways that "harsh injustices" can be inflicted upon outsiders. Indeed, its "failure to indicate why any group of people should think of themselves as a distinct or special people is a great political liability."[17] Among early twentieth-century theorists of the warfare state, Veblen included, such considerations were foremost in mind. As Joseph Gumplowicz observed, "satisfaction of needs and exploitation of the services of foreigners" are "the two fundamental social processes."[18]

His *Outlines of Sociology* added critically important international, imperial, and racial dimensions to what amounts to a quasi-Marxian theory of class exploitation. For Gumplowicz, natural desires to avoid irksome labor and availability of strangers for exploit combine to spur aggressiveness and amorality in international relations. His work offers what amounts to a material explanation for Carl Schmitt's famous friend-enemy distinction as the principal organizing difference of political life.

Veblen considers the phenomenon somewhat differently. By following his analysis, we can see links among ideas that characterize his political thinking. When aspiring warlords successfully claim "the good repute and the added power to be gained" from imperial enterprise, two crucial political forces come into play.[19] First, populations increasingly habituated to rule by a warlike crown will, "by award of the uncritical but ubiquitous sense of group solidarity," tend to identify with and take collective pride in their leader's conquests and triumphs. Loyal citizens perceive personal kingly triumphs as the reflected glory of their community's strength and power. In effect, he suggests, aggressively politicized populations will impute to themselves—no doubt with royal encouragement—the very powers they otherwise impute to the king's unique formidability. It is as if the mysterious logic of imputed power inverts itself, to the great ideological benefit of commanders in chief. President George W. Bush stands on an aircraft carrier in full fighter pilot array and citizens see themselves—for the moment anyway—reflected in his triumphant image.

Pride in kingly conquest spreads across the community. As it does, loyal citizens feel entitled to claim proportionate shares of emotional gratification. Veblen likened the inflated good feeling to psychic income, a politically passionate, if irrational, substitute for material reward. Such identification forms a vital part of the patriotic impulse.

A second, much more ominous political force is also at work. Predatory cultures teach people to think of rough treatment against strangers and enemies as reasonable behavior. Acts of power that might be worrisome within seem to bother us less when it comes to outsiders. "Gain at the cost of other communities, particularly communities at a distance, and more especially such as are felt to be aliens, is not objectionable to . . . standards of home-bred use and wont."[20] Moral provincialism emerges in the politics of seizure and predation—a precursor of latter-day imperialism that encourages suspension of criticism when it comes to application of force against foreigners. Recent American reluctance to embrace such institutions as the world court is partially understandable in these terms. Partisan political solidarity, the "uncritical sense of group solidarity," obstructs impulses favoring universalistic norms—the parental bent, for example—which look to the species' generic good.

Veblen is unusually clear on the implications of predatory relativism for the differential intensity of domestic and international conflict. But the idea also has implications for domestic political stability in class societies. Internal class differences give rise to exclusionary patterns of social stratification. These differences cause social and personal friction. The "prevalence of irritation and envy between classes and . . . emulation and disparagement between individuals" is a nagging political and social problem for unequal communities. The sense of group solidarity and foreign enmity helps to keep such domestic conflict in check. When forces of envy separate "culturally distinct communities," however, conflict intensifies; checks weaken. The scope of legitimate animosity and hostility widens. Politically, "the outcome is a state of aliency between . . . communities . . . which may on slight provocation rise to the pitch of manslaughter and seek relief in international hostilities."[21]

Long before it became fashionable for social scientists to warn that "People use politics to assert their identity," often taking identity from hostility to others, Veblen theorized that cultural symbols and divisions serve as fundamental sources of domestic political identity as well as international cleavage.[22] Once politically hardened, cultural divisions can assume primal emotional force. The resulting passions become ardent, efficient motivators of war. "The most capable dynastic statesmen and the shrewdest strategists of commercial patriotism," Veblen observed, "would be helpless to bring about a state of international manslaughter among civilized men except for the quasi-moral animosity that rises out of such discrepancies of 'culture.' "[23]

Though Veblen emphasized that technical progress contributed to accumulation of surpluses worth fighting for, predatory systems depended on more than self-earned agricultural and industrial wealth. As often as not, predatory communities enriched themselves on captured loot from military aggression. They lived off expropriation of other peoples' resources and industry. In this respect, the warlord was the first agent of predatory political power. And his ability to mobilize and galvanize perceptions of cultural difference furnished an especially potent ideological weapon. Call him king, general, seigneur, chief, or priest; the warlord stood for nothing so much as a system of internal political domination and aggressive foreign policy, a system based on honorific prowess demonstrated against external enemies.

Reputations for successful forays in external violence galvanized imputations of "personal force." Whole systems of symbolic politics glorified the leader's capacity to exhibit "the strong hand." "Epithets and titles used in addressing chieftains, and in the propitiation of kings and gods, very commonly impute a propensity for overbearing violence and an irresistible devastating force to the person who is to be propitiated."[24] Impressive ceremonials of power help to sanction royal or executive claims to stand as commander in chief. Ancient warlords left trails of brutal and parasitic habits, a host of illiberal traditions and legitimations, that later kings emulated and modern chief executives are wont to recall. As Tilly has observed, "The very logic by which a local lord extended or defended the perimeter within which he monopolized the means of violence . . . continued on a larger scale into the logic of war" pursued by modern political chieftains.[25] Here we can find some historic roots of what Rogers Smith calls "potent illiberal strains in American civic life and in political life generally."[26]

The Theory of the Leisure Class, a book widely celebrated for its satire of ruling class folly, constantly reiterates the unfunny claim that leisure class symbols function as icons of raw power, a power based initially on male seizure of foreign women as slaves. This is a power that is, for Veblen, unmistakably ugly, violent, brutal, and fierce. The book makes it clear that the cultural apparatus of leisure class pomp and circumstance, the whole lurid drapery of princely power, is much more than silly self-indulgence. It is cultural rationalization for conquest, killing, and human exploitation on ever widening scales. For Veblen, celebrations of barbarism and its heroes are mythic representations and transformations of the species' most deplorable, violent, and inhumane habits. The decisive fact of barbarism, after all, is its coercion. Barbarism is a culture of predatory violence, a system of institutions that endowed violence, and those most capable of inflicting it, with supreme honorific stature. Valorized by ceremony and ritual, barbaric culture makes "the taking of life—the killing of formidable competitors, whether brute or human—honorable in the highest degree"; hence it regularly favors "appreciation with a view to combat."[27]

As groups entered this predatory phase of culture, violent conflict with other humans, or other species, became the most accessible path for displaying socially valued contributions to communal life. Violence offered "the direction in which the most spectacular effect may be achieved by the individual."[28] The warlord's standing, his "high office of slaughter," is, therefore, a matter principally of honor symbolizing power, not a seeking after wealth and property for their own sakes. War, after all, is rooted fundamentally in politics, not economics. Successful brutality and predation led to wealth, to be sure. But the resulting trophies were just that: signs and symbols, vivid expressions "of the slaughterer's prepotence," that elusive, inscrutable inner force which emboldens the use of brawn and guile. It was this indwelling spirit, and its outward expression in violence, that people learned to fear and respect, that drew admiration, and that conferred high standing on its successful perpetrators.

Some of Veblen's most vivid political writing describes methods and examples of predatory rule, illustrations drawn from widely different epochs and systems. The blood lust of ancient eastern empires, for example—what he called the biblical empires—inspired some of his least satirical, least sterilized, most explicitly impassioned criticism. The rule of Babylonians, Persians, Assyrians, Israelites, Huns, Arabs, and Turks varied in ceremonial form and spiritual content. But they used violence in similar ways. Each drew economic sustenance and political stature from cruel subjection of neighboring agricultural populations. Other theorists, Joseph Gumplowicz, Fritz Oppenheimer, and Karl Marx, for example, emphasized economic causes of exploitation, the pumping of surplus labor from direct producers. Veblen, in contrast, stresses the political relation of unequal power as genesis of social order and stratification. Here the logic of political power combines economic exploitation, ritualized patterns of wasteful consumption, and systems of religious observance into singular structures of domination and exploitation. Equally critical to his analysis of domination are connections of exploit, waste, and ideology. Ancient desert kingdoms offer robust examples:

> There were great palaces and cities built by slave labor and corvee, embodying untold misery in conspicuously wasteful and tasteful show, and great monarchs whose boast it was that they were each and several the best friend or nearest relative of some irresponsible and supreme god, and whose dearest claim to pre-eminence was that they "walked on the faces of the black-head race." Seen in perspective and rated in any terms that have a workmanlike significance, these stupendous dynastic fabrics are as insignificant as they are large, and none of them is worth the least of the fussy little communities that came in time to make up the Hellenic world and its petty squabbles.[29]

These desert barbarisms featured "institutions proper to a large scale and to a powerful despotism and nobility resting on a servile people . . . in which the final arbiter is always irresponsible force and in which the all-pervading social relation is personal subservience and personal authority."[30] Irresponsibility and subservience may have appeared differently in later, more mature barbarism, but they were invariably present wherever military values and relations predominated. Underlying populations enjoyed little or no say in predatory decisions that affected their fate. Feudalism, for example, rested on smaller, more bounded agrarian systems. It was less imperial in thrust, but its central political features remained irresponsibility of power and subordination of underlying populations. As with older barbaric forms, a militaristic spirit informed feudal domination. It stamped the "regime of status" as a system of "compulsory cooperation" enforcing "subjection of man to his fellow man."[31] The emerging absolute monarchies, to which feudalism often gave rise, tended to replicate, albeit in changed form, similar patterns of coercive rule and territorial protectionism. Irresponsibility meant the same thing in all such cases. Dominant classes used resources and instruments of prevailing institutions for their own purposes—independent of the will of the dominated.[32] Even more, it meant that rulers felt free to use the dominated in ways answerable to no one but themselves and God, that ever-present "silent partner" in transactions of power. At the same time, "personal subservience" implied more or less willing compliance of the subjugated.

Fear and loyalty fuse within predatory cultures into complex habits of submission. For Veblen, these mixed habits converge around attitudes of self-debasement and acquiescence, submission and deference. He sees a self-investment in inferiority, but one constantly aware of threats and intimidation. Fear and loyalty work together. They subdue lurking sensibilities among the powerless to hold the powerful to account, much less to choose the power holders, or even more radically, to exercise social power directly.[33] Such habits are reflected in popular tolerance of elite secrecy and deception in contemporary democracies. Power to choose their leaders remains nominally with the people, but power's elusiveness remains a major prop of political culture. Ideologically, the unique inner capacities of the powerful are literally unaccountable, beyond tangible measure. Inexplicable, unfathomable, and ineffable, power is a phenomenon irreducible to calculations of weight or breadth. Paradoxically, imputed power is an abstraction of enormous cultural force, an imponderable whose effect we must nonetheless ponder in any account of political realities.

Popular demands for responsibility can carry only vague and uncertain applications in reference to such magical imputations. As Veblen explained, assumptions of responsibility entail judgments of knowable, comprehensible phenomena. People "do not pass appraisal on matters which lie beyond the reach of their knowledge and belief, nor do they formulate rules to govern the game of life beyond that limit." Responsibility, in other words, applies only within knowable bounds, what a senior White House advisor once mockingly called "the reality-based community."[34] Otherwise, power is free to create its own facts.

None of this means that Veblen believed predatory power was absolute or that it always operated beyond limit. Predatory ruling classes face constraints. Power might establish self-imposed limits. The general moral or religious character of the community might enliven power's sense of restraint. A dutiful sense of their strategic interests in conserving power could also lead rulers to weigh options with care. And of course countervailing powers can arise. Veblen did not think such limits were likely to be very effective, however. The will to power is too fluctuating, too dynamic, too subject to shifting expectations of emulative comparison, to prove a reliable source of self-control. And inasmuch as the community's moral code is saturated with predatory habits and the fighting spirit, moral restraints will be weak; in international relations, morals are beside the point anyway. Oppositional forces are the strongest candidates for checks on power—the spirit of insubordination come alive. A smart ruling class will be wary of doing things that might arouse rebellious spirits. In sum, Veblen suggests, the strategic interests of predatory power offer the most likely source of restraint on power, another sign of his radical realism.[35] But then how much can a ruling class yield to its subordinates? Class after all is an organizing premise of its power.

Class

If predation provides the stage for power's display, class provides its social framework. We can gauge Veblen's contribution here by a short comparison with Marx. At bottom, Marx and Veblen differed in their understanding of how the personal and the social comprise experience of class. Marx insisted that we should understand class in objective, impersonal economic terms. "Individuals are dealt with" in his work, he said, "only insofar as they are the personifications of economic categories."[36] Veblen not only understood his Marx, he certainly concurred with Marx—and with Weber too for that matter—about the impersonal quality of economic relations in bourgeois society. But Veblen did not believe, as Marx tended to, that capitalism brought a decisive rupture in the social psychology of precapitalist class relations. The impersonal or objective side of class tells only half, and, from a political viewpoint, not necessarily the more important half, of the story of predatory class relations.

Veblen recognized how modern economic classes rest structurally on impersonal, market-based factors. But he noticed something else. Capitalist class relations preserve illiberal residues of mastery and subordination born of older traditions of personalized rule and ascriptive status. As people experience class, they learn something of both features, the objective and the personal. Objective economic factors may decide the social structure and composition of class. But the social meanings, the texture, and ultimately the political consequences of class as a human experience, center on social and psychological orientations people feel at the individual level. Marx's view of class, suggested Veblen, is too one-sided, too invested in the objective economic facts, and too little concerned with those "matters beyond the reach of knowledge" through which subordinate populations fashion their spiritual lives.[37]

Veblen's approach can just as well be read as a critique of Tocqueville's model of democratic individualism—the idea of America as a society based on social equality. Like Marx, Tocqueville accented the novelty and modernity of democratic capitalism. For Tocqueville, democracy inspired feelings of generalized social equality. In this sense, both Tocqueville and Marx missed what Veblen insisted was a central fact of contemporary class relations: the continuously powerful shaping force of barbaric emulation in social and political consciousness. Indeed, archaic ascriptive views of civic identity are especially valuable to political elites bent on "fostering beliefs that a certain group is a distinctive and especially worthy people," a people legitimately entitled to mastery of others even as it remains structured by internal relations of inequality.[38] Veblen's class analysis reminds us of these continuities as well as ruptures in the evolution of modern social classes. It is a study of how individuals in various classes of bourgeois society continue to impute honorific, intimately personal qualities of prestige and worth to those who own the most, just as people once attributed the same kinds of personal qualities to representatives of militant leisure classes in feudal or aristocratic society. Veblen stresses deep-seated tendencies toward perpetuation of internalized feelings of subordination in the working class. In this way, his class theory is quite different from that of Marx or Tocqueville.

Veblen believed that the pedagogy of rank and class continues to be what for so many centuries it always was, a training ground in personal deference, loyalty, and obedience. A democratic gloss of civic equality may cover and shade the old outlooks, and they may even be curtailed by tendencies favoring insubordination. Still, venerable habits of subordination do not die. Capitalist ideology harbors older, darker motives and meanings, elements of an archaic iconography of mastery and subordination. Like Marx, Veblen understood how ancient and feudal predatory ruling classes not only lived off the wealth produced by their class inferiors but tried to control the internal state of mind, the interior social consciousness, of the ruled. Where leaders' self-esteem is a main currency of power, it could not be otherwise. Through elaborate rituals of command, service, and labor, premodern rulers continuously reinforced their subalterns' feelings of inferiority as well as their own felt sense of dominance. The workers' cultivated sense of personal, social inadequacy was and is a fundamental psychological condition of exploit and of their exploiters' much-desired prestige. And it has much, if not everything, to do with power's ability to rouse militant loyalties among workers to fight on its behalf.

Veblen's discussion of ideological control is, then, not a peculiar hallmark of his analysis of capitalism, any more than it is the case that predatory systems survived only by force. Combinations of force and fraud, coercion and ideas, were politically important long before modern business turned advertising and mass media to purposes of social control. The key point for Veblen is how much ideologies of power personalize claims to rule. He is interested in how abstract ideas of governance involve illusory imputations of power, insinuating themselves into direct, personal relations of mastery and subordination. Predatory ruling classes personalized not only their own higher claims to honor but their relations with the working classes in everyday life, reinforcing in the latter a steady and assured sense of inferiority and class indignity, especially by identifying industrial work in the minds of its practitioners with irksomeness, dishonor, lower intelligence, and brutishness, that is, with low, degraded social status.

Free labor markets did not expunge or wipe away all these ancient indignities. The age-old ill repute of manual labor held on, as a kind of low-boil defamation of the working class. It persists in modified religious and cultural garb, contaminating the rationalizing tendencies of technical work, reinforcing compliance among the exploited, enhancing receptivity to nonrational patriotic and religious appeals, and supporting the logic of exploitation. Lingering patterns of submission and inferiority imprint a strongly conservative bias on latter-day capitalist labor relations. In short, for Veblen, the lasting influence of degraded labor substantially curtailed the progressive implications of the handicraft era. Entailed here is Veblen's understanding of the intimate, face-to-face, personal web of relations through which predatory power often manifests itself. It is personal not only in the sense that relations between master and servant may be quite direct but in the deeper sense of the subaltern's internalization of subordination to others, who she perceives as intrinsically, even preternaturally, powerful and thus deserving of higher stature.

In a sense, Veblen broaches his own version of the "micro-power" relation that Michel Foucault systematically investigated in jail cells, hospital wards, and prison barracks. Veblen saw its precursors in a host of potent precapitalist social relations: lord and peasant, master and servant, priest and parishioner, man and wife—precursors that Foucault himself acknowledged.[39] Governance by impersonal markets (regime of contract) and impersonal law (constitutional democracy) did not close these spaces of personal rule. Modern power arrangements preserved them to support older habits of submission, notably in family and church, for example. This is not a novel insight, of course, but much of the unclaimed value of Veblen's approach is to give such traditional relations and understandings a considerably more prominent, less marginal place in the operations of modern democracy than either Marx or Tocqueville assigned them.

The larger social meaning of such notions for the evolution of social and political consciousness cannot be underestimated. They form seedbeds for popular submission to political authority and class privilege. Deep inside the social psychological mechanism of class societies, Veblen suggests, is the message that the mighty rule not because they are rich; the mighty are rich because they are personally indomitable. Their external wealth signifies their most prized personal possession: the mystique of those powerful and effective enough to acquire material riches. In the same way, the poor labor at what the culture defines as degrading jobs not because they lack income. They lack income because they perform what the culture defines as undignified, deplorable forms of work. And they do such work because they are weak and obsequious. People vulnerable to domination not only need to be ruled, they deserve to be ruled. Such people lack inner potency, militant spirit, strategic guile—all those virile manly qualities the culture deems essential for jobs that entail the master skills of command and control, force and fraud. In effect for Veblen, the human servant is to her master as brute matter is to the savage craftsman: a dull spiritless object upon which to place the stamp of the master's will.

Tragically, for Veblen, the poor and working class too often see themselves in just these ways, as passive, inert, without requisite personal force in a world that demands predatory aggressiveness as its chief human virtue.[40] Habituated to subordination in the domains of work and state, people develop deferential attitudes that overlap with and contaminate whatever beliefs they may have in political equality. This leads to a repressive tolerance among workers for their own subordination. It is a tolerance that prompts Veblen to question the viability of the most central premise of liberal democracy—self-knowledge of citizens and their capacity for insight into the real power implications of social relations.

Clearly, chances for impersonal government and responsible power have more limited prospects within Veblen's radical realist perspective than they do within more forgiving liberal frameworks, such as Tocqueville's. The latter envisions tighter links between civil and social equality, or between enlightened self-interest and shared responsibilities. As Veblen reads perceptions of social structure, people's imputations of qualitatively different personal forces arrayed by class discourage underlying populations from holding elites accountable. As crude empirical clues to Veblen's point consider the abysmal rates of American voting participation in presidential elections (50–55 percent)—a kind of symbolic expression of potential insubordination—or union membership—a considerably more active and militant expression of it—(8–10 percent of the private sector workforce).

Overall, as ascriptive imputations of personal force shape class perceptions, many in the lower class rarely even bother with the formal rituals of democracy. By the same token, we should never underestimate popular support for abstract symbols of flag and church. Shrewd politicians understandably tap into this fact. Presidential candidate Barack Obama did wear his flag pin, after all. Still, as celebrations of popular consent remain pro forma and unconvincing, insincerity can lead to the kind of cynical docility that Veblen describes in his examination of the American country town.[41] In any case, cynicism is not resistance, any more than gang violence is. Veblen sees such phenomena as functionally conservative in effect. He does not conceive of master-servant relations dialectically, as do Hegel and Marx. Nor does he explore what James C. Scott calls strategies and "weapons of the weak," the varied and subtle forms of symbolic or substantive resistance by which subordinate populations can inhibit a master's action.[42] Occasionally Veblen detects "passive resistance" from below, and he does entertain chances for a "spirit of insubordination." As we have seen, this libertarian streak, whose origins lie in prefeudal "pagan anarchism" and the handicraft era, developed into the liberal type of "the masterless man." Insubordination has potentially important democratic consequences, bursting out in such familiar acts of popular sabotage as strikes and protest movements.[43] But even acknowledging the spirit of insubordination, it is still the case that

Veblen offers no parallel to Montesquieu's shrewd eunuchs of *The Persian Letters*, or even to the subtle plays of resistance among Foucault's plebs.

Yet surely a man who can write *The Higher Learning in America* understands how the weak can passively subvert the powerful with wit, games, irony, and intelligence. The book, after all, is Veblen's literary revenge against the arbitrary rule of university presidents who sabotaged his career. And the fact is that Veblen always writes with the knowledge that the whole edifice of emulation depends on the subordinate's will to defer to the dominant. He never lets us forget that the ruling class has heavy needs of its own for psychic income. Its appetite for outward shows of deference, honor, and dignity is insatiable. But the fact remains that Veblen rarely, if ever, considers how servants might manipulate such needs for their own ends. As he prefers to see it, the tactical reactions and responses of weakness to power, or power's need to anticipate the reactions of the weak, count far less as political matters than the fundamental structure of mastery and domination itself, especially in preliberal, predatory systems. If "disorderly conduct" among underlying populations is not revolutionary, and usually it is not, Veblen does not think that it has much political significance as a threat to the system.[44] To say the least, Veblen held a constricted view of political possibilities. Servants may secretly mock their masters; they may exploit and manipulate ruling class needs for deference and ingratiation. But, Veblen seems implicitly to ask, so what?

He wants us to see that whatever the servant's plays of resistance, such strategies work themselves out within structured systems of control, the terms of which operate routinely to the disadvantage of underlying strata. For Veblen, institutionalized power carries much more political weight than occasional resistance among the discontented. The glass of resistance is half empty: class processes bring about subjective inferiority. The results are habits of subordination that deflect and contaminate psychic pressures arising from more generic human dispositions. The experience of class thwarts possibilities for free workmanship, social solidarity, and creative curiosity. Submission redirects their liberating potential toward traditions of loyalty, faith, patriotism, and war. The issues in this respect run very deep indeed.

As we have seen, among Veblen's most fundamental, least qualified assertions is the claim that human beings are purposeful creatures, subjective agents, beings that seek to use their creative energies and capacities for some "concrete, objective, impersonal end."[45] Veblen does not equate human purposefulness with freedom, but connections are unmistakable. Purpose, after all, requires a measure of freedom to have a chance for its realization. Veblen's work is an exploration of the range of purposes that people in a given culture choose, or that the powerful lead them to pursue. It is an examination of the ways that society develops and channels biologically impulsive generic ends, or deranges and contaminates those ends for the purposes of power.

Veblen offers no explicit defense of democratic, self-chosen ends. He tends to emphasize the cultural context of choice more than its free scope. In this sense his work anticipates such familiar concepts in political science as "mobilization of bias" and the various faces of ideological and structural power.[46] Veblen's ideas are obviously not those of a nascent liberal democrat. For him, the complex cultural factors that influence individual and social purpose are too dense and historical to permit naïve views of democratic deliberation, much less individual "rational choice." In the language of modern economic theory, Veblen's theory of choice is overwhelmingly "path dependent" and cumulative. Every choice is informed and conditioned by a history of previous choices and nonchoices, roads taken and not taken. But none of this means that Veblen conceives of people as automatons, far from it.

Veblen sees humans as beings who must face the world each day, challenged by its variable conditions and fluctuating dynamics, impelled to innovate and to adapt and thus to choose among variant and interrelated means and ends.[47] In this way, every society and every individual is a work in progress, and the stuff of such progress or regress as humans achieve lies within the domain of their selective, adaptive pursuit of choices and techniques. Thus are human beings distinctly teleological, purposeful beings. But the majority of these beings, as often as not, find themselves living in communities organized around the preferred ends of predatory ruling classes. As we have seen, Veblen defines the first purpose of the power seeker as precisely "the *conversion* to his own ends of energies previously directed to some other end by another agent."[48] From this standpoint, the basic meaning of class exploitation is denial to the exploited of their most distinctive human trait: self-directed use of their own energies and abilities to realize or to modify their own purposes in their own way. Inferior class position in Veblen entails structural denial of the capacity of individuals to pursue their potential for creative workmanship, adaptation, and curiosity, including possibilities of freely using industrial knowledge and technical prowess cumulatively developed by the species.[49]

To the extent then that premodern, illiberal cultures persuade their members to believe that they possess no legitimate capacity to author their own ends, or even to have important individual or social purposes of their own, apart from the social claims of ruling groups or those of "society as a whole," internalization of class identity and social-political integration become one and the same. Possessed of an instinct of workmanship that urges her to creative industry along her own lines, the servant or peasant nonetheless accepts conversion of her personal energies—or "labor power," as Marx defines it—to the higher purposes of her master. Social relations and processes that inform this conversion of human energies constitute the most damaging pathological human meaning of exploitation for Veblen. And this process is never less than intimately personal and psychological, in a word, habitual—even as it may unfold within systems of objective classes and impersonal market forces.

In this sense, Veblen's tendency to disregard the smaller resistances of everyday life, including much of the Sturm und Drang of conventional politics, is understandable. It is his way of highlighting the tragedy of personal subordination and exploitation, the regular thwarting of possibility suffered by a majority of the human species. C. Wright Mills captured the point precisely when he noted that Veblen's understanding of the relation between individual and community in predatory settings is that "what is good for the community is 'disserviceable to the individual.'"[50]

Mystification: Religion, Partisan Solidarity, and Patriotism

The burden of Veblen's class analysis is to turn study of subjection inward, to explain why the powerless so readily accept their lowly position. His discussion of emulation shows how forming social divisions and stratifications can be simultaneously dynamic and conservative—and this is no mean trick. But emulation has the defect of its advantage, for it also accentuates a potential, however small, for political conflict to erupt over stratification. Indeed if the powerful are to draw more than their share of self-esteem from honorific workings of class, they must face political dangers and risks. As the powerful have pressing needs for inflated psychic income, this psychic advantage can come only at the expense of psychic deformation of subordinate populations.

Precisely because emulation accentuates the authenticity and morality of subordination, systems based on predatory forms of emulation run risks that emulation itself might turn into harsher forms of envy, and even worse, class conflict. "Irritation and envy between classes" can become aggravated, politicized. In the history of the ancient and feudal worlds, peasant and agrarian revolts are anything but unknown. Neither is the spirit of insubordination foreign to modern workers. And there is always the lurking chance—distant as it might be—that underlying populations in different communities might come to see commonalities in their class situation as politically more important than affection for their social betters. Class conflict could, at least in theory, even spill over communal bounds and become a vibrant international force, as Marx expected it would.

From an ideological standpoint, effective social control in predatory systems demands more than a pacific channeling of emulative strains. Toleration of unequal social rank and power within, and especially the willingness to fight enemies beyond, need firmer, more general foundations of commonality and unity than social emulation can give. Predatory systems, too, must bridge gaps between social ranks; they must be more than crudely or coercively bound together. Class society must, as Marx argued, give itself the name of community. It must appeal to some higher unifying principle and authority, and promise some collective purpose or *telos*.

Moreover, especially in Veblen's instinctual sense, there are powerful psychological forces at work in politics. Veblen argues that the parental bent tends to push for institutionalized concern for the communal future, for what James Madison called "the permanent and aggregate interest of the community." No effective system of predation can defer needs to identify and reinforce the community's overall sense of internal harmony and its adherence to putative general interests. In short, legitimation best affirms the necessity of inequality when it can rationalize division as a necessary element of social, moral, and civic unity. Again, the problem and solution of ideology long predates capitalism.

Veblen's studies of precapitalist societies underscore the dual roles of religion and partisan solidarity—or its later version, patriotism—as bulwarks of power. Each appeals to a spirit of self-sacrifice, loyalty, and self-abnegation; each urges a willingness to give of one's self—indeed to give one's life—on behalf of a higher shared purpose. Partisan solidarity pulls us toward a sentimental love of place that helps to submerge and compensate for indignities of class. An outgrowth of humanity's generic sense of communal interest, joint occupation of space seems especially critical psychologically and socially to an experience of partisan solidarity. Sportsmanship, for example, aligns itself with the peculiarly local quality of predatory habits, and so we root for the home team. Patriotism gives such occupation a broader, though not necessarily deeper sense of political commonality. It not only historicizes social and political consciousness, it localizes, concentrates, and intensifies spiritual affinities for place-based community. It helps to form an "enclave consciousness."[51] Patriotism takes the arbitrariness of one's geographic birthplace and transfigures it into a moment of deepest human significance.[52] It supports and promotes a more or less human identification with a given community and a given place across generations, permitting and encouraging ancient ties and political unities, despite and across class differences. Thus warlords rank high in any predatory community's pantheon of heroes.

In the same way, religion takes us beyond the here and now, associating the individual's sense of her fate with particular expressions of a greater teleological design, God's will and plan, his universal scheme. Moreover, each of these ties promises a higher, spiritual realm of restraints on power, a kind of metaphysical machinery of responsibility that may well seem all the more effective for being intangible. Fears of a wrathful God chain god-fearing leaders to a sense of moral responsibility. That the force of such restraint is limited by the fact that rulers, or their priestly retinues, authorize themselves to interpret what God commands is an important qualification, no doubt. Still, religion teaches the important lesson that the ruler is himself ruled.

Few chieftains would responsibly urge their people to war without assurance of a higher alliance with almighty forces. Now, the higher sovereign may be present by his absence, but the absence speaks to an intangible and inscrutable supreme power that God-fearing rulers will not dare challenge, and that no equally inspired enemy can overrule. Thus the ruler's own personal habits of subordination to God doubtless do much to affirm the rightness of subordination throughout the ranks of society.[53]

Patriotism, or the spirit of partisan solidarity, works in similar ways. Intimately bound up with legends of aggressive action and/or longings for national revenge, patriotism is ambitious: it yearns for tests of collective superiority against all comers. So, as religion directs questions of responsible power upward toward God, patriotism directs issues of responsible power outward. Predatory responsibility is the leadership's imperative to defend the community against its enemies, to secure its military strength, to lead its forces into battle, to guard well its armament, force, and communal pride. Patriotism guides responsible power toward a heightened consciousness of the ill will of enemies, foreign and domestic. In making "the community" the ultimate object of responsibility, patriotism turns criticism of class interest in foreign policy into a matter of unseemly, quarrelsome discontent, or worse: the crass and unsavory acts of the disloyal.

Patriotism is, of course, more than flimflam. Embedded within venerable habits of predation, class, and emulation, patriotism is a potent political force that infuses the deprivations of war and class with a sense of partisan, civic solidarity, whose political effects never fail to impress Veblen. Once early economic development favored growth of a surplus product, and class, group, and individual self-seeking came to prevail over savage equality and solidarity, the community's economic interests, for Veblen, lost their joint or common character. Exploitation obviated them. Here is where Veblen and Hobbes agree on the falsity of notions of supreme good. One consequence is that social acceptance of internal exploit may not be forthcoming, even with threats of coercion. Loyalty is never automatic.

Political community provides essential means of solidarity. In the face of social cleavage and class division, *the community remains a community* because, for Veblen, it sustains a *common political reality and identity* for itself, amid a common sense of threat. The processes of imputation find their most centripetal social and political meanings right here. Imputation, after all, is a social relation binding the imputer and the imputed in collective understandings of what is worth valuing in the social relation itself. The political as patriotism is the magnification of emulation, the projection of inner strength to a ruling class, and from it to the spirit of an indomitable community. In this way, the political not only provides for that enlivened sense of oneness and security that is essential for successful warfare. It also permits collective enjoyment of the spirit of power. Patriotism allows a sense of public domain—however illusory—to live on in the civic imagination long after socioeconomic forces have divided the community by rank and class. As Rogers Smith notes, the construction of "civic identity" begins with "basic political imperatives . . . Political elites must find ways to persuade the people they aspire to govern that they are a 'people.'"[54] Within predatory systems, the people's public domain is obviously not a realm of active citizenship, nor is it a place for communal sharing of tangible resources. It is a place of common feeling and patriotic identity, a source of shared psychic income in celebration of collective feats of the militant group, a *res gloria*, if not a genuine *res publica*. So if, as Veblen argues, "it is only in its patriotic bearing that the political community continues to be a joint venture," this "patriotic bearing" ranks very high as a factor of social cohesion. It is of the greatest significance. Where "the collective prestige remains as virtually the sole community interest which can hold the sentiment of the group in a bond of solidarity," the "bond of solidarity"—partisan solidarity—is indispensable.[55]

Spiritual cords and sinews of patriotic habit bind predatory class relationships securely in place, strengthening habits of personal subordination, and easing identification of outsiders as enemies. They enable predation. The links may be intangible and spiritual, but Veblen never equated immateriality with impotence. Far from being merely epiphenomenal, politics, not least international politics, looms as both a crucial dependent and a crucial independent variable in Veblen's critique. On the one hand, politics is inextricably connected with the logic of predation and class; it infuses class-divided society with much of its collective rationale as a unified community, whose "defense" is a matter of joint interest. On the other hand, the political value of power encodes economic structure with honorific sanction, but even more, it supplies exploitative action itself with its main human motivation. Insofar as it is intimately associated with the crucial value of power, Veblen treated politics as both a means and an end of predatory human action.

Veblen and Coercive State Theory

Illiberal habits in predatory political cultures—predation, class, and mystification—developed long before the modern state system set into place and never faded away, not completely. They remained part of "the modernization of European institutions."[56] In essence, this meant for Veblen that emerging modern states and their politics were no more than partially modern and capitalist. Modern states and their leaders preserved quasi-feudal, predatory, combative inclinations. These states not only served business interests but advanced significant power claims on their own behalf. They possessed distinctively political interests in enhancing their own institutional power and prestige against rival states. Politics mattered because state officials were capable of doing more than taking orders from absentee owners. Political leaders retained the habit of "judging facts and events from the point of view of the fight." And the main "fight" to which political leaders addressed themselves was the international "fight," the struggle for power and prestige among states.[57]

To concentrate, as many writers have, on Veblen's description of state support for business enterprise in the American case is to lose sight of his broader comparative and international perspective, with its heavy accent on a power interpretation of the state. To take his comparative perspective seriously is to understand that Veblen ascribes characteristic or defining features of states to traditions and habits of intercommunal violence. Simply put, Veblen treats the state less as an economic institution than as a distinctively political one. His outlook resembles that of other early twentieth-century political sociologists and historians who also espoused coercive state theory. Max Weber is the most familiar of these writers, but others include historian Otto Hintze and sociologists Joseph Gumplowicz and Franz Oppenheimer. Michael Mann suggests they comprise a distinctively Austro-Germanic militarist school of state theory, one that places war at the heart of state formation and behavior.[58] Theda Skocpol describes their ideas differently. She spotlights their emphasis on the effect of international relations, rather than war per se, on state formation and development.[59] Hans Joas, meanwhile, objects to Mann's claim of a specifically German "militarist tradition" in social theory. Joas makes a reasonable point. Authors in this tradition concur on some things, but they disagree on others, and not all are Germans.⁶⁰ Still, there is probably enough agreement among members of this group to justify Skocpol's claim that such authors share a distinctive force-based or power/coercion interpretation of the state. One thing is certain. Their approach stands well apart from Marxist-class and liberal-contract models of government, and some of Veblen's key ideas bear a close resemblance to it.⁶¹

Political Ends, Economic Means

To explain the modern state's material base, Veblen looked, as any Marxist might, to economic forces and material changes. To explain the motives behind its genesis or evolution as an institution, however, he invoked, as Machiavelli might advise, older political and martial ambitions. In early modern Europe, it was "princely politics" that channeled fast-accelerating economic and industrial forces into support for state power. The dominant motivations were political; princes emulated one another's aspirations for power and prestige. More than anything they feared humiliation at a rival's hand. Princely politics was very personal, and nascent states became instruments of the resulting competition. These competitive political forces assumed a powerful and violent international character. First they took shape on the European stage; soon enough they assumed global proportions.

The ascending "princely politics" spawned competitive energies of armament and state building. To assure their martial strength, kings built states around new capacities of administrative and fiscal organization. The handicraft era's economic growth and technical development propelled political expansion and growth of state power. But the motivations for expanding coercion were primarily political. Veblen carefully distinguishes between political and economic factors to explain patterns of cumulative causation behind state formation in the handicraft era:

> What is known to economic history as the era of handicraft is for the purposes of the political historian spoken of as the era of state-making. The two designations may not cover precisely the same interval, but they coincide in a general way in point of dates, and the phenomena which have given rise to the two designations have

much more than an accidental connection. It is not simply that the development of handicraft happens to fall in the same general period that is characterized by the dynastic wars that went to the making of the larger states. The growth of handicraft had much to do with making the large states practicable and with supplying the material means of large-scale warfare; while the traffic in dynastic politics in that time had in its turn very much to do with bringing that era of industrial and commercial enterprise to an inglorious close.[62]

Princely expansion drove proclivities to war, and war pushed technology in militaristic directions. Meanwhile, an increasingly commercialized economy mediated between forces of state and industry. But if the early modern state had a *telos*, an inner logic or purpose propelling its growth and development, this end was not commerce. It was first and foremost the princes' purposeful "traffic in dynastic politics," a traffic they pursued through "large-scale warfare." Predatory power and honorific ambition always pervaded barbaric culture; now the emergent state tremendously enlarged their scope and breadth. It promised to valorize ancient interests in power and exploit on much greater scales, connecting them to new principles of national defense and security, the first stirrings of national-istic patriotism. For the purpose of understanding Veblen's political ideas, however, the key point about state formation in the handicraft era is that it finally compelled him to address politics head-on.

To explain the basic dynamics and consequences of social life in the handicraft era, Veblen could no longer simply subsume the political within the general category of barbarism. The old aggressive animus, once the preserve of tribal warlords and clan chieftains, now manifested itself within a novel institution, the state, that not only operated on a much wider scale but was a more destructive engine of war than anything the world had yet seen. "The growth of handicraft" did much to make "the large states practicable," Veblen observed, supplying them with "material means of large-scale warfare" that "ate up the sinews of industry."[63] Standing out as an institution that both accelerated and threatened further technical progress in the handicraft era, Veblen could not ignore the state. It demanded acknowledgment on its own political terms. At the same time, by constituting itself as the high domain of legalized force, the state also helped to rationalize increasingly indirect, abstract forms of business and administrative exploit. This contribution too he could not ignore.

In effect, predation was evolving; it was bringing about "a new scheme of institutions" to control and direct social and economic relationships. Predators took control of "powers and functions in the industrial community" and "decided" their use "*on other grounds* than workmanlike aptitude and special training."[64] These grounds were familiar predators' criteria: emulative power and its related processes of exploit. But the evolving political framework of the handicraft era looked more like a state than a tribe, clan, or manor. Whereas writers such as Gumplowicz and Fritz Oppenheimer linked earliest expressions of human plunder with "the state," Veblen is notably more cautious and deliberate. He locates the political roots of primal plunder in emulative motivations. But he distinguishes these primal forms, which he identified with "barbarism," from the specific and much later historic arrival of "the state." Veblen's state is an institution specific to the coming of the handicraft era. Indeed, even though ancient predatory habits are extremely important to his theory of the state, Veblen carefully avoids the concept of state in his discussions of primitive predation. The state hardly appears at all, for example, in *The Theory of the Leisure Class*. For purposes of situating Veblen's theory of state formation, then, the issue of how the category of "the state" appears in his analysis demands attention.

Institutions, Change, and Exploit

Veblen analyzes state formation in a definite historical context. He treats it not as a general conceptual abstraction, but as an evolutionary product of particular social and economic changes at a particular historical moment. As he explained, "The era of handcraft is for the political historian . . . the era of statemaking."[65] In this sense, Veblen's way of dealing with the state is entirely consistent with his method. He is, after all, a theorist pervasively concerned with the *genesis* of institutions. Too often, scholars have described his increasing interest in the state as a kind of ad hoc intellectual reaction to the coming of World War I.[66] True enough: he first treated the state in historical terms in *The Instinct of Workmanship*, which was published in 1914. But as we have seen throughout, clear indications of Veblen's thinking about power appear well before 1914. The more important point to note here, though, is that Veblen had substantial theoretical reasons for introducing the state as part of his analysis of the handicraft era. It is a considered analytical step: it addresses what Veblen recognized to be significant changes in the institutional arrangements and social experience of exploit.

Because it touches importantly on Veblen's evolutionary understanding of exploit, we need to underscore this argument. Veblen shared the coercive school's view of seizure as a political means to wealth, prestige, and power, but his decision to highlight the genesis of the modern state in the handicraft era also implies distinctions that Veblen seemed to recognize between contemporary and premodern forms of seizure, conquest, and plunder. Early exploiters used direct physical force. For all their different forms, Veblen suggests, the ruling groups of barbaric culture had not yet established, distinguished, or separated out for themselves a special institution—what Gumplowicz called "political means" for the organization of exploit. The larger structure of warrior culture itself embodied their "political means": status and class relations, pervasive martial obligations and insecurities, the animus of militant religion, and the whole logic of political domination that barbaric institutions legitimated and reflected in their illiberal habits. By concentrating on the specifically early modern roots of the state, Veblen draws what is for him an unusually sharp contrast with earlier types of barbaric exploit. Important things have changed, he suggests; they must be attended to, and on their own terms. Part of this change involves issues of scale. But there is more.

Other changes concerned the nature, modalities, and institutions of exploitation. Veblen associated these changes with a set of discrete but highly interrelated factors: the economically progressive capacities of the handicraft era; their material contribution to growth of state administration; the latter's impact on the rising scale and destructiveness of warfare; and not least, increasing concentration and urbanization of industrial and financial power in capitalist hands. All these elements contributed, for Veblen, to stimulating a shift toward indirect, more-pacified forms of economic exploitation via market mechanisms.

In sum, Veblen associated the modern state with a buoyant expansion of political and administrative institutions as well as economic power. This was a highly complex, mediated, and differentiated process of expansion. It rested on a new urban industrial and commercial base; expanding trade; improvements in means of communication and transportation; and impressive population growth. In other words, Veblen's insight into the state's contribution to basic changes in the structure and relationships of economic exploit in the handicraft era presented him with both a historical and a theoretical issue. It was this combination of historical and conceptual considerations that we believe awakened Veblen to the need to conceive of political institutions as a major organizing factor in the study of an increasingly pecuniary civilization. In short, Veblen turned to the state for theoretical reasons, not just because he sensed war coming.

Two broad themes converge: Veblen's understanding of state formation in the handicraft era, and the relation of that new institution to the complex of illiberal habits characteristic of older, precapitalist "political means." We have already considered the latter; now we explore the former a little more closely.

The State in the Handicraft Era

"By lineal descent," observed Veblen, the modern state and its powers "derived from the feudal establishments of the Middle Ages." "All that had gone before was not lost." The modern state was "modern only in the sense that it has been modernised out of the past," a form of political modernization that "has been necessarily incomplete."[67] Veblen reminds us not to ignore the grip of illiberal habits; he also cautions against underestimating the scope and depth of political changes that did occur. The resulting political institutions were "greatly altered" from the "mediaeval pattern by concessive adaptation to later exigencies or by a more or less revolutionary innovation."[68] Among these "later exigencies" none was more important to state formation than the impact of technical progress. A close second was the spread of commercial capitalist institutions, especially their price system. Indeed, these forces were inextricably interconnected.

Commercialization stimulated technical development, just as technical progress, in shipping and other industries, expanded the geographic range of commerce. The twinning of technical and commercial developments generated historically unprecedented quantum leaps in scale, efficiency, and lethality of the means of warfare. Progress in martial technologies during the first half of the era of handicraft was startling, exceeding "in material effect and in boldness of conception all the traceable improvements wrought in that line by all the warlike peoples of classical antiquity and all the fighting aggregations of Asia and Africa, from the beginning of the bronze age down to modern times."[69] This remarkable advance in "weapons and armour, defenses and warlike appliances" dramatically accelerated humanity's martial forces. They would culminate in the chilling statistics of death with which we began this chapter.[70]

Not that the kings and princes who sought enhanced military power aimed consciously to elaborate a new kind of political structure, much less a military industrial complex; their preoccupations lay with the old bloody business of dynastic war. "The aim of it all centered in princely dominion and prestige, and in unearned incomes" for the administrative and military staffs essential to more effective war making.[71] But in the face of a changing technical and commercial landscape, the "competitive enterprise of war and politics" required access to, and exploitation of, improved coercive powers that could only be unleashed by economic progress. In the process, monarchical states engineered new methods of political power and control. They conspicuously enlarged and refined institutions of bureaucratic, military, and fiscal power that functioned over an impressively greater range of land, wealth, and population.[72] In Veblen's words, these developments permitted competing royal powers "to extend an effectual coercion over larger distances and over larger aggregations of population and wealth; it became practicable, mechanically, to swing a larger political aggregation and to hold it together in closer coordination than before."[73]

In effect, a nascent international state system clustered around a competitive nexus of princely ambitions and relations, a system of political rivalries that itself became a compelling institutional source of military pressures. After all, individual states could make good on their national security and protection claims only by dint of their membership in an international system of states, one whose mutual threats constituted a fabric of common interests in each other's reason for being. "Any given governmental establishment at home is useful" as an institution of protection, Veblen observed, "only as against another governmental establishment elsewhere . . . The service so rendered by the constituted authorities in the aggregate takes on the character of a remedy for evils of their own creation."[74]

Thus modern states gained their coercive rationale and character not only from imperatives of domestic repression, as Perry Anderson argues, but perhaps even more from an aggressive, competitive rationality inherent in the international state system. This collective system of mutually hostile relations is thus key to understanding the militarism of the parts.[75] Without the mimetic, emulative contribution of other aggressive states, national defense aims would be nugatory.[76]

Of course, the pressures of an increasingly systematic political competition only amplified incentives to exploit the modernized means of war. But all this increasing technical competence and coercive efficiency came at a price. Kings eager to benefit from technical progress had to develop improved means to extract resources necessary to finance their militaristic projects. More than coincidentally, the same forces that provided new means of war also helped to forge novel material and administrative institutions to finance these very forces, a point strongly reinforced by Tilly's research on state formation.[77] As we have seen, the handicraft era encouraged growth of urban industrialism. With this development came new facilities and means of transportation and communication, and with these, increasingly elaborate government bureaucracies to extract state revenues from expanding flows of wealth in goods and gold. Improvements in shipbuilding, ports, and roads; the spread of printing; innovations in accounting, such as double-entry bookkeeping and rationalization of the price system—all these, fused with innovations in such basic tools of discipline as the watch and clock, stimulated expanding industry, capital, production, and population.[78] State-building monarchs took advantage of these developments for purposes of economic surveillance and extraction. Moreover, "the trade in arms and weapons was good at this time"; in the industrial towns, excellent profits were to be had in feeding royal demands for arms and means of coercion.[79] Responding to lucrative state-directed markets, handicraft era capitalists acted quite rationally. Even during these initial stages of capitalist development, the craftsmen-merchants sensed "little else than a pecuniary responsibility" to their community, or to their own interest as a class.[80]

Most important, because handicraft producers were also traders and sellers working in markets, their activities accelerated the spread of the price system, inspiring a revolution in economic organization that made it easier for kings to purchase and locate military resources, including mercenary troops, thus "enabling warlike operations to be carried on with greater facility at a greater distance than was feasible under the earlier rule of contributions in kind."[81] In this way, developments in monetized taxation and credit finance facilitated royal capacities to extract needed resources to pay for expanded war machines, as well as contributing to "concentration of wealth in fewer hands."[82]

A major feature of the new scale of political, military, and economic power, therefore, was a shift from the directly physical exploit typical of "contributions in kind" to an increasingly administrative, commercial, and abstract exploitation entailed by taxation of private wealth, with all that implied for emergent forms of record keeping, accounting, and budgeting. Whole new cadres of financial experts, lawyers, and administrative clerks arose to perform these roles. As "funds had become the sinews of war," kings, generals, bankers, and capitalists tightened their bonds.[83] Networks of financial, military, and political power solidified, though they never became so close—or so functionally rational—as to bar chances for fiscal crisis and economic exhaustion, whose potential grew along with the rising scale of war.[84]

Finally, through it all, as state apparatuses enlarged themselves in step with the military and imperial ambitions of their monarchical chiefs, predatory habits and sentiments "swamped the handicraft spirit and put abnegation and dependence on arbitrary power in the place of that initiative and pertinacious self-reliance that had made the era of handicraft."[85] States emerging from this complex of royal ambition, capitalist profitability, and industrial skill were a qualitatively new institution of power. Their political apparatus enabled governments to fight and conquer on vastly larger scales than ever before, and they enjoyed more effective purchase on the labor, skills, finances, and loyalty of domestic populations. Spokesmen for the crown, who gradually learned how to convert old solidarities into new patriotic appeals, anticipated developments in the ideology of nationalism, changes that would come in time to have a powerful democratic resonance. In short, Veblen's introduction of the state as a major actor in the narrative of the coming of pecuniary society illuminates the weight it assumed for him in a changing and ever more violent geopolitical landscape. The rising chieftains of business enterprise would have many reasons to exploit this new state system for their own purposes, but not even the absentee owners of later generations have necessarily yet learned how fully to harness its enlarged powers of violence, or wholly to subdue its potential for subordinating economic interests to militarism.

Several themes central to Veblen's political theory thus emerge from this survey. First, there is the firm insistence that ancient and illiberal habits of war and predation antedated development of modern states. These habits contributed greatly to the shaping of political and combative expectations. They influenced the design of modern states as governments became enlarged and formalized institutions of coercion. Veblen's claims along these lines separate him from Marxist as well as liberal theorists. They justify his consideration as a theorist of the coercive state.

Second, Veblen recognized that this new political institution, the state, was not simply an expression or condensation of material forces, although economic institutions and industrial factors played indispensable roles in its expansion. Monarchical ambitions and competitive political power stood behind modern state institutions. Whatever interests capitalists might—or might not—generate in respect to war—and Veblen clearly believed that business interests did generate imperial, aggressive interests—political relations among the new states produced their own statist reasons for war.

Finally, and perhaps most important, Veblen took the coming of the state very seriously, as a phenomenon of institutional change. He considered its historical genesis in the handicraft era to be a major institutional development, one that foreshadowed consequential changes in the political and economic character of exploitation as well as in the institutional relationships of increasingly specialized economic and political powers. The last point is especially relevant to the domestic and international political behavior of the ostensible democracies that evolved out of the dynastic state model.

7

OSTENSIBLE DEMOCRACY

For over two centuries democracy has been entangled with war, especially in the United States. Warfare and its threat have enlarged executive powers of military command, legitimated secrecy, spurred surveillance, distorted the economy, and militarized technological development. War making justified conscription, demanded loyalty, and exacted repression. Recent wars in Southeast Asia, Iraq, and Afghanistan eroded popular trust in government. The draft, for example, is now politically out-of-bounds. But the professionalized military that followed served only to loosen already tenuous controls on presidential war powers.[1]

None of this history would have shocked Veblen; he anticipated its main outlines. Still, he was not hopeless for democracy. He occasionally thought that democracy might actually subdue warrior legacies and pacify government, at least somewhat. Veblen was no liberal democrat, of course, but he had unmistakable democratic sympathies. Max Lerner greatly overstated the case when he asserted, "Veblen carefully avoids any reference to democratic ideals."[2] In fact, Veblen's discussions of pagan anarchism and the handicraft era give voice to several "democratic ideals," including self-government, representative assemblies, political freedom, rule of law, limitation of executive power, and not least, a defiant spirit of popular insubordination. One of his earliest essays even described constitutional democracy as a possible model for socialism. Not that he believed socialism was either imminent or inevitable.[3] The existing democracies were capitalist, and their underlying populations generally conservative in their politics. But capitalism did not completely stack political decks against social change. A more humane political economy was possible, if underlying populations fought to achieve it. It all depended on whether people chose this path, or rather, on how free citizens were to choose it at all. Here Veblen broached fundamental issues: How well did citizens and workers really know themselves and their own generic needs as human beings? Democracy expressed the will of public opinion, but how free is the public to form its own will? E. E. Schattschneider identified the American people as "semi-sovereign"; Veblen might have preferred the formulation "quasi-sovereign."

Some things, he believed, augured well for democracy. Technological modernization spurred matter-of-fact ways of thinking, habits hostile to "coercion, personal dominion, self-abasement, subjection, loyalty [and] suspicion."[4] Industrial progress might erode the grip of illiberal habits. Then citizens would see their interests more clearly and become more able to act in their defense. Democracy's chances would improve. An industrial republic might come about to let industrial forces serve popular interests and "fullness of life." But other factors affected human thinking as well. Many of these had counter-rational implications, inspiring deep Veblenian doubts about the freedom of public opinion to form itself. Human "reasoning," Veblen stated in one of his sharpest observations on political consciousness, "is largely controlled by other than logical, intellectual forces . . . the conclusion reached by public or class opinion is as much, or more, a matter of sentiment than of logical inference; and . . . the sentiment which animates men, singly or collectively, is as much, or more, an outcome of habit and native propensity as of calculated material interest."[5] Rational choice is not always so rational.

Democratic politics unfolded under a constraint of tensions between rationalization and sentiment, between sober insight into the present and a reactionary pull of illiberal habit.[6] Spiritually, democracy reflected the enduring influence of insubordinate, anarchistic legacies. But these libertarian trends are heavily constrained by atavistic ideas and institutions. Popular politics generated political forces of independence and insubordination—echoes of pagan anarchy and the handicraft era. But these are arrayed against and within the claims of society's major hierarchical institutions for control, subordination, emulation, and compliance. Like Imperial Germany, most contemporary political systems offer their own peculiar blend of irresponsible powers and democratic institutions, their own "distinctive form of the current compromise between the irresponsible autocracy of the mediaeval state and the autonomy of popular self-government."[7] Democracy has the potential to create a better world, but it is a potential substantially curtailed or sabotaged by habit and inertia. Democratic politics happens within this contradiction.

In this chapter we will consider how Veblen analyzed America's version of this "current compromise." He supported a certain notion of responsible democratic self-government, what he liked to call an "industrial republic." This is a possibility that government and business resist in the interest of their hold on power. Without forgetting Veblen's arguments about the independent impact of international relations, our focus here will be on how business regulates American political institutions domestically: state agendas, public opinion, and constitutional law. We will look at the business culture's impact on one particular aspect of popular consciousness, a cynical opportunism that, more for Veblen than most other observers of American politics, is a key preservative or stabilizer of the system. Our major concern throughout will be on the ways that pecuniary culture encourages citizens to emulate their rulers' predatory habits, subverting their democratic potential to use law as a means of nudging industry toward "furtherance of the life process taken impersonally."

Democracy, an Empirical Problem of Culture

Unlike most conventional democratic theorists, Veblen avoided purely conceptual, formal, or theoretical discussions of democracy. To understand democracy, for him, is not a matter of reconciling abstract principles, such as participation and authority, freedom and community, or obligation and liberty. Nor is it a question of proper institutional design. "Man's life is activity," Veblen insisted, "and as he acts, so he thinks and feels." This working principle informs Veblen's view of democracy, as it does all phases of his inquiry into human behavior. Democracy, too, is activity of a certain kind: popular political practices and expectations that persist and change within specific cultural settings, contexts shaped by ruling classes, prevailing institutions, and technical change. Democracy, in a Veblenian sense, comes down to what ordinary people really do and don't do to influence the exercise of institutional power. Such action, of course, is patterned by culture or habit. Tradition shapes or conditions what people experience as the possible range of action, just as it may counsel the wisdom of inaction. Culture also influences tensions between reason and sentiment that affect activity. Because the cultural frame is such an important part of democratic activity, it contains major clues to Veblen's understanding of American democratic life and its shortcomings.

With his firm cultural emphasis, Veblen wrote more like a classically minded political thinker than he is often given credit for. After all, "the effort to explain politics and public policy by political culture theory goes back to the very origins of political science."[8] The notion that politics reflects social habit is as old as Aristotle and as contemporary as the work of Robert Putnam.[9] If we take a self-proclaimed democracy to express in some way the self-understanding and activity of its citizens, it is reasonable that students of democracy should study the cultural arrangements and habits that make people what they are. Veblen treated modern democracy in just this way. It is a complex of institutions in and out of government that organizes and impedes action. The prevailing institutions work themselves out in concrete instances to fashion a particular compromise of statist, capitalist, and self-governing popular forces. What passes for democracy is a multi-institutional, cultural fact. It is a part of the broader institutional setting of action. But democracy is also its by-product. It is not purely, or even mainly, a political fact, especially if by political we narrow the focus to government and public administration. To grasp democracy, Veblen implies, political scientists need to appreciate its complex fullness, its relationships to society and economy and above all to history and tradition. They need to untangle its various elements, to identify and evaluate them in relation to the larger cultural and evolutionary matrix that forms the boundaries and content of popular political practice.

Above all, students of democracy should be aware of probabilities that "a certain characteristic tone or bias runs through the whole" of culture.[10] This "tone or bias" contributes "solidarity . . . mutual support . . . or re-enforcement" to the various social institutions; it infuses a given culture with its chances for coherence. As James K. Galbraith observes, Veblen emphasized the stability of social orders "dominated by a predatory and unproductive class" and a more or less coherent conservative bias.[11] For the U.S. case, Veblen saw hierarchical capitalist and statist tendencies as primary biases controlling, engaging, and limiting the nation's democratic activity. American democracy developed in their shadow and reflected many of their nondemocratic limitations.

Veblen was too sensitive to tension and variety in social life to reduce democratic culture to a single principle, such as equality, participation, or even business rule. He was more inclined to treat democracy as a mixed institutional type, though not in the traditional sense of a political order that fuses aspects of monarchy, aristocracy, and democracy. Veblen's understanding of mixture refers to the rather different, more temporal idea that cultures express conflicting patterns of change and resistance to change, and this resistance is especially reflective of embedded institutions, older and newer historical arrangements, as often as not working at cross-purposes. Institutions, especially political ones, function to organize the main social forces of dynamism and inertia in complex and contradictory ways. This Veblenian idea finds something of a contemporary expression in Orren and Skowronek's idea of "intercurrence." Though they do not mention Veblen in their work, what they propose is a notion remarkably akin to his approach: "Intercurrence depicts the organization of the polity seen strictly from an historical institutional point of view. It directs researchers to locate the historical construction of politics in the simultaneous operation of older and newer arrangements of governance, in controls asserted through multiple orderings of authority whose coordination with one another cannot be assumed and whose outward reach and impingements, including one another, are inherently problematic."[12]

In similar ways, we can appreciate Veblen's analysis by grasping how he thinks about political culture in three fluid or dynamic dimensions:

1. A prevailing set of historically evolved institutions, habits, arrangements, and controls
2. Current pressures and needs that arise especially from emerging material, environmental, and technical forces
3. Patterns of adaptation heavily influenced by orthodox habits of mind that operate to reconcile or adapt old arrangements to technical and social pressures, as often as not by thwarting, deflecting, or moderating such pressures, canalizing them into familiar forms.[13]

Veblen's concept of mixed government emphasizes both dynamic and inertial elements in social and economic life and the role government plays in mediating the resulting tensions. He offers no teleological promise that democracy will reach a balance or harmony of interests. Nor does he predict revolutionary ferment. Instead, Veblen anticipates a more or less stable order vulnerable to recurrent tensions, conflicts, and instabilities, ongoing strains between democratic, industrial, and anachronistic/predatory tendencies in culture. Maybe the system will reach a working balance, maybe not. The issue is empirical, not theoretical. Veblen's sense of indeterminacy amply illuminates his basic principle of modern democratic government. Democratic citizens everywhere aspire to some workable compromise between ideals of self-government and what he called the large-scale coercive principle.

From this standpoint, Veblen's early twentieth-century American democracy—and our own twenty-first-century version of it, for that matter—is a dynamic compound of forces moving at very different rates of speed. It includes a grudging eighteenth-century system of political institutions and even older illiberal habits; an exceptionally progressive technological system; an expanding business order dominated by large corporations; a financial system built on illusory forms of credit; and a warfare state with imperial and military ambitions. Democracy as it really exists, then, is a richly mixed compound of precapitalist, capitalist, imperial, and technocratic elements, perhaps even some protosocialist ones. It was and is a working synthesis of illiberal, liberal, and democratic habits. It is much more than a simple reflection of business interests, and Veblen understood that.

Those concerned for democratic prospects should do more than look to the past and present, however. Indeed, people should not, Veblen once noted, measure the future exclusively in terms of the past, for "the tempo of the present and of the calculable future is in many bearings very different from that which has ruled even the recent historical past."[14] The past is very powerful, he constantly reminded us. But the past is not all-powerful. An accelerating rate of change exerts significant pressures of its own. The outcome of collisions between past and future is not predictable with anything like mathematical certainty. Democracy is activity, which means that democracy itself is change. In this sense, Veblen was probably more ambivalent about democratic prospects than merely pessimistic. Or perhaps it is more accurate to say that he was both ambivalent and pessimistic, if that is possible. The ambivalence is aptly expressed in a term that he used in *The Nature of Peace* to describe the democracies of his day. "Ostensible democracies" he called them.

It is helpful to recall that the word "ostensible" comes from the Latin *ostensibilis*, a term with two linguistic roots, *ostendere*, which means "to show . . . against," and *tendere*, "to stretch." As usual, Veblen chose his words carefully. To indicate that a democracy is "ostensible" is to say that it makes a special show of its forms, rituals, and ceremonies. In the process it "stretches" its showy appearances to convey impressions that obscure darker truths. It is a matter of "what the older logicians . . . called *suppressio veri* and *suggestio falsi*." Suppress the truth and suggest the false.[15] That this principal was "the rule" of American "country town salesmanship" is more than coincidental. Veblen conceived of "the country town" as the American institution that had the greatest influence "in shaping public sentiment and giving character to public opinion."[16]

Veblen's Democratic Norm

Veblen's thoughts on democracy, like much of what he said about politics in general, come in scattered fragments. In later books, however, such as *Absentee Ownership* and *The Nature of Peace*, democracy becomes a more prominent and focused theme. Overall, it is fair to say that he was more prone to reflect on illiberal and nondemocratic aspects of "ostensible" democracies than he was to clarify political conditions for a fully realized democracy. Veblen thought of democracy at its best as a nonpolitical expression of economic modernization, a developed form of savagery, whose chief progressive dynamic was technical and industrial. Its historical realization thus depended on a willingness and capacity of underlying populations to abandon conventional politics and press for social control of the industrial system, to demand that society use industry to meet their broadly generic needs. In this connection, two features of democracy—impersonal law and public opinion—impressed Veblen as especially crucial elements of popular government. Considered together, law and opinion probably bring us as close as we are ever likely to get to a sense of what Veblen thought of as ingredients essential to democracy. This conclusion is especially warranted if we assess Veblen's treatment of these themes in the context of his consistent commitment to advancement "of the life process taken impersonally."

From democratic perspectives, it is as important as it is revealing that Veblen identifies impersonal standards of well-being with popular "common sense," a sensibility deriving from the instinct of workmanship and its related parental bent. Reflecting popular abhorrence of waste, Veblen heard such standards echoed "in the language of everyday life." Popular inclinations to criticize waste were one indicator of how "human intelligence has not yet gone into abeyance."[17] As industry and work come naturally to most people, their very difficulty a teacher of virtues, most people learn to value labor, conserve energy, and condemn waste. Such habits express the "economic conscience" that might someday motivate Veblen's industrial republic.

As noted earlier, barbarism made labor seem irksome, introducing leisure and excess as signs of prowess and privilege among ruling classes sheltered from industry. Many centuries passed before rulers could count on these habits to keep people quiet.[18] This is why Veblen thinks that his standpoint aligns with incipient inclinations among ordinary people to seek impersonal goods over personal benefits. As a feature of "common sense," Veblen implicitly suggests, the impersonal generic standpoint is a kind of popular or democratic inclination that flows directly from the species' productive and creative dispositions. Their influence leads us to satisfy the terms of our survival through socially valued labor, as in matriarchal savagery, pagan anarchy, and the industrial towns of the handicraft era. In such connections between "economic conscience" and "common sense," we get glimmers—though not much more than that—of Veblen's hope for democracy.[19] Building on them, we can cautiously sketch a Veblenian norm for democracy, a rough design of its progressive industrial bias.

In contrast with ostensible democracy's spectacle and display, industrial democracy promises only a sober, unsentimental public opinion that expresses itself through impersonal law. Opinion and law will guide forces of industry toward enhancement and fullness of life, impersonally understood. The whole system is merely an "unsanctified workaday arrangement for the common use of industrial ways and means."[20] It replaces glorification of power with a mundane, unflashy politics that decides the scope and content of generic needs, as these emerge from a yet-to-be-defined dialogue between public and expert opinion.[21]

Beyond obligations to define and satisfy generic material needs in noninvidious ways, a Veblenian industrial democracy would be libertarian. Following the quasi-anarchistic principle of live and let live, it would urge people to go their own way on issues of social or moral value. However, it would hardly be likely to forget the complex inheritance of the nation's past. So Americans would probably continue to fight "culture wars" over alternate conceptions of morality and value. Many citizens would continue to be discomfited by a "mechanistic mutilation of objective reality . . . and so fall back on the will to believe in the fog of occult and esoteric faiths."[22] Perhaps a general decline of atavistic sentiments would make these struggles between rationalists and believers less intense than they are now. Maybe the resulting democratic society would show as much regard for invidious and sentimental interests as contemporary capitalist democracies do for egalitarian values. All that can be said for sure is that industrial democracy would have its own distinctive biases and cultural tone. Public opinion and public law would be their reflection.

Democratic Opinion and Political Power

Though few of Veblen's critics have made much of it, he accepted the classical liberal idea that public opinion formed the basis of democratic society.[23] Veblen agreed that industrialization, business enterprise, the modern state, and universal suffrage favored growth of a mass democratic culture, one that nurtured movements and continuities in public opinion. The very fact that Veblen identified the great power of "the country town" with its impact on "public sentiment" speaks to this emphasis. And the fact that public opinion was a governing political fact meant that social relations and structures were now vulnerable to influence from more sources than the ruling class. Democracy is activity and activity has many causes and multiple possible directions.

Common opinion was now a force for elites to reckon with. Particularly important was the opinion of a working class, which Veblen believed—or hoped—through contact with the machine process, could become more sober, materialistic, and class conscious.[24] Social structures remained highly unequal; states were still hierarchical and militaristic. But now all classes, even the upper class, respected popular will, or at least claimed to respect it. Democracy introduced the unmistakable power of public opinion as the measure for judging conformity of institutions with popular aspirations. "Elder statesmen continued to direct" society from above, he wrote, but "it is the frame of mind of the common man that makes the foundation of society in the modern world."[25] Gone were the days when arrogant warlords and absolute monarchs could simply push working people around. Ordinary people now believed themselves to be legitimate rulers of society. Democratization implied a new populist logic of imputation: even as they continued to search for signs of prowess in their leaders, the people imputed political formidability to themselves. Besides, as James Galbraith notes, "the success of the predators depends in part on healthy prey. And to a degree, their prestige depends on it."[26]

Here are the roots of the idea of popular sovereignty, though Veblen saw too much of the old political illusion in it. He thought the notion ludicrous that "democratic citizens, each and several, by Grace of God hold sovereign dominion over the underlying population of which they each and several are abjectly servile components."[27] But he appreciated the fact that popular belief in democratic sovereignty had serious consequences. It meant, at least rhetorically, that political leaders must acknowledge that their authority is only on loan from the popular sovereign, a power delivered unto the leadership by consent of the governed. Veblen, however, sensed chances for more than mere symbolic maneuvers here. Consent gave the people an "eventual power of veto" over their leaders. Democracy made it, at the very least, "ceremonially necessary for the gentlemanly classes to consult the wishes of . . . their sovereign." But ceremony did not foreclose larger substantive implications. The principle of consent of the governed implied that the vital political power to say, "what may be safely done or left undone in society" depended on the "frame of mind of the common man."[28] At the same time, an impersonal and general constitutional law carefully channeled this new power of public opinion. Law defined conditions under which democratic power had effect, and in a variety of ways, could enlarge, but also limit, mute, or nullify that effect. In either case, Veblen took the democratic potential of constitutional law as seriously as he did public opinion.

Impersonal Law

In "Some Neglected Points in the Theory of Socialism" Veblen cited law's rationality and impersonality as the most distinctive feature of modern constitutional government.[29] Even more remarkably, he referred to it as a template for possible evolution of political into socialist democracy. "The whole system of modern constitutional government in its latest developed forms," he said, showed that democratic societies could establish principles of social organization distinct from previously dominant forms of military status and capitalist contract.[30] Constitutional democracy already differed from regimes based on ascriptive status. It made political power impersonal and legally responsible, at least formally. By abolishing capitalist property and establishing economic equality, social democracy could make further progressive moves. With military status and capitalist property in abeyance, ordinary people might fashion new communal foundations for democratic public law. Most important, this law would find its orientation in industrial, not emulative, ends.

Clearly written rules, prescribed limits of office and tenure, and public election meant that citizens of constitutional democracies were now freer to live and work under principles of responsible government. Even now, citizens are "subject not to the person of the public functionary, but to the powers vested in him."[31] Socialist democracy, giving reign to "economic conscience," would extend this principle to industrial life and economic planning. Promising something very different than to represent the emulative power desires of individuals, it would organize the collective voice and generic interests of the population, authorizing the state, through law, to take economic measures deemed necessary for the collective good. Constitutionally based socialist democracy would answer in the civic realm to the new institutional realities of collective power that had already overtaken the industrial order. As notable examples, Veblen cites two of the most confiscatory economic powers of existing democracies: "the right of eminent domain and the power to tax."

Still, a humane democratic socialism would have only modest pretensions. It would dispense with nationalism, patriotism, and imperialism, trashing the symbolic trappings of national glory. Industrial democracy "would be nothing to bluster and give off fumes about; nothing better than an unsanctified workaday arrangement for the common use of industrial ways and means."[32]

Coercion, Insubordination, and Conflict

On the face of it, it is hard to square Veblen's embrace of "impersonal law" with his critique of the coercive state and his anarchistic proclivities. Impersonal law unambiguously implies the state's coercive power. Law everywhere gives government authority to use force against citizens. Democracy—or the industrial republic—must preserve minimum elements of a coercive state. The question is how people might learn to neglect, as Veblen liked to put it, the state's warlike aspect, while learning how to channel democratic legal power toward humane generic ends. Veblen is painfully vague about all this. His inclinations to look to "fellowships of ungraded masterless men," "the rule of live and let live," or to "an anarchist republic of autonomous communes" are virtually useless as institutional clues. In quite un-Veblenian ways, they speak to aspiration, not activity.

Perhaps the closest Veblen came to even remote acknowledgment of the difficulties is a brief discussion of the Icelandic Republic, whose history he dated from the tenth to the thirteenth century. Veblen offers that distant form as the best example of a government that is not a state.[33] Gifted with the rare good luck of having avoided feudalism, he says, the Icelandic Republic lacked its coercive habits. It shed "powers for the Common Defense," and thus "subjection to personal rule." A "harmless and helpless national organization," the Icelandic Republic did not necessarily suspend all forms of force, but it curtailed the most dangerous agent of irresponsible power, executive war powers. The Icelandic Republic example—along with others such as pagan anarchy and handicraft era towns—suggests that Veblen was prone to distinguish internal from external forms of political force. He appeared to find economically necessary legal force acceptable; the coerciveness of militarism was not.

"Coercive authority" in militarized states supported power seeking, war making, predation, and exploit. It instilled a "sense of subordination" among citizens.[34] The economic policies of social democracy presumably enhanced the general welfare and enlarged conditions for free and reasonable work. Industrial republics favored equality and industry, not exploit.

To what extent, though, could Veblen's insubordinate citizens challenge law's definition of economic welfare? He offers no answers and no clues; he simply did not pursue the matter. All we can say is that Veblen probably envisioned—or at least should have seen—coercion and the spirit of insubordination as inevitably clashing principles of modern social democracy. Each contributes something valuable to the good of the whole. Coercion facilitates industrial coordination; insubordination preserves the human spirit. But if the claim that democracy has to reconcile principles of authority and resistance is unsurprising, the fact that Veblen recognized it is a little more so. Often charged with being a technocratic elitist, Veblen's political theory sees how challenging it is to balance authority and resistance. In fact, for all his regard for the logic of industrial rationality, Veblen issues a cautionary political caveat to aspiring collectivists: acknowledge "the spirit of insubordination," he insisted, because it is "an invaluable premise in any inquiry into the practicability or expediency of any system of control or any projected line of collective enterprise."[35] Socialist centralizers, beware!

Humans have an aptitude for "avoiding direct conflict with their competitors"; sometimes, though, conditions make conflict unavoidable, and so does "the spirit of insubordination."[36] Insubordinate citizens may well disagree with experts about how to use society's resources or about how to organize the industrial process. Democratic citizens could justifiably rouse themselves in compelling ways. In pagan anarchy and the handicraft era towns, after all, active resistance to authority and "the spirit of insubordination" were vital civic forces. And popular traditions and culture have long supported habits of opposition.[37] Rebellious habits also characterize the "masterless man." Indeed, Veblen held that the "ancient ideals of insubordination" form the very "substance of . . . free institutions" in the Anglo-American tradition, a tradition always capable of "re-asserting itself in democratic discontent."[38]

Veblen's sympathies for insubordination are equally visible in his praise for such radical groups as the Industrial Workers of the World, and in his deepest hope that contact with mechanization would stimulate wider circles of insubordination among workers. Beyond these examples, it is worth remembering that he not only reluctantly supported U.S. entry into World War I, he advocated violent overthrow of the German ruling class at its conclusion.[39] He also admired Russian peasants for defeating

western capitalist states when the latter tried to reverse the Soviet revolution by force.[40] Most important, he was quite prepared to concede that a
break with capitalism might compel a head-on collision of class interests.

The end of business enterprise would not necessarily arrive through "the
innocuous shape of unstudied neglect," Veblen warned. Chances were
good that in a class confrontation, business would use "all the coercive
agencies of law and order to uphold the ancient rights of ownership."
The underlying population would be left with no choice but to take "an
uncompromising stand." At that critical point, a "recourse to forcible
measures is . . . scarcely open to question. History teaches that in such a
quarrel the recourse has always been to force."[41] Veblen, it appears, was
quite prepared to draw distinctions between emulative combat, in which
fighting served to enhance personalized power and class predation, and
ideological conflict, which aimed to bring irresponsible power to heel, or
to bring about a more just and rational society. In short, while he abhorred
violence Veblen was neither a pacifist nor in principle opposed to political
conflict and coercive political power. He was, once again, a radical realist.

Appreciating Veblen's nuanced view of political force helps to explain
why he despaired of the lack of insubordination in ostensible democracy.
He lamented that citizens too rarely challenge predatory authority in
serious ways; they exercised too little of their presumed sovereignty. And
such contests usually have limited structural effects when they do break
out. Most citizens veer toward political passivity. Quiescence is a stronger
habit than insubordination. Intensity of mass participation, "the violence
of faction," is simply not the problem of democracy James Madison
thought it was. Opinion mattered, but its potential for transformation
into insurgency was small.

Illiberal Habits and Democratic Opinion

Public opinion emerged as the great democratic force of the
nineteenth century. But much of its content was neither modern nor
enlightened. The newly emergent popular opinion embraced many illiberal habits and old ideas. For Veblen, as we have seen, there are few more
salient facts about democracy than this one. Habits of predemocratic social
deference, ascriptive status, and class subordination persisted well into the

new age.[42] These drew strength from the fact that modern patriots and rising nationalists learned how to bind national populations with atavistic themes. At the same time, religious belief was far from exhausted, and emulative aspirations received boosts from capitalist salesmanship. "The masterless man" would find his place within such conservative institutions as the warfare state, business enterprise, the military, and the church. So have many masterless women more recently. In nineteenth- and twentieth-century mass culture, habits of deference, patriotism, patriarchy, and racism held their own, shaping and narrowing experiences of liberal freedom and democratic expectation. Money mattered above all perhaps, but it is crucial for a Veblenian analysis of democratic opinion that the putative measure of monetary values remained tied, however obscurely, to ancient claims for honorific power. For Veblen, American business culture used money to gauge levels of imputed power. It was, as people on Wall Street like to say, a way of keeping score. Money gave the ancient appeal of formidability a bright golden sheen. But the prevailing pecuniary "bias or bent" still leaned toward ends that were ultimately "invidious, personal, emulative, looking to differential values in respect of personal force or competitive success . . . to gradations in respect of comparative potency, validity, authenticity, propriety, reputability, decency."[43]

In all these ways, much that was old was still venerated; the people greeted political novelty, but not without measures of caution and reserve. In essence, liberal individualism sustained itself with older bonds of loyalty, community, and convention. Liberalism and its values, including its more populist and democratic aspects, developed within institutional frameworks whose conservative contents were healthier and more lively that most liberals and conservatives thought. Veblen understood the progressive novelty of liberalism. But he also sensed that, like any new ideological or political form, it shared cultural space with older verities. In the wake of political modernization and democratization, "All that had gone before was not lost, many things were carried over." Such views explain why conservatives like Ernest Dewey might claim Veblen as a closet ally.

As we saw earlier, Veblen believed modern political systems depended on a shifting, incontinent balance of illiberal, liberal, and even postliberal or democratic tendencies. In cases such as Imperial Germany and Japan, illiberal habits clearly predominated, although even authoritarian states featured notable social democratic tendencies. England and the United States enjoyed decidedly more-liberal political institutions, but illiberal habits persisted. England had its monarchy and its empire. America had a growing empire too, including a string of bloody conquests, participation in a series of foreign and domestic wars, not to mention slavery, Native American genocide, and their racist legacies. Each of these political orders, in its own way, represented, as did Imperial Germany, a "distinctive form of the current compromise between the irresponsible autocracy of the mediaeval State and the autonomy of popular self-government."[44]

Adding to the difficulty of gauging the complex balance of forces, political and business leaders could use new media of communication, such as radio and film, to mix messages and conflate symbols.[45] Development of mass communications, especially fields such as public relations and opinion management, engaged new cadres of opinion technicians. New experts in salesmanship became adept at melding old sentiments and new desires into effective symbols and compliant patterns of public opinion. What could be more indigenous to twentieth-century American democracy, for example, than its pledge of allegiance, a loyalty device that came into the political culture only in the 1890s.[46] Explore the root meanings of the term allegiance and one discovers, as Veblen understood, a reference to the Latin term *ligare*, "to bind," as in relationships of vassal and lord. The pledge of allegiance lent democratic veneer to an essentially feudal ceremony of subordination.

Economic and technical rationalization, on the other hand, could lead democratic opinion in more radical directions. Most important, Veblen understood that democratic trends affected political expectations at all social levels. Industrialization, corporate expansion, and growing state power led to a dynamic mass democratic culture, a political order governed by swings as well as continuities of public opinion. At a minimum, popular claims to power implied that system legitimacy demanded an appearance of popular control. In practice, events turned not only on abstract ideological claims. The public's vigilance still counted, especially its ability to issue credible threats of insubordination. Docile populations would make easier pickings for warrior politicians and corporate salesmen; insubordinate ones could make trouble, and Veblen appreciated the conflicting possibilities. In *The Nature of Peace*, for example, he crafted an impressively balanced assessment of democratic opinion. Remarking on popular opinion in Western Europe, his statement applies with equal force to the North American case. In the ostensible democracies, Veblen wrote, citizens believe that they

> urgently need freedom to live their own life in their own way, or rather to live within the bonds of convention which they have come in for by use and wont, or at least they believe that such freedom is essential to any life that shall be quite worthwhile. So also they have a felt need for security from arbitrary interference in their pursuit of a livelihood and in the free control of their own pecuniary concerns. And they want a voice in the management of their joint interests, whether as a nation or in a minor civil group. In short, they want personal, pecuniary, and political liberty, free from all direction or inhibition from without. They are also much concerned to maintain favorable economic conditions for themselves and their children. And last, but chiefly rather than least, they commonly are hide-bound patriots inspired with an intractable felt need of national prestige.[47]

This is a finely calibrated judgment. As befits a population with cultural and political roots in the handicraft era, modern democratic citizens desire freedom to live their own way, albeit within "bonds of convention," which they have learned to accept. In order to provide well for themselves and their families, they expect opportunities to earn and spend money freely. They also expect to influence government, to which they remain patriotically loyal. In short, modern democracy nurtures citizens who are, at once, anxious for freedom but habituated to hierarchies. Protective of their freedom, and jealous of their place in society, they compete for recognition, income, and power within institutions framed by state and business. Pocketbook issues remain central. But social integration still draws heavily from patriotism, family, and religion. Together, these are "the bonds of convention" through which people aim for and control their pecuniary and political aspirations.

The prevailing culture celebrates private gratifications and public loyalties, but it hardly blocks all grounds for public complaint. "Pecuniary competition, when carried to its ideal pitch works the lower industrial classes to exhaustion," and while fatigue minimizes activism, economic disappointment leads to irritation and frayed populist tempers.[48] The elections of 1932, 1992, 2008, and 2010 supply ample evidence. Besides, as corporations grow larger and more hierarchical, "the authority of ownership" threatens to become more "coercive," its "harsh aloofness" becoming more like "irresponsible tyranny," with "none of the genial traits that may relieve even a relatively ruthless despotism." In response, labor can grow "sullen" and "unenthusiastic," producing, as it often did in the English case, "a grudging disloyalty" and class friction.[49]

Holding coercion in reserve, business can avoid corrosive tendencies with higher pay and mass entertainment. As James Galbraith reminds us, "Contrary to Marx, in Veblen's scheme of things the industrial orders are not driven to the point of subsistence."[50] Rewards and gratifications abound. The allure of sports, along with the cheerful product of new radio and film companies, not to mention an endless assortment of emulative consumer goods, favors a "politically salutary dissipation" in the underlying population. Religious spirit and patriotic pride lend their support to the going order too. All these forces help to lift "the common man's afterthought into the upper air, instead of letting it run along the ground of material fact, where it do might do mischief."[51] But even patriots and the faithful have limits. Hard times still create bad feelings and political trouble.

Summing up, for Veblen, the overall pattern of democratic opinion adds up to an occasionally irritated or impatient inclination to accept the going order, with a measure of freedom reserved for periodic complaint and episodes of insubordination. On occasion the public will insist on improvements and a political redress of grievances, although it figures to be intolerant of radical alternatives. Generally, it will display impressive patience before it demands reform. In short, democratic public opinion is likely to be apolitical and to trend conservative, albeit somewhat peevishly and inconsistently so, willing on occasion to dissent, but not to express expectations that push much beyond the secure outlines of the status quo.

For elder statesmen and absentee owners, this main drift of opinion is reassuring, though power continues to spur uncertainties. Where the very status of master is assimilated to the "prevalent habit of judging facts and events from the standpoint of the fight," conflict is built into the logic and relations of power. Power always looks for the next fight.[52] In this sense, elites are unwise to overlook the public's potential volatility. The spirit of insubordination remains a lingering and dangerous variable. As Alex Carey advises, private and public power-holders in the early twentieth century wanted very much to eliminate this risk factor from American democracy.[53]

For Veblen, these risks were most effectively and smoothly limited through popular acceptance of those "bonds of convention" that formed the conservative boundaries of normal life. But the visibility and audibility of power in democracy means that power elites must accept an inevitable degree of risk. The more politically aware or "alert" public opinion becomes, the smaller the "the margin of tolerance" for failures and abuses chargeable to "elder statesmen" and absentee owners. "If brought to a sufficiently sharp test" there is always a chance that "popular sentiment would stubbornly assert its paramount dominion." It might even take "an uncompromising stand."[54] Popular sovereignty gave the citizenry an "eventual power of veto" over its political leadership. Even more than constitutional law, this belief makes elites sensitive to consultation with the public.[55] The Bush administration's sales effort to gin up public support for its Iraq invasion illustrates the point. In fact, the trend is so strong and even global that Veblen saw its effects at work in Imperial Germany, where the authorities regularly saw fit to cloak realities of power behind a façade of democratic-sounding legalism.[56] Yet if support from public opinion was now a functional requisite for maintenance of concentrated powers in both dynastic states and "ostensible democracies," there was still a definable difference in their basic patterns of rule. In the democratic commonwealth "the common man has to be managed rather than driven," wrote Veblen, "and it is pleasanter to be managed than to be driven. Chicane is a more humane art than corporal punishment."[57]

Exploit in democratic society demanded and received subtle techniques of control. Novel principles and practices of public management, drawn from the fast-rising disciplines of business administration and industrial relations, followed in the wake of corporate capitalism.[58] These developments suggested the advent of smoother and cleverer styles of political leadership. Ruling classes began to appear less aloof from public opinion and shop-floor discontents and more willing to cater to popular moods, even as they nudged and guided public opinion into relatively innocuous zones of dissent. Having become a strategic variable, a target of control in elite calculations of power, public opinion, Veblen suggested, stood to lose much of its spontaneity, its self-generating capacity for insubordination, its effective sovereignty. "It is the constant care of the pillars of society to see that . . . antiquities of the human spirit"—the sentimental values of emulation, business as usual, patriotism, and religion—are not overly "sterilized" by clear thinking. It is worth remembering, he noted, that in "all the Christian nations," families, churches, and schools forge "bonds of convention" very early. Before teaching their children how to read and write, Americans insist that a "child must first learn to say his prayers and salute the flag."[59]

Bound by duty to God and country, public opinion and political participation still matter, but as limited and contained factors, fluidly and strategically dynamic, to be sure, but within a matrix of conservative habits and obligations. In this matrix, corporate and state powers function as the de facto, material constitution of the political system, the old juridical constitution of supposedly balanced powers remaining more myth than reality. The cumulative effect explains much about how constitutional democracy becomes "ostensible democracy." As Sheldon Wolin recently noted,

> democracy as we know it in the self-styled "advanced industrial democracies" has been constituted, that is, given forms, structure, boundaries. Constitutional democracy is fitted to a constitution. It is not democratic or democratized constitutionalism because it is democracy without the demos (the people) as actor. Its politics is based not, as its defenders allege, upon "representative democracy" but on various representations of democracy: democracy as represented as public opinion polls, electronic town meetings and phone-ins, and as votes. In sum, a constitution regulates the amount of democratic politics that is let in.[60]

In Veblenian terms, Wolin's contained democracy is an absentee democracy, the political counterpart of absentee ownership.[61] But the phenomenon of absenteeism has very different implications in the economy and the state. In the economy, absentee owners disengage themselves from contact with industry and tangible property, invoking paper claims to draw real profits. Absenteeism connotes economic power to exploit. In absentee democracy, the remoteness of the absentee citizen has opposite implications. It reflects the public's lack of power and strength and the citizens' structural vulnerability to predation. Absenteeism in the public sphere defines the status of what Veblen implied was an insubstantial citizenship, a status of nominal, fictive equality. This illusory equality lacks the pecuniary content, the economic power, upon which state officials confer genuine respect, access, and acknowledgment. Ordinary citizens are insubstantial, connected to power vicariously, through television screens, computer monitors, opinion polls, and political advertising, by the whole remarkable technology of democratic ostensibility and quasi-sovereignty. In all these ways, Veblen argues, "a numerical minority—under ten percent of the population—constitutes a conclusive pecuniary majority." And "barring a slight and intermittent mutter of discontent, this arrangement has . . . the cordial approval of popular sentiment."[62]

As early as *The Theory of Business Enterprise*, Veblen makes it clear that the business takeover of government depends as much on exclusion of citizens as it does on the absentee owners' immediate grip on the state.[63] For purposes of maintaining illusions of popular sovereignty, absentee democracy is an indispensable condition of absentee ownership. Above all, though, the surest way to limit the scope and volume of political demand is to reign in popular expectations of democratic power itself, to curtail the idea that government might be responsible for—or be capable of—meeting tangible economic needs. Or, at least, government should define such needs in terms the state and the absentee owners are prepared to grant.[64]

Law and the Sabotage of Opinion

To limit the scope of public opinion to business-based assumptions and themes, Veblen gave substantial credit to the conservative cast of American law. It is not only that the Constitution endorses absentee democracy. Economically speaking, the venerable document ignores the subject of material need altogether, turning a blind eye to industry. At the same time, it legitimates business's freedom to coerce by withholding from people economic rights to make claims for work or access to needed resources. The Constitution treats economic life as if it were exclusively a matter of ownership and property right, disregarding legal possibilities that might flow from treating industry as a domain of vital needs or self-regulating labor. It glides over issues of needs and work, leaving them in a kind of legal limbo. Because needs and industry form the two primary aspects of economic activity, their constitutional omission has enormous ideological and practical implications. At the very least, it discourages working people from developing a constitutional consciousness of their material interests.

For Veblen, it is not so much the Constitution as a legal or juridical document that is at issue here. He understood that power has a habit of bending laws and rules to fit its requirements. What matters more is that the underlying population learns to revere the Constitution as their fundamental document of freedom. Americans impute to it a kind of divine sanction and spiritual significance, believing that it offers final words on how a good society is properly organized. Many, indeed probably most, Americans believe that what the framers took to be natural and right in 1787 is the main fount of wisdom for what ought to be done today.[65] Historical preconceptions become eternal convictions. As Veblen put it, today's "principles of law and morals" are " 'immemorially ancient' and 'eternally right and good.' " And they have been "ever since they became ingrained by habit and presently reduced to documentary statement in modern times . . . from A.D. 1776 or 1787, according as one may prefer to see it."[66] Even liberals, who insist that judges interpret the Constitution in response to evolving needs and conditions, tend to gauge the limits of policy change against the sacred principles. In short, the Constitution's ideological importance is that its once-upon-a-time historical norms and ideas enter into public consciousness as universal, natural standards. They implicitly establish what most people take to be legitimate legal boundaries of respectable economic and political thought. Consider industry first.

As far as the economy is concerned, the Constitution elaborates rules that protect the conduct of private business and financial relations. But it largely ignores the material implications of those relationships. The basic law's focus on securing private property and "the obligations of contract" says nothing about securing metabolic needs of real human beings. For this, the individual is left to her own devices. The Constitution endorses rights of contract; it nowhere mentions human claims to work, food, or shelter. It gives Congress powers to regulate interstate commerce. But it omits substantive criteria that indicate how "commerce"—much less "industry"—should function to meet terms of social responsibility or "the general welfare."[67] It confers patent and copyright protections upon inventors and authors—but these rules essentially give temporary monopolies to their owners. They are matters more of business than industry. In fact, the Constitution mainly sweeps matters of workmanship and industry under the rug.[68]

In this respect, American constitutional law resembles what Veblen considered one of the chief hallmarks of barbarism. Leisure class barbarians also shoved industry and workers into the obscure background of their aristocratic culture. In comparable ways, the American Constitution pushes virtually the whole human experience of labor into a dusky legal background of common law, much of it feudal in origin.[69] The big exception is slavery. The Constitution sanctioned the slave trade until 1808, even giving southern states rights to count their slaves as three-fifths of a person for purposes of "representation."[70] Of course, the Constitution is silent on the subject of business corporations too; it certainly mentions private property, but not absentee ownership. Only when corporations became major economic actors in the post–Civil War era, did lawyers, legislators, and judges carve out special, highly protected niches for corporate enterprise, endowing the new business institution with artificial personhood. This novel entitlement included an array of rights and privileges that allowed corporations to swing their economic powers with far greater force than any person could. That American law first saw fit to endow a group of enslaved human beings with a weird and repressive kind of fractional personhood, only later to bestow full-blown artificial personhood upon a category of economic institutions, speaks volumes not only about political connections between law and power, but also about the remarkable versatility of American legal imagination.[71]

Much the same can be said about relations between the basic law and human economic needs. That "no person may be deprived of life, liberty, or property without due process of law" is a familiar and sacred constitutional rule. But no other human material need—for shelter, food, clothing, or health care—is granted equivalent status. Yet these needs are the requisites of a sustained life. Thus the principle of due process carries the defect of its virtue. Although the Constitution prohibits physical coercion between persons, it does not forbid some people from peacefully depriving others of material resources they require to live. That is, it nowhere addresses itself to the problem of economic power, the "power to withhold from others what they need."[72] To the contrary, the Constitution's security for private property protects precisely the power to deprive. Like industry, human economic needs are not "a legal metaphysically competent reality." Bracketed by the constitutional system, their satisfaction, like control of industry, is subcontracted to corporate persons and absentee owners.[73]

In all this, Veblen wants us to appreciate the law for what it teaches us to ignore. This is another expression of that which is absent from American democracy. But this is not only an ideological matter. As suggested above, coercion is involved too. Constitutional and statutory law protect absentee owners' freedom routinely to charge people whatever the traffic will bear to meet their elemental economic needs. In effect, when it comes to basic human needs, the power to deprive is the power to compel. This is not coercion at gunpoint. But experiences of hunger, homelessness, or lack of health care will drive people to do whatever they have to do to assure that they and their families will survive, including accepting whatever wages business is prepared to pay. In this sense, the law supports economic power to coerce and deprive much more than it protects people from the pressure of economic coercion, especially poorer people, who find it difficult at best to meet their needs through the wage and price systems. Indeed, "such coercion" is "in point of legal reality, no coercion" at all, even in "cases where the pressure is severe enough to result in insolvency, sickness, or death." In American law, violence is prohibited, but "pecuniary pressure can not be barred."[74]

As powerful as the democratic warfare state is, Veblen reminds us how much coercive power American society regularly displays internally through private and market institutions. In fact, business exerts most of the coercions in domestic life outside the state, where it is legally displaced into the price system, whose obligations citizens can never take lightly, especially not in pecuniary America.[75] It rarely occurs to most people to question how the legal presumptions of business enterprise govern everyday life, or how "the life process taken impersonally" is affected or thwarted by the law's "pecuniary bias." In this view—which can seem natural to a people who have learned to believe it—citizens routinely see coercion as a feature of political, not economic, life. In contrast with the coercive state, the business enterprise economy is free and open, rife with opportunities, scarce in coercions. But as much as its opportunistic freedom invites optimism,

American business can also encourage cynicism, a hard-boiled attitude toward life that forms another vital piece of the American democratic spirit.

Opportunism and the Spirit of Evasion

Americans believe in business, but Veblen did not think they are completely naïve. He sensed how their affection for commerce is coarsened by something rougher—a hard-won sense of how they think the world really works.[76] Belief in the system can be tough-minded, to a fault. Often cynically opportunistic, Americans are much less captivated by economic theories than by hopes of making a fast buck, often feeling there is little wrong in cutting corners to get something for nothing. It is not that industriousness, patriotic loyalty, religion, and moral feeling do not have solid foundations in the culture, or that all Americans are crooks. Veblen believed most ordinary people are reasonably honest. It is just that prevailing norms of civic virtue and religious righteousness do not necessarily inhibit other less honorable forms of behavior. This sense of tolerance for evasion lends a kind of amoral uplift to popular acceptance of business and state power.[77] In short, for Veblen, cynicism and opportunism are peculiarly salient factors in the makeup of American opinion.

In an economy dominated by giant corporations, whose connections to the state confer advantages unavailable to small business and workers, "the little guy" often thinks that the roots of inequality lie less in hard-earned moral virtues than in questionable patterns of influence. "It's not what you know," after all, "it's who you know." If big business buys influence and reaps rewards, if politicians live high on the hog, then average folks deserve chances to seize their own advantages in their own ways. Civility and honesty are all right as far as they go, but "nice guys finish last," and "you do what you have to do." In the machine politician's classic phrase, "I seen my opportunities and I took 'em."[78] "Honest graft" is there to be had—and so you take it! That is the American way. "They are sitting out there waiting to give you their money," shouts the star real estate salesman to an inept sales crew in David Mamet's screenplay *Glengarry Glen Ross*, "Are you man enough to take it?"[79] Or, in Veblen's version of the same dictum: why not "take a chance with the legalities and moralities . . . when there is easy money in sight and no one is looking."[80]

Nowhere are such sentiments more rife than in the quintessential American business of real estate, that "enterprise in 'futures,' designed to get something for nothing from the unwary, of whom it is said that there is one born every minute."[81] Long before twenty-first-century wizards of Wall Street finance persuaded themselves—not to mention buyers of subprime mortgages—that real estate values only rise, Veblen captured the essential truth of American country town life as a self-deluded quest for hyperinflation of real estate values, lifted ever "farther off the level of actual ground-values." So deep runs this pattern, he suggested, "that there is no help for it," for it "is worked out by uniform circumstances over which there is no control." Recurrent speculative fever "falls in with things" American; it "answers to the enduring aspirations of the community."[82]

For Veblen, in effect, Jefferson had it wrong. The scourge of local corruption actually spread from the country towns to the city, not the other way around. Both fascinated and repelled by its crude opportunism, Veblen took the country town's aggressive, amoral spirit more seriously than other social scientists of his time or today. It was, for him, a living, corrupting influence in everyday life, coarsening habits and debasing expectations. Its opportunistic ethos is part of the toll of surviving in the squeeze among pecuniary pressures, a constitutionally weakened democracy, and bountiful opportunities to make a fast buck. To meet the terms of monetary pressure and to reap its gains, Americans became a people whose forces of competitive emulation are barely contained by their legal system. For such a people, much of the spirit of the laws has to do with avoiding laws, or with gaming them. Americans learn that to play by the rules is to play smart: to seek out and exploit every loophole, and to be ever on the hunt for new ones. In their cynical opportunism, Veblen suggests, Americans forged a doubling of meaning that wrapped legality and extralegality, morality and amorality, into complex webs of activity that sully prevailing norms even as they reinforce them. In effect, Americans sacrifice the progressive implications of insubordination when they adopt its most wily, aggressive, and individualistic forms, the cynical opportunism that feeds off of, rather than challenges, competitive emulation. Cynicism, in short, dramatically limits the boundaries of democratic aspiration.

People see through the democratic swindle, or think they do. Their hardened insight then becomes justification for conduct at the obscure, blurry margins of legality and morality. Veblen sees Americans as a people who cope with the pressures of living in a brutally competitive culture by letting its very unfairness and injustice become tacit justification for their own playing fast and loose with rules whose legitimacy they accept, but whose fairness they question. Such conduct has its own psychic satisfactions; at least there is the knowing sense that one is not a sucker, that one will not be had. That "self-preservation knows no moral law" is one of Veblen's working principles of everyday life in fiercely competitive America.

Again, it is not that all Americans are lawbreakers, or that we would all be Bernard Madoff, if we could. But there is a rough-hewn common sense in the culture that advises that a little crookedness is part of the price of success. And it is a reasonable price to pay for reaping whatever advantages we can grab at each niche in the social order. As Veblen captures the conventional wisdom, "It will not do for an honest man to let the rogues get away with the best." "A sound principle" for people intoxicated by the sweet smell of success is to grab the main chance "and, if worse comes to worse, let the courts determine tomorrow, under protest, just what the law allows, and therefore what the moral code exacts." Besides, "the courts will be wise enough to see that the law is not allowed to . . . impede . . . business-as-usual."[83]

Such notions did not just float about in the slick American air. For Veblen, they had deep roots in America's material experience of frontier development and country town boosterism, whose dominant feature was aggressive private seizure of public wealth. Only quasi-organized and barely regulated, America's rural development showed little scruple for niceties of human or animal life, nature, or the guiding hand of public law. Violent seizures of human beings, extermination of native populations and species, and massive grabbing of public resources lay behind the fiercely opportunistic frame of mind, the knowing sense that with as much force, luck, and cunning as technical skill, a person could become a "substantial citizen." In this climate of rip and run, belief in "equal opportunity" nurtured a form of life "whose rules . . . call to mind the rules governing games of skill, [with] about the same degree of scruple that is commonly to be had" at the gaming table.[84] Indeed, it is arguably the case that Las Vegas casinos monitor their gaming tables more scrupulously than U.S. regulatory agencies monitor American business and finance. It is easier to cheat outside the casinos than in them.

But then the point is that cheating is not so much outside the rules, as it is part of the rules, anticipated and encouraged by laws chock full of loopholes, gaps, and spaces, a host of carefully sewn fissures designed to support a kind of economic freedom that only gradually shades over into outright flimflam and fraud. This cynical opportunism, nowhere more evident to Veblen than in America's country towns, shaped a popular outlook that looked askance on law, government and public policy, even as it stimulated faith in luck, sharp practice, and "the main chance." After all, "What the law allows can not be far wrong."[85] Even so simple a word as "is" remains vulnerable to legalistic interpretation, a recent president suggested, caught by his enemies in the snare of his own lies.

What might one expect, Veblen asked, of a culture whose original country towns were "the perfect flower of self-help and cupidity," organized and managed by their founders "with a view to speculation in real estate"? The country town might build a church on solid foundations. Its "code of morality" was made of more slippery stuff, based less on faith in the hereafter than on inflated promises of rising land values here and ever after. The resulting code of practices "is quite sharp, meticulous; but solvency always has a sedative value."[86] Today's state lotteries, betting pools, and Internet gambling sites, not to mention Wall Street's stunning array of options for sophisticated wagering and hedging, illustrate gaming habits whose grain runs deep and wide.

Opportunism, in short, supplies spring and lift to commonplace hopes. In Veblenian perspectives, Las Vegas more than Hollywood bears consideration as cultural capital of the national dreamscape. Uglier moral implications also follow. Embedded in the opportunism of seizure is a learned tolerance for habits of predation and human exploitation, including racism and sexism. Destruction of native populations, enslavement of Africans and their offspring, and domination of women affected moral sensibilities in ways that would pay dividends of support for later imperial ventures.[87]

Conclusion

Veblen's critique of American democracy exposes a political system that pacifies and irritates more than it activates the population. Or perhaps it is more accurate to say that, for Veblen, it is a political system that activates people in the misbegotten direction of emulative and pecuniary competition. It plainly does not encourage their political identification as a majority of industrious citizens. The underlying population more or less accepts its triple role as insubstantial citizen, productive worker, and opportunist. Its acquiescence permits absentee owners and state officials with a minimum of friction to convert popular energies to their own predatory purposes. In this sense, the American political system provides considerably more room for emulation than for representation. It encourages ordinary people to identify much more with their leaders than it compels the leaders to fight for popular interests against those of power and wealth. In the end, Veblen's analysis points to the conclusion that American democracy is a system of exploit more than a system of self-government.

Emulation works to keep citizens and workers dedicated to habits of mind and patterns of action that allow rulers to convert the fruits of the population's work into the profits and taxes that finance absentee ownership and war. Emulation, the people's identification with their rulers' canons of value, keeps them from recognizing themselves as an economic majority, one whose material interests diverge significantly from those of their rulers. Emulation becomes the enemy of self-consciousness, and as Andrew Bacevich has observed, "the absence of self-awareness . . . forms an enduring element of the American character."[88] Thus does emulation provide emotional fuel for the sabotage of democracy. People who closely identify with the personalized values and patterns of behavior of their rulers will have a hard time deciphering clues to their independent political identity, clues that lie within their own generic needs as human beings, clues that are routinely masked by the politics of keeping up appearances.

Veblen's exploration of the politics of emulation, especially the incipient compatibilities among capitalism, democracy, and cynicism, is among his most valuable contributions to the study of American ideology and institutions. Challenging Abraham Lincoln's famous quip about the limits of popular manipulation—"you cannot fool all the people all the time"—Veblen observed that "in a case where the people in question are sedulously fooling themselves all the time the politicians can come near achieving that ideal result."[89] With this claim Veblen questions the most fundamental premise of democracy—citizens' ability to know and to advance their own needs. Closely identifying with the opportunistic sentiments of absentee ownership, ordinary people lose a sense of themselves and their class. They learn to abjure possibilities for alternative forms of life, community, work, and politics. Like that battered class of nineteenth-century America, the small farmers, today's workers end up as "good losers . . . gracefully accepting the turn of things," all the while continuing "to count on meeting with better luck or making a shrewder play next time." For all these reasons, Veblen concluded, "The common man does not know himself." In this alienation from self-knowledge, the chance for people to make democratic common cause withers. "The American tradition stands in the way."[90]

8

VEBLEN AND POLITICS: AN OVERVIEW

Thorstein Veblen will never be a popular thinker, not even among intellectuals, perhaps especially among politically motivated intellectuals. His refusal to offer program or ideology leaves him few friends among those anxious to defend, reform, or attack the status quo. Conservatives, who might otherwise appreciate his assessment of tradition, find little to celebrate in his critique of pecuniary culture. Liberals may welcome his criticism of corporations, but they take little comfort from his skepticism of reform. Veblen's hatred of exploit makes him a natural ally of Marxists, but his analysis of political consciousness offers few hopes for proletarian radicalism. His aversion to belief in teleology distances Veblen from ideologues of all stripes. Not even the postmodernists can discover in Veblen a true hero, for his claims about the species' generic needs suggest impatience with the particular, provincial, parochial, or partisan view. But the absence of ideology and program in Veblen should not be mistaken for an absence of political thought. Veblen's thought was political in the specific sense that he founded his critical theory on an account of exploit that made power—its aspiration and glorification—pivotal to the development of institutions.

Indeed, Veblen's main preoccupation is the study of how exploitative and emulative institutions thwart human industry and fullness of life. The quest for power, its prestige, and, especially in democratic societies, its disguise, reflects the historic or traditional influence of what Veblen took to be emulative habits of mind and predatory habits of action. Together, these habits inform his critical sense of the political. They go a long way to explain the darkly pessimistic, unforgiving strain in his thought. But Veblenian pessimism is at least partly offset by an intriguingly subtle analysis of multiple lines of possible tension, resistance, and conflict in contemporary democratic societies. The roots of such possibilities lay in Veblen's ideas of economic conscience and its ally, the instinct of workmanship, ideas freighted with moral as well as political significance. Unfortunately, the moral dimension in Veblen's basic ideas is at best problematic and undeveloped; at worst, it is inconsistent and opaque. To inquire into such difficulties is an important part of coming to grips with the elusiveness of the political in Veblen's thought.

Politics and the Economic Conscience: Veblen's Janus-like Method

Veblen never treated politics as a discrete subject because he did not think that politics was a distinctive or autonomous field of human activity. For him, politics was one type of pragmatic, exploitative, power-driven behavior, similar in competitive spirit and aggressive motivation to kindred activities such as warfare, sports, and business. These are all fields in which he observed the principal motivations and habits to be those of predation, pragmatism, and mystification. And Veblen considered politics, like other forms of the predatory and sportsmanlike, from a dual point of view, both in its own honorific terms of power and from the more generic standpoint of the industrial life process: these are, in sum, the ceremonial and industrial dimensions of Veblen's thought.

Methodologically, the implications of these contrasting patterns of honorific and material culture become most visible and are best understood through the recurrent and shifting comparisons that mark his work. Veblen oscillates in his perspective, regularly adjusting his point of view between symbolic and material positions. Indeed, one of the great difficulties in reading Veblen lies in learning how to engage with his analytical and literary habit of changing perspectives. Most major theorists sustain a reasonably uniform and consistent point of view: thus Marx's material dialectic, Weber's focus on authority and legitimacy, Machiavelli's preoccupation with strategy, or Locke's interest in the balance between rights and authority. The consistency of Veblen's point of view, however, lies in the alternating conceptual rhythm of its shifting, fugue-like movement. Its themes constantly run ahead of, into, and behind one another. They exist in relationships of contrapuntal juxtaposition and overlap, as point and counterpoint, theme and countertheme. He consistently sets exploitative institutions within the industrial and technical domain of the life process, seemingly giving primacy to material factors. Yet Veblen never fails to add that the material life process is stamped by the restrictive context and frame-work of honorific culture and institutions. But as soon as we follow Veblen to see the effects of atavistic cultural habits, we are instantly reminded of how brute material processes tax the ancient verities, compelling more or less awkward institutional adjustments as the price of survival. And just when we are led by Veblen to discover the cumulative effects of technical change on established institutions, we are forced once again to confront how such institutions resist and thwart matter-of-fact adaptation to material demands: on and on, world without end.

"The particular point of view, or the particular characteristic that is pitched upon as definitive in the classification of the facts of life depends on the interest from which a discrimination of the facts is sought."[1] Veblen makes this point in reference to perception of class and culture. But it serves also as a valuable methodological clue to Veblen's own ambiguous relation to relativism and chances for popular resistance. Veblen is surely relativist in his appreciation of the impact of culture and industrial life process on human values and norms. Even the norms and practices of science change, after all. But Veblen is relativist in more subtle and engaging ways. His oscillating points of view on culture and industry reveal a mind that refuses analytically to conflate cultural and material phenomena. He treats each in ways that encourage readers to see how much each is inside the other, how each is closely affected by the other, yet how each remains elusively distinct from the other. Veblen changes and shifts his point of view because, for him, it is the best way to express the ambiguities and overlaps that follow the reciprocal or dialectal interplay between material and cultural life. But matters become more complicated still when we realize that while habits of culture evolve and change, the effective motivations of generic life process, the core source of Veblen's moral outlook and critique, the source of whatever hope he has for the species, remain more or less fixed and eternal in their compulsion. Throughout his analysis of the dynamics of cultural and material life, Veblen never wavers from a belief that within the sensibility of "the instinct of workmanship," there is an unvarying standard for "economic truth."

This standard of "economic conscience" looks conspicuously and self-consciously beyond "the existing circumstances of individual habit and social custom," beyond the prevailing "canons of usage and conventional decency." Veblen's standard looks to assess critically and dispassionately whether current economic and political practices and expenditures "result in a net gain in comfort or in the fullness of life" or "enhance human life on the whole . . . the life process taken impersonally."[2]

In effect, Veblen completely embraces relativism in respect to habits of thought and practice, including scientific thought. In reference to the perspective of generic human needs, though, the human imperatives that drive or motivate the life process, Veblen is unrepentantly universalistic. Veblen examines particular societies or cultures—the specific constellations of their habits and institutions—from an outside position that recognizes differentiation and specificity among singular cases, but within a frame governed by the idea that human beings share fundamental biological or metabolic commonalities and needs. It is a position that specifies comparison and contrast as the proper working method of analysis. It is why Veblen is so much a comparativist at heart. But Veblen's outside stance has a profoundly ambiguous meaning for social science. It reflects a quite relativist, constructivist recognition of what C. Wright Mills called "the human variety." But Veblen's sense of this outside or estranged position also manifests the objective pull and strain of "economic conscience," a stance committed to the "economic truth" of a nonwasteful expenditure of resources and satisfaction of generic human needs.

Yet for all his insistence on generic human interests, the idea remains for Veblen never more than a hypothesis. He never claims more for generic need than the status of tentative conclusion drawn from his reading of current biology, anthropology, and history. He doubtless believes in the truth of the related hypothesis of economic conscience, but he never asks readers to accept it as empirical truth, one available to some kind of exacting intersubjective test. His appeal is to something considerably less precise or rigorous than science; it is to "a dispassionate common sense." The great trouble, of course, is that Veblen rarely finds in his social inquiry a "common sense" that is distinguishable from passions, sentiments, and conventional canons of decency. Here is a main clue, perhaps, to the many charges of confusion in Veblen's thought. The epistemological status of the key critical concept in Veblen stands in contradiction with the very substantive analysis it is meant to expose. Dispassionate common sense is just what prevailing institutions seek to complicate and mediate with an array of chronically dissatisfied and highly personal longings and passions. So what sense does it make to speak of a "dispassionate common sense"? Not much, it would seem. We thus reach a point of acute vulnerability and weakness in Veblen's theoretical structure. Its critical standpoint is undermined by the substance that it explicates. But without this critical standpoint, the analysis loses most of its force. Lev Dobrianski's powerful critique along these lines has much merit, though his own answer of a divine foundation for morality would hardly convince Veblen.

To read Veblen as we think he intends to be understood is both to recognize the humility of his position on issues of "economic truth or adequacy" and to accept the fact that he is speaking from an external position that understands generic, metabolic interests of human beings apart from variable canons of convention. Such a position will inevitably induce its own sense of intellectual dissatisfaction among those looking for certainty, just as it will among those certain that there is no certainty. But if this equivocal reading of Veblen has any merit, it will cast doubt on views of his work, such as the one recently advanced by Helge Peukert, to the effect that Veblen "formulated a postmodern epistemology" or that "he deconstructed the concept of objective knowledge."[3]

Veblen was relativist in his view of custom, culture, and mores. To the extent, however, that he worked with a hypothetical construct of "economic truth," one that exists outside social institutions, his stance hardly adds up to a deconstruction of objective knowledge. Peukert's interpretation imputes contemporary understandings to an author who wrote decades before the postmodern demiurge. It reduces Veblen's oscillating viewpoints to a singular position, at the cost of ignoring or suppressing his belief in the impersonal, objective, generic interests of the species, the very standpoint that governs, however vulnerably, his whole critique of culture. As critics have complained from the beginning of his career, Veblen failed to explain his claims about "fullness of life" or "generic" interests. Nor did he reveal the substantive or formal methodological requirements necessary for a "dispassionate" analysis of their content. These are serious problems, to say the least. An undefended criterion of objective value makes for a slender defense against charges of weak, unsystematic, or wishful thinking. Even sympathetic interpretations of Veblen have to acknowledge this radical weakness in his thought. And the deep flaw here cannot be evaded by efforts to tuck his theory under a postmodern tent that would not be pitched until well more than a half century after his death. There is no getting around it: on very serious issues Veblen stands guilty of the very tendency toward opaque, unpersuasive formulations that he so frequently faults in others.[+]

We think that a balanced view of Veblen can reasonably take him to be an economic sociologist who is at the same time a sociological economist. The economic sociologist looks to the ways that industry and technology shape human life and give it sustenance. The sociological economist looks to the way that culture both reflects material forces and works back on them, as often as not distorting and wasting economic potential with ritualistic and honorific claims, the rituals of ceremony that draw the fruits of industry away from producer classes to serve the aspirations of exploitative ones. To understand this dualistic relation between the economic and social aspects of culture—the industrial and ceremonial aspects of institutions—is to begin to see how and where the political really emerges in Veblen's thought. It is, after all, a set of essentially political motives that animate the ceremonial in Veblen's theory of social structure.

The State and Politics

It is true that Veblen does not make the study of formal political systems a central focus of his work. But this generalization deserves qualification. It is a more accurate comment about such acknowledged early classics as *The Theory of the Leisure Class* than it is about such less familiar books as *The Nature of Peace* or *Absentee Ownership*, where the subject of the state looms very large. But even accepting the element of truth in generalizations about Veblen's indifference to formal government, it is important not to ignore the often specific and important things that he does have to say about overtly political institutions. He treats the executive of the state, for example, more in the manner of James Madison than Karl

Marx, that is, as an institution imbued with warlike habits and proclivities that can clash with or even undermine business interests, much less democratic ones. Moreover, Veblen explored the terrain of legitimation, public opinion, and mass communications in democratic societies in ways that prefigured major concerns of twentieth-century political science. And long before today's interest in identity politics and conflicts of culture, he recognized that political combat in democratic states might well come to a head over spiritual and sentimental matters that are not easily reduced to ideologies of economic interest. Veblen, in short, understood how much contemporary political life is concerned with sentiments, values, habits, and institutions that long predate capitalism. This is an idea that has only recently begun to influence contemporary political scientists, but it is among Veblen's basic premises.

For the most part Veblen stressed the ways that predatory habits reinforced and stabilized unequal social structures. But he also saw how resilient popular claims to insubordination and recalcitrance can vitalize political combat and resistance in modern democracy. Indeed, in some notable ways Veblen's political thought echoes the Jeffersonian spirit of American localism and its defense. Thus he often described local councils and municipal governments as distant reflections of ancient self-governing savage communities, institutions drawn toward industry, material survival, and the instinct of workmanship more than to war and predation. Veblen's descriptions of the villages of pagan anarchy and the early industrial towns of the handicraft era resonate with deep-felt appreciation for connections between popular self-government and properly conducted industry. It is a mark of the depth of Veblen's critique of the business takeover of "the American country town" that it stands out as the only extended critique of a local political form in all of his work. Local governments come off rather better in Veblen than does the large, ambitious state. Veblen admired the skepticism of David Hume, but Hume's original defense of the large republic, which influenced Madison, was not among Hume's legacies that Veblen cherished.

Democracy and Sources of Popular Resistance

The easiest way to dismiss such suggestions is merely to quote Veblen's observation that "Representative government means, chiefly, representation of business interests." This claim can hardly be rendered consistent with appreciation for the array of public-interest, social-movement, and ideological-cause groups representing themselves in contemporary democracies, movements that certainly had forbearers in Veblen's own day: populists, progressive reformers, the feminist and temperance movements, and union radicalism. Veblen's point thus seems overstated for his own day and time, and even more so for today. But Veblen meant exactly what he said; his qualification is worth remembering, for the word "chiefly" suggests strong bias, not ironclad inevitability. Veblen was doing more than playing it safe. He understood that government has more to do than satisfy business interests. His point was that even when it entertains nonbusiness civic or social functions, government remains "under . . . surveillance of the business interests"; hence it rarely happens that modern governments will "persist" in policies "detrimental or not ostensibly subservient" to major business interests.[5]

In short, Veblen understood that empirically sensitive models of capitalist democracy required conceptual space for other than business considerations to be pressed and represented. Some of these were popular, others martial and statist and hardly democratic. If martial and diplomatic interests politicized policy at the highest levels of executive power, public opinion might politicize it from below. And the texture, composition, and direction of public opinion could be, for Veblen, a curiously complex phenomenon.

In *The Theory of the Leisure Class*, of course, he advanced the strongest case for the idea that ruling class values and standards permeate the lower or subordinate social ranks. The leisure class, he insisted, will "determine, in general outline, what scheme of life the community shall accept as decent or honorific; and it is their office by precept and example to set forth this scheme of social salvation in its highest, ideal form."[6] But much else that Veblen said about the state departed from, or at least notably qualified, this Gramscian-like emphasis on the ruling class's hegemony of ideas. To be reminded of such qualifications may be a particularly appropriate way to conclude this study of Veblen's political ideas. For as much as we have stressed the strain of realist political pessimism in Veblen, his ideas also contain germs of hope, albeit slight, for more democratic possibilities. Each of these themes is more or less familiar in Veblen scholarship. Pulling them together, however, permits us to draw a more complete picture of Veblen's thinking on democratic change.

At various moments in his work, Veblen saw multiple or plural factors favoring popular resistance to predatory politics and ideological mystification. The most obvious and widely noted in the literature is the famous thesis, advanced in *The Theory of Business Enterprise*, that contact with the machine process would lead workers gradually to develop a more sober, impersonal, even radical political consciousness. This machine-induced attitude, reflecting an increasingly matter-of-fact scientific outlook, might strengthen labor's resistance to nationalist propaganda and religious flim-flam. A more rational working class could then generate sufficient power from below to support moves toward some kind of socialist technocratic rule of industry, founded on a popular base. In this respect the machine rationalization thesis matches up well with Veblen's later idea of a "soviet of engineers." For in *The Engineers and the Price System*, it is the techni-cians who might lead the changeover to technocratic socialism, but only with mass support from the kind of politically rational working class that Veblen identified in 1904. It is this argument of course that prompts many Veblen critics to charge him with crimes of utopianism or elitism.

Yet in writings published both before and after the arguments of 1904, Veblen was characteristically cautious in his appraisals of working class radicalism. In fact, considered as a whole, Veblen's collected observations about working class militancy suggest that his rationalization hypothesis of 1904 stands out as an exception to his greater ambivalence and skepti-cism in respect to working class militancy. Throughout his career, Veblen was generally dubious about workers' potential to shed their sentimental attachments to God, nation, and free enterprise. He refused to rule out such a development, consistently holding that it was possible, if unlikely. Thus even in his last, arguably most dour assessment of American democ-racy, *Absentee Ownership*, Veblen did not rule out chances for a "red line of cleavage" to develop between absentee owners and the economic majority over issues of "management of productive industry."[7] Such a class politics from below, were it to emerge, would likely be driven not by claims for "equity in the distribution of incomes," but by issues of "expediency" in the use of industrial resources. Some vindication for Veblen's assess-ment is visible in the battles over resource planning in the New Deal, but perhaps even more in environmental critiques of pollution, waste, and global warming today, though the social base of such criticism is much less the working class than the middle and professional classes, including substantial elements of the scientific community.

In contrast, much earlier in his career Veblen weighed the chances for an egalitarian thrust in democracy more positively. "Some Neglected Points in the Theory of Socialism" (1892) not only described constitutional democracy as a possible blueprint for a working socialism; it also identified class envy among workers as a potentially powerful egalitarian sentiment, one that might culminate in a "readjustment" of social relationships "adverse to the interests of those who possess more, and adverse to the possibility of legitimately possessing or enjoying 'more.'"[8] Especially notable in this imagined possibility for socialism is that it drew not from the sober, mechanized political consciousness that Veblen described in 1904. It reflected instead the idea that sentimental and passionate interests in emulation and envy could provoke an attack on capital. In that sense, Veblen was not, at least at some points in his life, averse to seeing progressive potential within passionately driven, sentimental politics.

As he observed in reference to Marx, because human reasoning is "largely controlled by other than logical, intellectual forces," it is sensible to conclude that the views expressed in "public or class opinion" are "as much or more a matter of sentiment than of logical inference." While such an observation precludes "asserting *a priori* that that the class interest of the working class will bring them to take stand against the propertied class," it remains possible that workers "will go forward," on the basis of their class passions, and "enforce a new deal" that puts an end to "class discrepancies" as well as "international animosity and dynastic politics." Then again, perhaps not; the proletariat's "training in subservience" could just as well prevail, the sentiment of subordination being the stronger political force. All Veblen would say is that either outcome, or some even murkier combination of diverse or mixed trends, is within the range of historic possibility. The eventual result would depend on the usual suspects: "habit . . . native propensity and the range of stimuli to which the proletariat are exposed."[9]

This argument about class militancy is framed by Veblen's engagement with the Marxism and socialism of his day. But, as we have seen, Veblen did not think of mass or democratic politics only in terms of class. He also entertained the thesis that traditions and habits of premodern peasant communities, modified and altered by the rise of liberalism in the handicraft era, gave rise to a novel "spirit of insubordination," personified by the historic character of "the masterless man."

This fighting, defiant "spirit of insubordination" is more than anything else the anarchistic antagonist of cultural drives toward power and exploit. Mastery aims at conversion of another's energies and purposes to those of the exploiter. The "spirit of insubordination" stands against power: it renounces hierarchy, disrespects authority, and opposes mastery. The spirit of insubordination claims self-respect based on individual autonomy and independence. It demands liberty to act, to work, to create, and to live sufficiently and fully against the constraining controls and carrots of authority. In a sense, the spirit of insubordination is the self-guiding instinct of workmanship energized for civic action, eager to repel fiat control of individuals' capacity for self-directed activity. Insubordination is for Veblen the potential negation of predatory power.

With his idea of a "spirit of insubordination," Veblen outlines a "red line of political cleavage" over the proper boundaries of authority and hierarchy as organizational principles of social structure. Veblen, who has too often been seen as offering only a class-oriented critique of capitalism, also modeled a theory of political conflict over power as such. In this respect, Veblen anticipated, however vaguely or ambiguously, how a politics of power and assertive rights might develop in league with or even distinct from a politics of class resistance. The development of an aggressive, insubordinate liberal politics of rights, a kind of politics that has characterized the American left since the 1960s, and not always for the good of the left as a whole, illustrates this second possible path. It is worth remembering, after all, that Veblen associated the spirit of insubordination in his own day as much as anything else with the cause of restless and masterless women, with the liberating thrust of the feminist movement for "a self-directing, self-centered life," one that would embrace women's "direct participation in the affairs of the community, civil or industrial."[10] Substitute for women people of color, gays, Native Americans, or college students, and one has a fair description of the American new left as it developed in the late twentieth century, a left that has fundamentally occupied itself with issues of liberty, power, and self-expression far more than it has with issues of workmanship, economic power, and control of industry.

Finally, beyond class and power as possible "red lines of cleavage" in democratic society, Veblen added one more "good cause" for people "to be restive" about in the emergent order of advanced, technically innovative capitalism: the coldly implacable scientific cast of modernity itself.[11] That humanity has a strongly spiritual bent is a theme that persists across Veblen's works. This spiritual bent is reflected in our strong collective reluctance to abandon animistic and teleological habits of mind. But the spiritual bent also expresses human creativity that manifests itself in mythmaking and the creative arts. Some of it reflects the urgings of intelligence itself, the profound human longing to explain the inexplicable, to find meaning and purpose in the mystery of existence. Humans for Veblen are prone by their savage legacy to embrace enchanted explanations of things, to be repulsed by the cool materialistic distancing of life and spirit. There is good Veblenian reason to expect that rationalization will not result in wholesale disenchantment, that humans will continue to lay claim to their spiritual selves, to their metaphysical habits of mind and practice, to religions, symbols, rituals, and myths, and to defend forcefully their claims against rationalization and secularization. The revival of global religious sentiment in the twenty-first century would not surprise Veblen. Nor would the fact that important elements of both liberal and conservative movements embrace spiritual meanings or derive political strength from religious identities. Advocates of conservative and liberal causes alike invoke religious themes. Both sides in the Iranian political crisis of 2009, for example, drew inspiration from understandings of Islam.[12] Radical tendencies among certain green and ecofeminist groups also offer mythic and spiritual appeals. Analytically apart then from issues of class and power, technical rationality itself often inspires resistance in the name of metaphysical or spiritual values. In this sense, the whole litany of claims to govern based on scientific expertise—claims advanced by planners, technocrats, administrators, and experts, what Foucault called "power knowledge"—constitutes for Veblen yet another cleavage point in the emergent political relations of advanced democracy.

If we consider his works as a whole from a political point of view, it would not overstate the case by very much to suggest that Thorstein Veblen was in certain ways more alert to the multiple possibilities of popular friction in the machinery of modern society than was Max Weber, for whom the "the masses" were mainly incapable of self-directed action. In this sense, Veblen's catalogue of potential civic discontents in modern democratic orders offers a valuable guide to the dynamics of the multiple conflict and cleavage lines of contemporary politics. And, in contrast with Karl Marx, Veblen treated the issue of authority as a source of political conflict connected with but also independent of class issues. Veblen caught the quasi-anarchistic spirit of populist antiauthoritarianism that ebbs and flows in the interstices of modern bureaucratic orders and that from time to time animates popular political consciousness and action. The Tea Party is an obvious recent example.

Conclusion

For all its weaknesses and gaps, Veblen's thinking about politics and power has intellectual value. Among its greatest defects are a conspicuous reluctance to approach political matters in a systematic way; a tendency to overstress brute forces of change and inertia at the expense of popular movements of resistance and change; to avoid close study of the interior processes of government, administration, and politics; and to demure from the kind of exacting empirical inquiry that might shed light on the detailed relations of corporate power, popular forces, and the state. At far too many crucial moments in his political discussions, Veblen abandons the field, preferring to let a pointed or acute observation stand without supplying the probing analysis necessary to support, explain, or qualify it. Throughout this study, as we have alluded to such problems, which the copious Veblen literature has amply and duly noted, we have also given Veblen's political ideas more credit than it has been the habit of most scholars to give. Readers will, of course, judge for themselves whether we have leaned too far on Veblen's behalf.

Still, the last thing Veblen would want is an overstatement of his relevance to a world that has changed dramatically since his seven decades of history came to their end in 1929. In notable respects, both the spirit of insubordination and the religious spirit have grown stronger in recent decades, while the claims, powers, and legitimacy of the welfare state have eroded. Technology has accelerated material and social change to rates of speed that would have impressed Veblen himself. German history proved every bit as calamitous as Veblen feared, but contemporary Germany is among the least warlike states. Meanwhile, the Soviet experiment in socialism, which he found so intriguing, has come to an inglorious end. America has grown more warlike; Islam has replaced Christianity as the most dynamic religious force in the quasi-modern world; and China looms as the society whose contradictory marriage of authoritarian politics and economic liberalization features the most unstable and perilous compound of institutions among the major nation states. Nowadays, it is such global phenomena as poverty, environmental stress, and nuclear weapons proliferation that rank among chief threats to the species.

Facing these and other potential crises, Veblen would despair to think that social science did not evolve theories and insights to grasp such developments on their own demanding terms. Yet for all his location in his own epoch, which was marked by the full upsurge of modern industrial capitalism, imperialism, and global war, Veblen's work offers categories and forms of critical theory that remain suggestive as illuminations of this day and time. Perhaps above all, Veblen's preoccupation with the cultural and technical evolution of the species establishes a benchmark for a nonpatriotic, universalistic social science whose guiding interest is the generic well-being of the species rather than the invidious claims of any nation or political system. Veblen's perspective is at last a richly human one and asks more of our shared humanity than can be claimed by any presumed difference. At a time of so many heightened threats to the planet and all its inhabitants, Veblen's generic approach to the life process places first things first, the claims of life before the claims of power. In its exploration of the difference between the interests of power and the interests of life, Veblen's critique of politics is a source of ideas to be reckoned with.

NOTES

1. Introduction

1. Fisher, 1995, 2004, ch. 1.
2. Veblen, 1997, 443.
3. Benhabib, 1996; Mansbridge, 1983.
4. Veblen, 1969a, 16.
5. Veblen, 1997, 20.
6. Ibid., 320.
7. Veblen, 1979, 90–91.
8. Gattone, 2006, 38–41.
9. Much has been written of late about a "new institutionalism" in political science, particularly its emphasis on "the informal conventions . . . that shape political behavior; its refusal to take political institutions at face value; and its rejection of 'determinism' in favor of an historical, evolutionary approach" (Lowndes, 2009, 92; Orren and Skowronek, 2004; Orren, 1991). In fact, Veblen's "institutionalism" embodied each of these habits of mind long before they became fashionable in contemporary political studies.
10. Though Randall Collins (1974, 148) barely mentions him in his account of "the conflict tradition" in sociology, by the criteria outlined in his essay, Veblen was very much a "conflict theorist," who, like Machiavelli, embraced a "capacity for naturalistic realism." That is, he focused on such issues as elite ambition, power, and honor, the creation of unequal and exploitative social orders, and their legitimation by codes of morality, codes that are given life by "deception, especially through the deliberate staging of dramatic gestures . . . especially of the externals of religion." On the importance of deception and mystification in Veblen's theory, see Dugger, 1989, 156–158.
11. Perhaps it would be most accurate to say that for Veblen, political science needs to become an evolutionary-minded political anthropology.

12. Veblen, 1978, 399–400.

13. Spindler, 2002, 63.

14. Patsouras, 2004, 170.

15. Galbraith, 2008, 127.

16. Gambs, 1946, 22.

17. Nitzan, 1998, 173–174, emphasis in original.

18. Ferrarotti, 1992, 117.

19. Diggins, 2000, xxviii.

20. Draper, 1977, 20.

21. Veblen, 1997, 9.

22. Veblen, 1979, 30.

23. At the time of his death, Leon Ardzrooni, a close friend, found among his papers an unsigned note in Veblen's penciled script. Among its contents was the following declaration of self-effacement: "It is also my wish, in case of death, to be cremated if it can conveniently be done, as expeditiously and inexpensively as may be, without ritual or ceremony of any kind; that my ashes be thrown into the sea; that no tombstone, slab, epitaph, effigy, tablet, inscription, or monument of any name or nature, be set up in my memory or name in any place or at any time; that no obituary, memorial, portrait, or biography of me, nor any letters written to or by me be printed or published, or in any way re-produced, copied, or circulated" (Dorfman, 1934, 504).

24. Veblen, 1969g, 96.

25. Edgell, 2001, 30–32.

26. Cited in Tilman, 1992, 9.

27. Ibid., 9, 8.

28. Ibid.; Bartley and Yoneda, 1994.

29. Fueling eccentric images of Veblen, but adding new levels of psychopathology to the mix, is David Riesman's *Thorstein Veblen: A Critical Interpretation* (1953). Using Dorfman as his chief biographical source, Riesman offers a psychoanalytic view of Veblen as a man permanently damaged by a supposedly cold and distanced relation with his father, a portrait that reveals rather more about Riesman's "academic liberalism in the 1950s that it did Veblen" (Tilman, 1992, 167; Bartley and Yoneda, 1994, 590–591).

30. Dorfman, 1934, 518.

31. Ibid., 7.

32. Lerner, 2002, 65.

33. Evidence exists that Veblen had what we would today call two "meaningful relationships" aside from that with his first wife, Ellen. These were with a graduate student at Chicago, Sarah Hardy, at a time when his first marriage was beyond repair, and then later, with his second wife, "Babe" Bradley (Jorgensen and Jorgensen, 1999). No direct evidence exists that Veblen ever entertained dalliances with his colleagues' wives. Such stories are the stuff of legend and myth.

34. Mills, 1953, vi, viii–ix.

35. Tilman, 1992, 4–5; Edgell, 2001. In their fascinating account of Veblen's life at his summer retreat on Washington Island, Wisconsin, Russell and Sylvia Bartley (2007)

shed valuable light on Veblen's convivial relations with his island neighbors as well as his gifts as a cheerful teacher of very young children.

36. Jorgensen and Jorgensen, 1999, 15.

37. Ibid., 10.

38. Ibid.

39. Veblen's stepdaughter Becky noted in her diary that "people who called (her father) a philanderer just didn't know him . . . He was, in his way of life, meticulously careful, neat, considerate and responsible, as far as his frail health permitted." Cited in Jorgensen and Jorgensen, 1999, n. 17, 254–255.

40. Edgell, 2001, 3; Veblen, 1990, 320.

41. Veblen, 1990, 320.

42. Edgell, 2001, 4.

43. According to Tom Veblen, Thorstein's grandnephew, Thomas Veblen decided to move from Wisconsin because Nerstrand, Minnesota, offered more abundant opportunities. "Nerstrand had it all: good land, nearby markets. No rocks. No trees. Good water." It also had "Valdris Valley Norwegians. But that wasn't the end of it. The market town of Northfield, 11 miles west of Nerstrand, had an excellent normal school. There the children could learn to write and speak good English while absorbing science, the liberal arts, history, and mathematics. In up-and-coming Northfield, associating with 'Yankees,' the children would learn what it took to succeed in America and in doing so would be exposed to opportunities beyond farming." The authors would like to thank Mr. Veblen for permission to cite from his work in progress, *Going Viking*.

44. Dorfman, 1934, 12; Edgell, 2001, 13.

45. Dorfman, 1934, 41.

46. Porter and Sumner battled over the latter's right to use Herbert Spencer's *Study of Sociology* in his courses. Porter, a religious traditionalist, could not abide Sumner's Darwinian embrace of evolutionary theory. A month before Veblen was awarded his doctorate, the Yale faculty approved curricular changes that markedly diminished "the distinctively theological features of the university" (Dorfman, 1934, 43–44).

47. For example, the highly regarded economist James Laurence Laughlin, who would later teach Veblen at Cornell and bring him to Chicago, had to leave a temporary position at Harvard to work as an insurance agent before he could find his way back to a university post (Viano, 2009, 39).

48. Ibid.

49. Bartley and Yoneda, 1994, 601; Jorgensen and Jorgensen, 1999.

50. Veblen's revenge upon Rainey was to pen "A Study in Total Depravity," a satirical account of the bureaucratization of the university at the hands of businessmen, their methods, and their college president toadies. To spare his career, friends convinced Veblen not to publish the book. Persuaded of the usefulness of restraint, Veblen held off until 1918, when the book finally appeared under its less sardonic title *The Higher Learning in America: A Memorandum on the Conduct of Universities by Businessmen*.

51. Jorgensen and Jorgensen, 1999, 65–131.

52. Veblen's career at the Department of Agriculture ended when he aroused Secretary Herbert Hoover's wrath for a suggestion that to increase farm output, members of the Industrial Workers of the World should be employed as farmhands. The Jorgensens (1999, 157) write: "Hoover . . . was outraged. Veblen's paper was returned, with a note stating that the government would *never* deal with the I.W.W. Veblen's response was to leave Washington," suspecting that food-packing interests controlled the department.

53. Bartley and Bartley, 2007, 18–30, 52, n. 117.

54. Veblen, 1964q, 319–336; 1964i, 423–436.

55. Dorfman (1934, 57) reports that in his youth, Veblen identified with the Democratic Party, especially its advocacy of free trade, but the older Veblen avoided even the most formal kinds of political participation, such as voting. According to the Jorgensens, Veblen "once ducked into the woods for an hour or two when another faculty member planned to shepherd him to the polls to vote for a local candidate" (1999, 148).

56. Dos Passos, 1964, 113.

57. Mitchell, 2002, 45.

2. Social Science and Politics

1. Riesman and Lynd, 1960, 547.

2. This chapter and the one that follows, where we examine the critics' charges in greater detail, owe considerable debts to Tilman's original analysis of Veblen's critics (1992). The arguments we advance here, however, represent an interpretation developed specifically in relation to the political aspects of Veblen's thought.

3. In the words of Veblen's best student, Wesley Clair Mitchell (1936, xix), "Veblen repudiates preaching. As an evolutionist his office is to understand; not to praise, or blame, or lead us into righteousness. From his point of view, any notions he may entertain concerning what is right and wrong are vestiges of the cultural environment to which he has been exposed. They have no authority, and it would be a futile impertinence to try to impose them on others." Morton S. White (1957, 90), who quotes these words, questions the sharpness of Mitchell's distinction, claiming instead that Veblen knew very well that "most of his readers construed the fundamental ethical good as precisely the service of human life and well-being on the whole." But although the contention that human beings harbor such dispositions is an idea central to Veblen's social theory, he never claimed to have proved this notion once and for all, nor did he believe anyone ever could. In this sense, Mitchell is quite correct to emphasize Veblen's reluctance to pose as an authoritative source on moral or political questions.

4. See Bell, 1963; Stabile, 1984; Knoedler and Mayhew, 1999; Tilman, 1996a. *The Engineers* is actually not so much an integrated study of its subject but a collection of related articles, originally penned in a generally accessible, polemical style, for the political magazine *The Dial*, at the end of World War I. This fact alone ought to give students pause before drawing conclusions about its place in the Veblen canon.

5. Because it has created more political animus against his work than perhaps any other single item in the Veblen corpus, some sympathetic Veblen analysts wish that he had not written the book at all. But the book cannot be ignored or explained away. The question is whether it is possible to develop a credible explanation of its relation with the rest of his work, or whether it is fairly seen as an aberration, without significant analytic or doctrinal roots in earlier writings. Perhaps it is best understood as a whimsical expression of a major thinker's idiosyncratic personality, a work that marks a moment of unusual, naïve optimism before he abandoned all hope of structural change in American society. Or, as we think more likely, its pessimism about the probability of an engineer-led revolt only foreshadows the generally dark view of the future that pervaded his last book, *Absentee Ownership* (1923). See Tilman, 1996a, 167–197.

6. Charles Gattone (2006, 37), for one, cogently argues that Veblen's point in *The Engineers* was precisely "to demonstrate the improbability" that technical experts could supervise a social revolution in America and the new industrial order that might result from it. The idea of a soviet of engineers is, for Gattone, best understood as a hypothetical or a counterfactual, one that Veblen used to illustrate the critical point that "although the engineers were the only possible contenders for this new position of authority, their ability to fulfill this role was embarrassingly insufficient. Rather than acting as a united, class conscious group capable of collectively managing the industrial order, the engineers were a passive and individualistic lot," loyal employees of the business class.

7. Veblen, 1964p, 318.

8. Cited in Therborn, 1977, 86.

9. Adorno, 1967.

10. Veblen believed that people tend to conceive of pragmatic action in two ways: as goal-oriented action directed by human interest and advantage, and as technical industrial activity, whose product may or may not immediately be useful or of advantage to the producer. The former includes political and ideological action, while the latter may be undertaken under conditions of labor exploitation. The former implies a degree of freedom, while workmanship may be expressed even under conditions of intense servitude. Veblen makes it clear that unless otherwise specified, he intends the term to be used in the first sense (1969a, 13, n. 9).

11. 1969a, 20.

12. Ibid., 20, 19; 1957. Francesca Viano's new work on the importance of Veblen's brief time at Cornell University sheds valuable light on the various intellectual influences that shaped his scientific outlook, not only there but also at Johns Hopkins. Veblen took classes at Hopkins with the historian Herbert Baxter Adams, under whose influence he became familiar with the emerging movement of professional historiography, or historical analysis shorn of traditional preoccupations with "reformist engagement." Cornell's faculty in history, political science, and economics, on the other hand, was more beholden to the reform ideal of developing fact-based analyses of social problems, devoting themselves to cultivation of "professional expertise" that was "meant to guide political action" but "not become one with it." Except for the handful of

policy recommendations he made during his stay at the Department of Agriculture, Veblen let his critical analysis speak for itself. So while he deferred from the guidance of policymakers, his work reflected "a combination of social inquiry, moralizing attitudes, and institutional historiography" that he learned at Cornell (Viano, 2009, 43).

13. What Veblen once said about scientists' business sense applies to their political sense too: "a competent scientist or scholar well endowed with [political] sense is as rare as a devout scientist—almost as rare as a white blackbird" (1957, 109).

14. Among Veblen's sympathetic critics, Helen Liebel (1965, 209, 215) has argued that he believed the methods of the natural and social sciences are incommensurable, a view contradicted later in her essay, when she more accurately concludes that "Veblen believed that he was above all else a scientist because he did not hesitate to apply what he believed was a social-science-logic, free of anthropomorphism, one which stressed brute causation and selective adaptation." To the extent Veblen's social theory understood "brute causation and selective adaptation" as basic elements of Darwinian science, it is difficult to see how he could have drawn sharp distinctions between methods appropriate to the natural and social sciences. The more telling point is that Veblen recognized that all modes of science ultimately rest on metaphysical preconditions, which resist empirical proof. In this sense, his consistent point of view was to stress the socially constructed quality of scientific knowledge (Gattone, 2006, 38–39).

15. Veblen, 1969a, 19.

16. Weber, 1948b. In an interesting and provocative reading of *The Higher Learning*, Eyüp Özveren (2007, 17–22) suggests that Veblen understood the chief motive for learning in terms of a competition with the self, drawing an analogy with Joseph Schumpeter's entrepreneurial theory of "the logic of creative destruction." Our view is that Özveren mistakenly reads an emulative motive into a form of action that Veblen regards as anything but emulative or competitive. Veblen's theory of idle curiosity nowhere mentions or alludes to competitive emulation as a motive for theory, stressing instead the work-based and private intellectual satisfaction that derives from finding better answers for their own sake. This is not to say that scientists are immune from competitive and egoistic motives, only that Veblen himself resists assigning an inherent link between idle curiosity and emulation. We thank Professor Özveren for permission to cite his essay.

17. Veblen, 1964e, 226.

18. Ibid., 219–231.

19. Veblen, 1997, 29.

20. Ibid., 24, 29.

21. Machiavelli, 1961; Huntington, 1981, 75; Morgenthau, 1962a, 311–312; Niebuhr, 1932.

22. Veblen, 1997, 156.

23. Mills, 1953, xi.

24. Huntington, 1981, 3.

25. Veblen, 1997, 160.

26. Bartley and Bartley, 2004, 2.

27. Veblen, 1979, 99.

28. Veblen 1990; 1964l, 207.

29. White, 1957, 207.

30. Ibid.

31. Dugger, 1984, 982; Dugger and Sherman, 2000.

32. Sherman, 2003, 3.

33. Baumgartner and Jones, 1993, 4.

34. Veblen, 1997, 19.

35. Ayres, 1937.

36. Ross, 1991, 213; Gattone, 2006, 38–41.

37. Dos Passos, 1964, 113.

38. Kariel, 1966.

39. For two insightful efforts to identify Veblen's foreshadowing of postmodernism, see Meštrović (2003) and Peukert (2001). Meštrović, however, tends to overstate Veblen's critique of the machine process, while Peukert's emphasis on Veblen's relativism does not attend fully enough to Veblen's claims about the possibility of objective knowledge concerning "the life process taken impersonally."

40. See, e.g., Adorno, 1967; Bell, 1990; Dobriansky, 1957; Diggins, 2000.

41. Diggins, 2000.

42. Dorothy Ross goes so far as to call Veblen "the American Gramsci" (1991, 207).

43. Diggins, 2000, xxxi.

44. Meštrović, 2003.

3. The Assorted Politics of Veblen Criticism

1. On this score James K. Galbraith adds the important historical observation that the Cold War "era evidently had room for only two grand visions. One was that of Marx . . . the other was that of Hayek and Friedman." One posited revolution as the definitive outcome of capitalism; the other envisioned the free market as a rational mechanism favoring economic equilibrium and the best of all possible material outcomes. Neither has proven accurate. "Veblen's vision of an essentially stable order, yet dominated by a predatory and unproductive class, was plainly too subversive for the marketers, yet it was too cynical for the Marxists. And so it was effectively squeezed out of existence between them" (Galbraith, 2008, 128).

2. Veblen, 1979, 9.

3. Tilman, 1992, 46–60; Knight, 1920, 1941, 1956, 1960; Gattone, 2006, 38–45.

4. Knight, 1956, 18.

5. Knight, 1969, 226.

6. Veblen, 1997, 18.

7. Dewey, 1959, 180, 171.

8. Veblen, 1990, 25.

9. Seckler, 1975.

10. Ibid., 54–55.

11. Veblen, 1969b.

12. Dobriansky, 1957.

13. Strauss (1953), as far as we know, never dealt with Veblen specifically, though Veblen is a prime example of the historicist and relativist sins of modernism about which Strauss regularly complained.

14. Tilman, 1992, 73–75.

15. Dobriansky, 1957, 249, 256.

16. Veblen, 1979, 7.

17. Veblen, 1990, ch. 1; 1957, ch. 1.

18. Thus, as Veblen put it, a "close relation" subsists between "the norm of economic merit," which favors "the material furtherance . . . of life,"—that is, "human life on the whole . . . the life process taken impersonally"—and "the ethical norm of conduct" (1964d, 81–82; 1979, 109).

19. Veblen, 1979, 7.

20. Veblen, 1990, 318–319.

21. Dugger, 1984, 972.

22. Shannon, 1996.

23. *New York Times*, 19 April 2005, A9.

24. Shannon, 1996, viii–ix.

25. Veblen, 1979, 99.

26. Dobriansky, 1957, 350.

27. Ibid., 345.

28. Tilman, 1996c, 200.

29. Ross, 1991; Friedmann, 1987; Ricci, 1984; J. Scott, 1998; Hearn, 1985; Seidelman, 1985; Graham, 1976; Habermas, 1970.

30. Shields, 1952, 106.

31. Buxton, 1985.

32. Ibid., 17.

33. Parsons, 1966, 240, 258.

34. Parsons, 1968, 84.

35. G. H. Mead, 1964, 360.

36. Schneider, 1949; Tilman, 1992, 184; Gambs, 1946, 33–34, 40.

37. Mannheim, 1950.

38. Weber, 1948b, 115–128.

39. Bell, 1963, 638; Adorno, 1967.

40. Ignatieff, 2003; Rieff, 2003; Rosen, 2003.

41. Bell, 1960; Lipset, 1960; Fukuyama, 1992. In fairness, Fukuyama has since modified some of the stronger claims he advanced earlier about "the end of history." See, e.g., Fukuyama, 2006.

42. Jacoby, 1999.

43. Adorno, 1967, 393. Or, in Dos Passos's apt phrase, "Veblen asked too many questions, suffered from a constitutional inability to say yes" (1964, 114).

44. Horkheimer, 1941, 371.

45. Veblen, 1978, 323–324.

46. As Bernard Rosenberg interpreted Veblen's value, "most of" the latter's "brilliance is dissipated when the rationalist in him wins out over the skeptic" (1956, 87).

47. It is, after all, in that supposedly utopian tract *The Engineers and the Price System* that Veblen cautioned against expectations that technicians will lead a revolt (1983, 128).

48. Thus Ross calls Veblen "the American Gramsci" (1991, 207); see also Diggins, 2000.

49. Marcuse, 1964, 3.

50. Veblen, 1957; Plotkin, 2010.

51. Veblen, 1969g, 96; 1964e, 226–231.

52. See, e.g., Veblen, 1969a, 4.

53. Ibid., 26; Veblen, 1990, 333–334.

54. Hobson, 1936; Sweezy, 1957, 1958; Davis, 1968; Dowd, 2000.

55. Baran, 1957, 89–90.

56. Cutler, 1938.

57. Landsman, 1957, 345.

58. Rosenberg, 1956, 76.

59. Ibid., 77.

60. Cited in Tilman, 1992, 247.

61. Hodder, 1956; Patsouras, 2004; Tilman, 1996a.

62. Stabile, 1984, 183.

63. Veblen makes precisely this criticism of Marx. See Veblen, 1969d, 413–418.

64. Veblen, 1983, 128–129.

65. Braverman, 1975.

66. Interestingly Stabile acknowledges Diggins' analysis of the relationship between animism and alienation in Veblen, but it seems not to have played any role in shaping his own interpretation. Stabile, 1984, 188 and 285 n. 26.

67. Stabile, 1984, 191, italics added.

68. Veblen, 1990, 31.

69. Ibid., li.

70. Veblen, 1964c, 32–49; 1964d, 78–96. The line of argument in these essays stresses linkages between animism and the reification of power, predation, and enslavement of women. A somewhat different explanation stresses the religious, priestly origins of exploit. See Veblen, 1990, 147–160.

71. Notably, Stabile ignores the gendered basis of Veblen's theory of power, but it is an aspect of the theory that remains keenly important.

72. For an interesting analysis of the narcissistic aspects of Veblen's theory of envy and power, see Meštrović, 2003, 1–17.

73. Knoedler and Mayhew, 1999; Rutherford, 1992; Stabile, 1984.

74. Cited in Tilman, 1992, 170.

75. Diggins, 2000, xxxi.

76. Cutler, 1938; Corey, 1937.

77. Sweezy, 1958; Rosenberg, 1956.

78. Diggins, 2000, xxxi.

79. Marcuse, 1964, 5, xi.

80. Veblen, 1919, 16.

81. Lloyd, 1997.

82. Ibid., 4.

83. Something of the painful uncertainty of late twentieth-century Marxian praxis might be seen in the fact that a writer like Donald Stabile can explain Veblen's political flaws by his removal from the factory floor, while Lloyd roots the problem in the errors of Veblenian theory itself. Neither is prepared to accept the fact that Veblen never set himself the problem of fomenting political revolution.

84. Lloyd, 1997, 64.

85. As Paul Bush (1999) has carefully noted, scholars divide into at least three sets of views on the question of Veblen's understanding of science and the fact-value distinction. One is that Veblen is to be taken at his word as a dispassionate, value-free scientist, a positivist, in effect. This view, partially adopted by Lloyd, has earlier precedents in the work of Seckler (1975) and substantially in the scholarship of Geoffrey Hodgson, neither of whom Lloyd cites, and whose interpretations of Veblen are far removed from Lloyd's Leninist reading. A second, more critical position also adumbrates some of what Lloyd argues, insisting that while Veblen favored positivistic science, he lacked the discipline to stay the course, thus falling into normative statements that are inconsistent with his scientific proclamations. This view is held by such conservative critics as Cummings (1899) and Knight (1960), as well as by the liberal David Riesman (1953). A third view, Bush's own, is that Veblen's claims to dispassionate science, or as Lloyd would have it, Veblen's positivism, expresses a deliberately ironic stance. Veblen regularly contrasts his objectivity claims and normative judgments in order precisely to undermine sharp distinctions between fact and value, which positivism proclaimed. Though sympathetic with this last perspective, as we suggested in the previous chapter, Veblen's ironic posture toward the fact-value distinction in science also reflects his radical realist critique of power. On this point, see also Ross (1991, 213–215) and M. S. White (1957, 206–207).

86. Veblen, 1969h, 38; 1969a, 17.

4. The Politics of Power and Predation

1. Veblen, 1969b, 56–81.

2. Veblen (1997, 171) suggests, for example, that it may well have been in the "moral penumbra" of the slave trade that the founders of the American enterprise "learned how not to let its right hand know what its left hand is doing; and there is always something to be done that is best done with the left hand."

3. In the last twenty years or so, scholars working in the subfield of American political development (APD) *have* begun to focus on the evolution of political institutions as well as on the continuing influence of past arrangements of governance on

contemporary political patterns, a historical phenomenon that Orren and Skowronek call "intercurrence." Remarkably, these authors highlight the fact that they and their colleagues in APD "stumbled onto this common ground without any apparent guidance from prior theory." It is one of the intellectual costs of Veblen's effacement by political science that it took the profession the better part of a century to recapture the characteristically Veblenian insights that "the institutions of a polity are not created or recreated all at once, in accordance with a single ordering principle," and that political analysis needs to be anchored "in terms that are irreducibly historical and institutional" (Orren and Skowronek, 2004, 112–113).

4. Russell Bartely, personal communication, January 2009.

5. Bush, 2002, 3.

6. Veblen, 1997, 24.

7. Veblen, 1979, 10.

8. Weber, 1948b, 59; Morgenthau, 1967, 25.

9. Schattschneider, 1960, 2.

10. For Nietzsche's influence on Weber and Morgenthau, see Diggins, 1996, 129–131; Frei, 2001, 98–108. Veblen certainly acknowledged Marx's contribution to contemporary thought, but nowhere in his work, to the best of our knowledge, does he show any familiarity with Nietzsche.

11. Veblen, 1979, 19.

12. Meštrović, 2003.

13. Veblen, 1979, 19.

14. Ibid., 97–101; 1990, 25–27.

15. Veblen, 1964d, 82.

16. Veblen, 1979, 15.

17. Ibid., 22–24.

18. Morgenthau, 1962a, 3–4.

19. Diggins (2000, 76–77) argues that Veblen failed to provide such an explanation; we argue that Veblen's account of the evolution of power constitutes precisely that answer.

20. Meinecke, 1998, 4, 7, 11.

21. Veblen, 1990, 316.

22. Meinecke, 1998, 11.

23. Veblen, 1964f, 175–193.

24. For discussions of the Darwinian influence on Veblen, see Tilman, 1996, chs. 2–3; Hodgson, 1992, 2001; Wiltgen, 1990; Dugger and Sherman, 2000; Murphey, 1990, vii–xlv; Russett, 1976, ch. 6; Harris, 1934; Murphree, 1959. Also see Bowler, 2003; Crook, 1994.

25. Veblen, 1979, 98–99.

26. Veblen, 1964d, 83–84.

27. Edelman, 1964, 5, 9.

28. Veblen, 1997, 20.

29. Diggins, 2000, xiv.

30. Veblen, 1979, Preface, 1–3.

31. Ibid., 11–12.

32. Veblen, 1964d, 85.

33. Veblen, 1979, 12.

34. Meinecke, 1998, 4.

35. Diggins, 2000, 75.

36. Veblen, 1979, 12–13.

37. Adorno, 1967, 84, 86.

38. Our use of gendered pronouns is, of course, quite deliberate here. It reflects Veblen's theory that the beginnings of male exploitation of women constituted the crucial change from exploitation directed at animate phenomena in the environment to the social relations of human beings themselves (1979, ch. 2).

39. Of course, as noted earlier, self-generated purpose, for Veblen, does not imply a distinctively individual purpose but rather a shared sense of purpose that arises more or less spontaneously out of communal need, life, and industry.

40. Veblen, 1979, 22–24.

41. Not surprisingly, Veblen argued that human technical or industrial proficiency is best achieved under "circumstances of moderate exigence." "Great stress" and pressure tend to encourage "crudity of technique" (1990, 33–34).

42. In drawing such distinctions, Veblen described categories that he believed were developed by primitive peoples. But, in effect, he also offered what amounted to pure or ideal types of human action that underpin the substance of his critical social theory. In practice, exploit and industry mix in variant ways, each reflecting and embracing attributes of the other. They are not discrete forms of human activity, especially where predatory habits become controlling social norms. See, e.g., 1990, Preface, p. li. In contrast to the view taken here, Meštrović (2003, 8–9) argues, incorrectly, we think, that Veblen understood the human agent to split industrial and barbaric habits into "separate, logic-tight compartments." The point at issue is one of origins and evolutionary patterns. Exploit developed out of industry, in domains of human experience that industrial experience did not seem able to control. But exploit can retain elements of workmanship, just as workmanship can include aspects of exploit.

43. Veblen, 1979, 20.

44. Ibid.

45. Ibid., 17–18.

46. Ibid.

47. Weber, 1978, 1:242. Veblen is, if anything, less insistent than Weber on performance or empirical success to secure legitimate authority." See, e.g., Veblen, 1997, 116.

48. Veblen, 1997, 114.

5. Savagery and Its Anarchistic Legacies

1. Veblen, 1979, 19.

2. Ibid., 6–7.

3. Veblen, 1990, 177.

4. Ibid., ch. 2.

5. Veblen, 1964d, 84; 1917, 198; 1969f, 315–316.

6. Veblen, 1964d, 78.

7. As Gordon S. Wood observes, "For centuries it was assumed that most people would not work unless they had to. 'Everybody but an idiot,' declared the English agricultural writer Arthur Young . . . 'knows that the lower class must be kept poor or they will never be industrious'" (Wood, 2009, 324).

8. Veblen, 1964d, 78.

9. Banfield, 1974; Murray, 1984; L. M. Mead, 1986, 1992.

10. Veblen, 1964d, 78.

11. Ibid.

12. This is exactly why Veblen believed that if "ostensible democracy" could be stripped of its "metaphysical figment of sovereignty," the remainder would be "nothing better . . . than an unsanctified workaday arrangement for the common use of industrial ways and means" (1997, 28).

13. Veblen, 1964d, 85.

14. Veblen, 1990, 92–100.

15. Kropotkin, n.d. We can find no instance where Veblen discusses or even mentions Kropotkin's work. On connections between Kropotkin and Veblen, see Dugger, 1984.

16. Bartley and Yoneda, 1994, 602.

17. Shiva, 2000, 74; Sandilands, 1999; Mies, 2001; Plant, 1991.

18. Evans, 1993, 177.

19. Veblen, 1990, 93–94.

20. Edgell, 2001, 90.

21. Veblen, 1964g, 18–19; 1990, 90.

22. Crook, 1994, 145.

23. Veblen, 1969e, 231–251; 1964h, 143.

24. Edgell, 2001, 90. In his first sketches of savagery, Veblen was prone to suggest that savage human nature was "proto-anthropoid," belonging possibly to a "sub-human . . . cultural stage" (1979, 360–361). We do not find this evolutionary distinction in other Veblen texts.

25. Diggins, 2000, 68, 72. He suggests, correctly we believe, that Veblen's conception of savagery presupposed neither the natural goodness of man nor his immunity from alienation.

26. Veblen, 1990, 177.

27. "Most fighting" among the earliest humans, reports one historian, "was, as it is now among contemporary hunting and gathering people, a sporadic, highly personalized affair, homicidal in intent and, occasionally, in effect, but lacking a sustained economic and political motivation beyond that of revenge and, sometimes, women" (O'Connell, 1989, 25).

28. Veblen, 1990, 123–124.

29. Veblen, 1964d, 81.

30. Veblen, 1990, 178–180.

31. Influenced by John Diggins, Warren Samuels put the point well when he observed, "In a sense, Veblen was principally a student of ideology, and a most profound one indeed" (1979, 456).

32. Diggins, 2000, 97.

33. Veblen, 1990, 12.

34. Edgell, 2001, 90–91.

35. Merchant, 1991, 260–261.

36. *New York Times*, 18 February 2004; *Harvard Crimson*, 13 February 2005.

37. Veblen, 1979, 358; Eby, 1992.

38. Veblen, 1979, 358.

39. Ibid., 357.

40. Ibid., 358.

41. Veblen, 1954, 13.

42. England also greatly benefited from the geographic advantage of its relative separation from much of the political intrigue and warfare of mainland Europe. So did the United States, if less directly, later. See Veblen, 1954, ch. 4; 1997, 121–122.

43. Veblen, 1954, 17.

44. Adorno, 1967, 88.

45. Echoing his early Kantean influence, Veblen observed that "the premises and logic of the machine technology" are "in every man's mind" (1954, 190).

46. Ibid., 326.

47. Ibid., 325

48. As Veblen's observations about maternal savagery anticipated aspects of contemporary ecofeminism, his discussion of pagan anarchy foreshadows the related but distinct "small-is-beautiful" tradition of convivial, decentralist technology. See, e.g., Illich, 1973; Schumacher, 1973; Lovins, 1977; Sale, 1980.

49. Machiavelli, 1961, 101.

50. Machiavelli, 1961; Montesquieu, 1949; Pocock, 1975.

51. Veblen noted that advanced industrial systems may include groups living in small communities, but such groups would have to live peaceably together across whatever boundaries divided them because "a large and diversified industrial scheme is impossible except in a community of some size" (Veblen, 1954, 108). Power, whether responsible or not, would necessarily have to become more centralized.

52. Neumann, 1956, 10.

53. Veblen, 1954, 312–314. On the importance of the police power to the substance and sweep of royal claims to authoritative control of their populations and territories, see Dubber, 2005.

54. Veblen, 1954, 323.

55. Ibid., 46. Veblen's characterization of "neighborly surveillance" as the effective source of communal order not only echoes familiar anarchist themes but also anticipates certain contemporary liberal and feminist notions of the productive, creative aspects of community power. See Lynd, 1956; Stone, 1989; Parsons, 1966; Arendt, 1972; Young,

1996; Mansbridge, 1983. Critics of Veblen, e.g., Parsons (1968) and Davis (1945), who charge that he had no concept of order relevant to peaceable, nonrepressive societies, ignore Veblen's clear emphasis on normative controls in pagan anarchy.

56. Veblen's thinking here resembles Max Weber's more familiar notion of "neighborhood" as an "unsentimental brotherhood" (Weber, 1978, 1:361).

57. Sennett, 1970.

58. Veblen, 1954, 327. The idea bears some resemblance to what Foucault (2007, 194–202) calls popular "counter-conduct."

59. Veblen, 1954, 14.

60. Ibid., 329.

61. Ibid., 329; 1979, 98.

62. Weber, 1978, 1:329.

63. Veblen, 1954, 329.

64. Ibid. 329, n. 1.

65. Ibid., 46.

66. Ibid.

67. Lynd, 1956; Sennett, 1970.

68. M. Anderson, 2000, 316, 313. See also the account of Hans Morgenthau's experience of rising anti-Semitism in the little German town of Coburg, in Frei, 2001, ch. 1.

69. Veblen, 1954, 326–327.

70. *New York Times*, 14 June 2008, 1.

71. Veblen, 1990, 297–298.

72. Ibid., 276.

73. Veblen, 1997, 44–45. This celebration of self-liberation suggests that Max Lerner overstated the case when he observed that Veblen did not appreciate "that freedom too has its dynamism in history." Clearly, "political values" were not always "marginal" in Veblen's work (Lerner, 1948, 40).

74. Veblen, 1990, 276.

75. See Marcuse (1941, 416), for whom critical reason found its locus in the emergent liberal spirit of insubordination.

76. Gumplowicz, 1980.

77. Veblen, 1990, 276.

78. Veblen, 1997, 47.

79. Ibid. See also Oppenheimer, 1975, 89–90.

80. Marx, 1967, chs. 26–28.

81. Orren, 1991, 13.

82. Veblen, 1997, 50.

83. Veblen, 1954, 196.

84. Macpherson, 1962; Thompson, 1964, 1975.

85. Edgell, 2001, 123.

86. Veblen, 1997, 28.

87. Veblen, 1990, 297.

88. Veblen, 1954, 327. Perhaps the success of conservative, neoliberal, and right-wing populist movements in the United States and elsewhere—the Tea Party movement most recently—owes a good deal to this "restless casting back" for local control and more convivial political institutions. Conservatives may have manipulated such longings in the interest of emancipating both business interests and the warfare state. Still, as Veblen suggests, one would be naïve not to acknowledge the popular appeal of "an alternative compromise" to that offered by absentee bureaucratic liberalism.

6. Illiberal Habits, War, and State Formation

1. Veblen, 1954.

2. Tilly, 1992, 67. Michael Mann estimates that from 500 B.C. to the present day, "the average state has been engaged in at least one open, organized war with another state in about 50 per cent of years" (Mann, 1988, 130–131).

3. O'Connell, 1989, 144.

4. Veblen, 1997, 23.

5. Beyond identifying the state with political interests in mastery, violence, and war, Veblen's evolutionary method precluded him from giving a formal, uniform definition of the state. This is exactly why his theory suggests the need for an evolutionary-minded, historically sensitive, and comparative political science.

6. Veblen, 1978, 300.

7. Veblen, 1917, 27.

8. Almond, 1990, 285.

9. Edgell, 2001, 131.

10. James K. Galbraith, 2008, 127.

11. Observing the ability of leaders to get their populations whipped up for war, Veblen adds the cautionary note that such emotions get roiled "at least for the time being" (Veblen, 1917, 22). Glorification of war may have a relatively short half-life. Popular patience usually soon runs thin.

12. The model suggested here differs in certain respects form Dugger's important and useful analysis of Veblen's theory of power. First, Dugger's model is a functional analysis of modern corporate power rather than a formulation of Veblen's political thought. Second, his model rightly stresses the general patterns of the contamination of the instincts in Veblen's theory, a contamination that flows largely from the workings of power. The four processes Dugger describes—contamination, subordination, emulation, and mystification—play crucial roles in Veblen's analysis of precapitalist power relations, and we will allude to them below, but the emphasis of our model is historical, cultural, and, if you will, evolutionary, rather than formal. That is, we are stressing the historical features and legacy of illiberal, precapitalist habits of power that define a predatory model. The two approaches are not inconsistent, but they do handle the problem from different points of view. See Dugger, 1989, and the pithy summary in Tilman, 1992, 284–285.

13. Veblen, 1997, 20.

14. Dowd 2000; Gambs, 1946; Sweezy, 1958.

15. Veblen, 1917, 12–17; 1954, ch. 3; 302–332.

16. See, e.g., Ngai, 2004; Daniels, 2004; Tichenor, 2002.

17. R. Smith, 1997, 9–10.

18. Gumplowicz, 1980, 205.

19. Veblen, 1954, 48.

20. Ibid.

21. Ibid., 138.

22. Huntington, 1996, 21; Castells, 1997; R. Smith, 1997.

23. Veblen, 1954, 138.

24. Veblen, 1979, 18.

25. Tilly, 1985, 185.

26. R. Smith, 1997, 10.

27. Veblen, 1979, 18–19.

28. Veblen, 1964d, 93.

29. Veblen, 1990, 168. Historical evidence suggests that Veblen may have overesti-mated the humanity of the classical age, which is the "only (previous) historical period whose level of militarization of social life . . . approaches our own," especially if the case of Rome is considered in addition to that of Sparta and the often-warring Greek city-states (Mann, 1988, 135).

30. Veblen, 1990, 168.

31. Veblen, 1969c, 402.

32. Veblen's notion of irresponsibility, as applied here and throughout his work, reflects his normative position, opposing exploit in favor of self-guided industry, in which agents are free to use their own energies for their own self-guided ends. In this respect, Veblen's conception of irresponsibility exists outside, or astride, the self-understanding of power relations among inhabitants of the system being described. The difference does matter. Within the terms of reference of the powerful, irresponsibility would consist of behavior that was at odds with or dysfunctional regarding the prevailing ruling-class consensus on appropriate action. Such terms may prove sufficiently ambiguous to cause conflict within the class. For example, if one segment of a ruling class, against the resis-tance of other members of the class, opted to open up channels of popular voice, its opponents might well deem such openings an act of class treason, much as elements of the U.S. business class in the 1930s indicted the Roosevelt administration for its support of labor's collective bargaining rights. Conversely, such openings might be seen by their advocates as both a socially enlightened and a politically wise bid to assure class control in the long run. Veblen certainly understands the ambiguous dynamic of strategic maneuver within ruling classes, along with the internal conception of class responsibility that it implies. But a transcultural normative framework determines his and our use of the term "responsibility," not the local understandings of the ruling classes that he studies. We thank Russell Bartley for stressing the importance of this distinction.

33. A notable exception to Veblen's sense of acquiescence and passivity in subordi-nate populations is the potential for a criminal subculture of gang violence to develop (1979, 250).

34. Veblen, 1919, 6; Danner, 2005, 73.

35. The idea that power may sometimes sense its own limitations surfaces especially in *Imperial Germany* and in *The Nature of Peace*. In the former, for example, Veblen describes part of Prussian political strategy with respect to the German working class in terms of co-optation: provision of a strong social-security system solidified working class loyalty to the regime (1954, 215). The somewhat restraining hand of strategic interest also plays a role in Veblen's remarkable discussion of a "peace without honor" strategy for the allies in World War I. An analysis of a hypothetical submission of the United States, Great Britain, and France to German rule, this chapter is, in essence, a comparative anatomy of imperial oppression, where the severity of physical intimidation by conquerors is shrewdly calibrated by the dominator's assessment of its own strategic requirements. Brutality is applied or relaxed in relation to strategic interest. Morals have little more to do with imperatives of empire than to legitimize them (1917, ch. 4). For a classic realist discussion of the uneasy relation of power to moral restraint, see Meinecke, 1998, ch. 1.

36. Marx, 1967, 10.

37. Marx, of course, insisted upon the difference between "class-in-itself" and "class-for-itself," so he was hardly unaware of the problem of conservative tendencies in working class consciousness. But he also believed that, whatever its current deficiencies might be, the political consciousness of labor was educable—that is, in a revolutionary direction—through experience and intense union and political party work. Veblen was more skeptical; indeed, he doubted it, as he gave considerably more credit to the feudal holdover of emulation in working class consciousness. See especially Veblen's essays on socialism and Marx, 1969d, 387–456.

38. R. Smith, 1997, 6.

39. Foucault, 2007.

40. In his play *Angels in America*, Tony Kushner penned a classic formulation of the idea that claims to personal power control perceptions and valorizations of status and identity, placing it in the absurdly rational words of a fictionalized Roy Cohn. Cohn's futile denial of his own homosexuality resounds with a boast about the power basis of his nongay status. Rejecting his physician's insistence that a diagnosis of AIDS implicates his gayness, Cohen replies, "You think these are names that tell you who someone sleeps with, but they don't tell you that . . . Like all labels they tell you one thing and one thing only: where does an individual fit in the food chain, in the pecking order? Not ideology, or sexual taste, but something much simpler: clout . . . Now to someone who doesn't understand this, homosexual is what I am because I have sex with other men. But really this is wrong. Homosexuals are not men who sleep with other men. Homosexuals are men who in fifteen years of trying cannot get a puissant antidiscrimination bill through City Council. Homosexuals are men who know nobody and nobody knows. Who have zero clout. Does this sound like me, Henry?" (Kushner, 1993, 45).

41. Veblen, 1997, 142–165; 1954, 332–340.

42. Scott, 1985.

43. Veblen, 1997, 44–45; 1919, 39.

44. Veblen, 1983, 106. This view amounts to a different way of stating Veblen's basic idea that the most consequential changes in social life and institutions develop slowly and cumulatively, not through conscious, much less revolutionary, political action.

45. Veblen, 1979, 15.

46. Schattschneider, 1960; Bachrach and Baratz, 1970; Lukes, 1974; cf. Veblen, 1990, 177. For a critical view of such approaches, see Hayward, 2000.

47. Liebel, 1965, 208. For a different, psychological interpretation of Veblen's complex view of agency, see Meštrović, 2003, 11–12.

48. Veblen, 1979, 13, italics added.

49. Dugger, 1989.

50. Mills, 1953, xii.

51. Plotkin, 1991.

52. Satirically, Veblen suggests that to understand the arbitrariness of human identification with place it is useful to draw an analogy with clams: though it is a matter of sheer chance where the young clam finds "a resting place for the sole of his feet," this place is, nonetheless, " 'his own, his native land' etc." Less satirically, Veblen goes on to note that the organic analogy of the clam does not quite suit the human case. For it is not really "the accident of domicile" that lends power to human associations with place, nor does "mere legal citizenship." Individuals, after all, can hold multiple civic loyalties; they may become hyphenate citizens of a given community, or obtain dual citizenship. Place-based identities thus originate not in nature but in "conventions, legal or customary." Militant loyalties to place, suggests Veblen, emerge out of traditions of invidious comparison with other groups. They are a kind of quasi-tropismatic "reflex" of the habit of sectarian animosity itself, a habit that contaminates putative tendencies humans might have to identify with the generic interests of the species (Veblen, 1917, 134–136). Veblen's analysis parallels Carl Schmitt's assertion that general human equality is "neutralized through the definitive exclusion of all those who do not belong to the state, or of those who remain outside it" (Schmitt, 1988, 12). See also Smith, 1997, on the general theme of the partisan constitution of civic identity.

53. Veblen did not see religion as a wholly conservative, repressive phenomenon. Also associated with altruistic and communal values deriving from the parental bent, religion could serve noninvidious human interests, such as "brotherly love," charity, social justice, and environmental protection. See Veblen, 1964l, 200–218; 1979, 334; Patsouras, 2004, 232–233. Bernard Rosenberg, by contrast, insists that religion was among the serious "blind spots" in Veblen's theory (1956, 49).

54. R. Smith, 1997, 9.

55. Veblen, 1954, 53–54.

56. Veblen, 1997, 21.

57. Veblen, 1979, 19.

58. Mann, 1988. Randall Collins (1974, 168) offers a similar view of "the German tradition of historiography," suggesting that it "was oriented towards conflict, but along military rather than economic lines."

59. Skocpol and Amenta, 1985.

60. Joas, 2003, 141–162. Weber, of course, defined the state by its claim to a "*monopoly of the legitimate use of physical force* within a given territory" (1948a, 78, emphasis in original), but he was far more circumspect than Gumplowicz (1980) and Oppenheimer (1975) in attributing imperial or expansionist power motives to all states (Weber, 1948b, 159–179). By the same token, Gumplowicz and Oppenheimer believed the state to be born in the struggles of ancient warrior bands to extract unpaid labor from foreign populations. The motive force in primal plunder was a presumed natural desire to seize unearned consumption goods. What Veblen called the "irksomeness of labor" was a crucial assumption for Gumplowicz, who believed aversion to labor to be a cardinal feature of human nature (1980, 205). Veblen's critique of a natural aversion to labor is, as we have argued, basic to his political theory of power. Oppenheimer, by contrast, accepted Gumplowicz's economic explanation for plunder, but he insisted on drawing a sharp, Veblen-like distinction between labor—a legitimate "economic means" to wealth—and predatory plunder—"the political means"—which, as in Gumplowicz, are identified with the state (Oppenheimer, 1975, 12–13).

61. Gabriel Almond (1990, 189–218) defends pluralist political science, but not Marxism, from charges of social and economic reductionism, insisting that major pluralist authors do reserve substantial autonomy for state actors. What Almond tends to ignore, however, is that classic pluralist discussions of the autonomy of political actors typically include the careful reservation that prevailing social relations and social structures provide a framework that must not be challenged. See, e.g., Dahl, 1961, 94; Truman, 1951, 249–261; Schattschneider, 1960, chs. 4, 7.

62. Veblen, 1990, 268–269. On this point, Veblen agreed completely with Hintze and Weber. Indeed, if anything, Veblen argued that the warfare, national security, and foreign policy aspects of the state tended to influence domestic politics at least as much as, if not more than, domestic political considerations conduced to warlike foreign policies. In this sense, William Appleton Williams is right to argue that Veblen avoids "the basic error of trying to analyze . . . foreign policy . . . in terms of a simple reaction to outside stimuli." But in light of Veblen's insistence on the state system as critical to the warlike character of individual states, it muddles Veblen's view of the reciprocal relationships here to insist, as Willams also does, "that Veblen's *central proposition* is that foreign policy is intimately connected with domestic policy" (Williams, 1957, 112, emphasis added). His "central proposition" is, in fact, different. It is to emphasize the inseparability of these forces, as they are locked into patterns of self-reinforcing causation.

63. Veblen, 1990, 268–269.

64. Ibid., 146, emphasis added.

65. Veblen, 1990, 268.

66. Arthur Davis, for example, lauded Veblen for his examination of the state during and after World War I, calling his "postwar essays on international relations . . . so incisive and penetrating . . . that many of them are as relevant today as they were when written" (Davis, 1957, 97). One sees this theme even more strongly in a recent survey

of Veblen's ideas, which claims that compared with his politically sensitive wartime writings, Veblen's earlier scholarship is marked by a "wry distance from the social issues he is considering" (Spindler, 2002, 61).

67. Veblen, 1997, 21. Huntington (1968) argues that America's noncentralized or "tudor polity" is an example of attenuated modernization that departs from the more centralist, national template of European states, a legacy of the fact that Britain's greatest political influence on American institutions was felt before the growth of centralized parliamentary power in the eighteenth century. Veblen's notion of incomplete modernization suggests that the feudal inheritance was strong even in the more centralized, unitary states of Europe, although it was manifest not in patterns of representation, but in diplomacy and war making.

68. Veblen, 1917, 9; 1997, 21.

69. Veblen, 1990, 270; McNeill, 1982; Machiavelli, 2003; Braudel, 1973, 290–295; Parker, 1996, ch. 1.

70. Veblen, 1990, 269–270.

71. Veblen, 1997, 22. As an example of the personal ambition Veblen had in mind, consider the remarks of Frederick II of Prussia, who described his motivations for war with Austria in the following terms: "These were the reasons that prevailed upon me to wage war against Theresa of Austria . . . Ambition, advantage, my desire to make a name for myself—these swayed me, and war was resolved upon." Citing this statement, Michael Mann remarks on how Frederick identified his rivals as specific personalities— "rival states are personally named—another indication of the geo-political privacy of these dynasts" (Mann, 1988, 154). Upon observing President George W. Bush's handling of foreign affairs, a White House advisor similarly noted "that things haven't changed all that much since foreign affairs were the affairs of kings—how they got along or didn't, determined the fate of nations" (cited in Suskind, 2006, 109).

72. Tilly, 1992; Braudel, 1973, 325–372; McNeill, 1982, chs. 4–6. Not all states followed the same fiscal-military strategy, of course. In the eighteenth century, for example, English military power, especially the British navy, benefited from establishment of a strong central bank to help finance the substantial costs of expansion and modernization. In contrast, French naval development lagged in part because France lacked a central bank with its power to channel credit to military purposes (McNeill, 1982, 180).

73. Veblen, 1990, 269.

74. Veblen, 1917, 78, 140, 197, 206ff., 217, 282, 299, 310, 366–367. Charles Tilly (1985, 171) recently advanced a remarkably similar argument, suggesting the analogy of racketeering as apt for understanding how local strongmen, aspiring monarchs, and belligerent chief executives frequently make offers of protection that their populations cannot refuse. For Veblen, as for Tilly, the state is "an enterprise in intimidation" precisely because "the state is useful for disturbing the peace."

75. Tilly, 1985, 170; P. Anderson, 1979.

76. "Global power," as George Modelski has written, "strengthened those states that attained it relatively to all other political . . . organizations. What is more, other

states competing in the global power game developed similar organizational forms and similar hardiness: they too became nation-states—in a defensive reaction, because forced to take issue with or to confront a global power . . . or in imitation of its obvious success." Cited in Tilly, 1985, 185; see also S. Smith, 1989, on this point.

77. Tilly, 1992; P. Anderson, 1979, pt.1; King, 1986, ch. 2; Peacock and Wiseman, 1961.

78. Braudel, 1973, chs. 6–8.

79. Veblen, 1990, 271.

80. Ibid., 271. For a fascinating discussion of how state military and administrative rationality stimulated the growth and efficiency of the U.S. machine-tools industry in the nineteenth century, see M. R. Smith, 1977, 24–42.

81. Veblen, 1990, 272.

82. Ibid., 272–273.

83. Ibid.

84. As Louis Mumford concluded, "The coalition of money power with political power was one of the decisive marks of monarchic or despotic absolutism; and the more dependent the military machine became on technical inventions and mass production of weapons, the greater the immediate profits to the national economic system— even though in the long run succeeding generations would find these putative gains offset by the cost of reparations, repairs, and replacements, to say nothing of human wretchedness" (Mumford, 1964, 242).

85. Veblen, 1990, 273. On this point, Tilly's work (1992) represents a significant advancement beyond Veblen. Tilly shows clearly how the expansion of the means of coercion and extraction by centralizing monarchs frequently generated political resistance from insubordinate classes, conflicts which, over the long haul, led to substantial institutional changes: growth of parliaments, limits on taxation and conscription, popular suffrage, increased levels of domestic spending, the welfare state, and an overall pattern of civilianization of western European states. The striking exception to Tilly's thesis, of course, is the United States, whose historical trajectory toward a more militarized national-security state has been unmistakable, especially in the Cold War and post–Cold War eras. Tilly does not analyze the United States, but Veblenian explanations would doubtless focus on the imperial aspirations of its absentee owners and state officialdom. See also McNeill, 1982, ch. 5.

7. Ostensible Democracy

1. Melman, 1970, 1974; Barnet, 1972; Bacevich, 2002, 2005; L. Fisher, 1995, 2004; Blum 1995; Greider, 1998; Boggs, 2003; Schlesinger, 2004; Yoo, 2005; Raskin and LeVan, 2005.

2. Lerner, 1948, 36.

3. Veblen, 1969c, 387–408.

4. Veblen, 1954, 268–269.

5. Veblen, 1969d, 441.

6. Veblen, 1990, 344–345. Veblen's emphasis on the continuing influence of traditional attachments within the otherwise sober institutions of capitalist democracy is at odds with Joseph Schumpeter's fear—deeply influenced by his Weberian analysis of rationalistic capitalism—that rationalism would spawn radical challenges to traditional patterns of political and economic inequality. Such anxieties led Schumpeter to lionize charismatic capitalist entrepreneurs, and to work up the apologetics of democratic elitism as a conservative political arrangement to restrain the tide of mass democracy, an idea with abundant influence in mid-twentieth-century American political science (Schumpeter, 1962, 131–133; Scheuerman, 1999, 189 passim).

7. Veblen, 1954, 230.

8. Almond, 1990, 138.

9. Putnam, Leonardi, and Raffaella, 1993; Putnam, 2000.

10. Veblen, 1990, 177. Veblen stressed that cultures featuring a more or less consistent or homogeneous bias—America's pecuniary culture, for example—were likely to be "stable." Those, which, like early twentieth-century imperial Germany and Japan, featured contradictory "cultural elements," such as technical rationalization coupled with an overtly authoritarian, militaristic state, were more likely to experience significant dislocation and turbulence. The latter societies were in "an unstable or transitional phase," likely to experience internal serious conflict over directions, a level of stress and strain that foreshadowed grievous problems for the world at large. 1954, 271; 1964j, 248–266.

11. Veblen, 1990, 177; James K. Galbraith, 2008, 128.

12. Orren and Skowronek, 2004, 113.

13. As Veblen once answered a critic, "for the purpose of my inquiry—an inquiry as to why and how the habits of life and of thought come to be modified," factors such as "customs, conventions, and methods of industry" must be considered along with such physical aspects of the situation as climate and topography. And all these "vary incontinently" (1964g, 22). That is, such variance and change are unstoppable; they are constantly at work.

14. Veblen, 1917, 102. It is not clear that Veblen always thought the increasing rate of technical and economic change would support progressive possibilities, though on balance it would seem that he did. He observed that most people had little liking for a disenchanted world. They resisted "all this mechanistic mutilation of objective reality into mere inert dimensions . . . Laymen seek respite in the fog of occult and esoteric faiths and cults, and so fall back on the will to believe things of which the senses transmit no evidence" (1954, 333).

15. Veblen, 1997, 159.

16. Ibid., 142.

17. Veblen, 1979, 98; 1997, 16.

18. Veblen, 1964c, 32–49; 1964d, 78–96.

19. On this score, Veblen is liable to serious charges of overstating his own subjective viewpoint, imputing to people in general views that are his own. This is a serious problem, and Veblen's defense rests on his instinct theory; reject that, and the normative

structure of Veblenian theory collapses. By this point, most readers will have made up their own mind on that point.

20. Veblen, 1997, 28.

21. In *The Engineers and the Price System*, Veblen argues that a main part of the technicians' responsibility in the industrial republic will be "to know and take care of the community's habitual need and use of consumable goods," and he carefully adds that a special quasi-political(?) role will fall to "the 'consulting economist,'" whose "place in the scheme is analogous to the part which legal counsel now plays in the maneuvers of diplomatists and statesmen" (1983, 148, 136). Obviously, Veblen envisions a technical division of labor among experts, but one that leaves agonizingly open the issue of the political division between experts and public opinion. He offers no clues to his preferred institutional design.

22. Veblen, 1990, 333–334.

23. Mill, 1951; Tocqueville, 1945; MacIver, 1947.

24. Veblen, 1978, 344–345.

25. Veblen, 1919, 16.

26. James K. Galbraith, 2008, 127.

27. Veblen, 1997, 26–27.

28. Veblen, 1919, 126.

29. Veblen, 1969c, 387–408.

30. Ibid., 403.

31. Ibid., 404.

32. Ibid., 404; Veblen, 1997, 28.

33. Veblen, 1917, 12–14. Curiously, Veblen's discussion of the Icelandic Republic in *The Nature of Peace* omits any mention of "pagan anarchy," or the communes of the handicraft era, as other examples of relatively noncoercive or less coercive political forms. Perhaps the omission reflects the fact that Veblen's focus in *The Nature of Peace* was the state system, and as we saw in the last chapter, that system was an outgrowth of the handicraft era. Pagan anarchy and the handicraft era industrial towns were not yet examples of states, but then neither was the Icelandic Republic. But that is just a guess. It is one of the frustrations of Veblen's episodic, discontinuous discussion of political institutions that such connections remain implicit, undeveloped promises of his frequently suggestive, but too often inchoate, political thought.

34. Veblen, 1917, 11–14.

35. Veblen, 1954, 328, n. 1.

36. Veblen, 1964d, 86.

37. In Ralph Miliband's (1977, 44) words, "Tradition is not a monolith . . . there is in most societies a tradition of dissent as well as a tradition of conformity . . . Traditional ways are never uniformly conservative," a point well worth remembering in a Veblenian context, which tends to stress the conservative more than the insubordinate aspects of tradition.

38. Veblen, 1954, 251.

39. Veblen, 1917, 242.

40. Veblen, 1997, 252–253.

41. Veblen, 1917, 363–365. Arendt (1972, 147–148) argues that once mass support for ruling groups disintegrates, "revolutions are possible but not necessary." For "where commands are no longer obeyed, the means of violence are of no use." Veblen anticipated Arendt's point with his notion that an accumulation of neglect for predatory institutions was the strongest factor making for progressive change; but he clearly had doubts about the outcome in a situation where popular will encountered the physical force of a threatened ruling minority. Indeed, as she acknowledged, "Violence can always destroy power" (Arendt, 1972, 152).

42. Though Veblen's influence is not to be found in the study, Rogers Smith's excellent work on "conflicting visions of citizenship" in the United States establishes solid empirical grounding for Veblen's point about the persistence of illiberal ascriptive statuses in America's quasi-egalitarian political culture (R. Smith, 1997).

43. Veblen, 1990, 177; 1979, 26. Most people in capitalist society assessed others' social position by the latter's "acquisition and accumulation of goods." Yet even in the pecuniary era, Veblen cautioned, "the highest honors within human reach may . . . yet be . . . gained by an unfolding of extraordinary predatory efficiency in war, or by a quasi-predatory efficiency in statecraft" (1979, 30).

44. Veblen, 1954, 230.

45. Veblen, 1997, 318–319; 1964k, 450–453.

46. Curiously, the pledge came into prominence through the efforts of, and may well have been written by, Francis Bellamy, brother of the socialist Edward Bellamy, author of *Looking Backward*, a book Veblen much admired. "The Pledge was published in . . . *The Youth's Companion*, the leading family magazine and the *Reader's Digest* of its day. Its owner and editor, Daniel Ford, had hired Francis in 1891 as his assistant when Francis was pressured into leaving his Baptist church in Boston because of his socialist sermons." For Francis Bellamy, the pledge's keynote was its commitment to "the republic," a term which conveyed "the concise political word for the Nation—the One Nation which the Civil War was fought to prove. To make that One Nation idea clear, we must specify that it is indivisible, as Webster and Lincoln used to repeat in their great speeches." Notwithstanding Bellamy's egalitarian, democratic sympathies, the pledge had become by the 1950s, when Congress added the words "under God," "a patriotic oath and a public prayer" (Baer, 1992). Any socialist overtones were long gone. Reflective of its now more ancient religious and patriotic meanings, Congress clarified how it expected citizens to express their allegiance to flag and country. In 1942 Congress required "That the pledge of allegiance to the flag . . . be rendered by standing with the right hand over the heart; extending the right hand, palm upward, toward the flag at the words 'to the flag' and holding this position until the end, when the hand drops to the side. However, civilians will always show full respect to the flag when the pledge is given by merely standing at attention, men removing the headdress. Persons in uniform shall render the military salute." Cited in *Elk Grove Unified School District et al. v. Newdow et al.*, U.S. Supreme Court, 542 U.S. 1 (2004).

47. Veblen, 1917, 132.

48. Veblen, 1990, 178.

49. Veblen, 1954, 134.

50. James K. Galbraith, 2008, 127.

51. Veblen, 1964k, 452–453; 1954, 142. For all these amusements and entertainments, of course, the common man would be expected to pay, not excluding taxes to fund patriotic display, and charitable contributions to finance the various houses of worship, not to mention public subsidies for today's professional sports stadia. After all, because it is workers who are "to be relieved of afterthought, it is only reasonable" that they "should pay the cost."

52. Veblen, 1979, 19.

53. Carey, 1997.

54. Veblen, 1964g, 16; 1954, 252.

55. Veblen, 1919, 126.

56. "Shamefulness of servitude" had in fact become so much a part of the increasingly democratic ethos in Europe, that even where the dynastic State stood firm, "it will no longer do to display its character openly as an organization of servitude based on subjection." Thus the German State presented itself as "the people legally united as an independent power" (1954, 169–170).

57. Veblen, 1919, 127.

58. Chandler, 1977; Stabile, 1984; Braverman, 1975.

59. Veblen, 1997, 282.

60. Wolin, 1996, 34; 2008. And as Andre Gorz (1985, 76) adds, "Politics should never be confused with executive power, with administration, in other words, with the state. If it is not a means of expression which transmits the aspirations of civil society to the government . . . then politics loses its autonomy, and goes into decline." In Veblen's terms, democracy then becomes "ostensible."

61. Plotkin and Scheuerman, 1994, 103–105.

62. Veblen, 1917, 154–155.

63. Veblen, 1978, 286–287.

64. Arthur Davis (1968, 305) claimed that Veblen overstated the ideological power of cultural lag and anachronistic ideas while understating the role of "vested interest rationality" and class planning in the control of underlying populations. While this idea might be a useful Veblenian counterweight to Marxian tendencies to overstate capitalist political rationality, Veblen's political thinking, said Davis, overlooks "conscious exploitation of society by Big Business" (Davis, 1957, 93). The arguments here may be read as, in part, an answer to Davis's criticism. For a review of Davis's shifting perceptions of Veblen, see Tilman, 1992, 223.

65. Dahl, 2002.

66. Veblen, 1997, 15.

67. The preponderance of what American law has to say about the social responsibilities of ownership is based on old common law principles and the advent of modern administrative law, which derives primarily from the commerce clause. A working conser-

vative majority on the Supreme Court has, however, recently curtailed Congress's power to make national social policy based on the commerce clause, insisting that Congress has overreached in its interpretation of "inter-state commerce." See, e.g., *United States v. Morrison* 529 U.S. 598 (2000); *United States v. Lopez*, 514 U.S. 549 (1995).

68. Veblen, 1978, 275. Industrial institutions and activities, Veblen cautioned, "are not often recognized as institutions, in great part because they do not immediately concern the ruling class, and are, therefore, seldom the subject of legislation or of deliberate convention. When they do receive attention they are commonly approached from the pecuniary or business side; that being the side or phase of economic life that chiefly occupies men's deliberations in our time, especially the deliberations of the upper classes" (1979, 208).

69. Orren, 1991.

70. Wills, 2003.

71. The irony is even more glaring when we remember that the source of the law's personification of the corporation was the very same amendment—the Fourteenth—that was designed ostensibly to secure "equal protection of the laws" to newly freed slaves. That the corporations enjoyed their protection much earlier and with less political difficulty than the ex-slaves did will come as little surprise. More, the amendment did little to liberate women. See Foner, 1998, chs. 5–6; Horwitz, 1992; Sklar, 1988; Lustig, 1982; R. Smith, 1997, 222–225.

72. Commons, 1968, 52.

73. Veblen, 1978, 276, 278.

74. Veblen, 1978, 276, 274.

75. Indeed, "nowhere else," Veblen observed, "has the sacredness of pecuniary obligations so permeated the common sense of the community, and nowhere else does pecuniary obligation come so near to being the only form of obligation that has the unqualified sanction of current common sense. Here, as nowhere else, do obligations and claims of the most diverse kinds, domestic, social and civil, tend to take the pecuniary form and admit of being fully discharged on a monetary valuation" (1978, 272). For a contemporary statement of this theme, see Charles Lindblom's (1984) notion of "the market as prison."

76. Peter Sloterdijk's *Critique of Cynical Reason* (1987) is an important work that bears consideration in this context. Sloterdijk's conception of cynicism as "enlightened false consciousness"—deriving from his study of Weimar—bears a different historical stamp and a different orientation to political enlightenment than Veblen's. As "that state of consciousness that follows after naive ideologies and their enlightenment" (p. 5) have been exhausted, its reference point is the dissolution of radical hopes in the twentieth century. Veblen's conception, rooted in a distinctive American brand of barely regulated nineteenth-century capitalism, situates its cynicism in a petty bourgeois culture of opportunism, attitudes endemic to a society whose faith in the main chance enables an opportunistic cynicism that is rooted not in historical failure but that draws from faith in the future, a hard-bitten faith oftentimes, but one that continues to cultivate its opportunities. For a study of Sloterdijk's theme as it worked

out in a depleted American industrial town, see Dandaneau, 1996. In the instance of Flint, Michigan, worker acceptance of the new "reality" of global competition and "dependent de-industrialization" displayed a harsh, grim edge, with considerably less of Veblen's belief in luck as a possible way out. Also in contrast with Veblen, Samuel P. Huntington's (1981) perspective on cynicism in American political culture claims that it grows out of a deep-seated liberal aversion to power in a society that cannot dispense with power. For Huntington, cynicism has specifically political foundations, becoming a way by which Americans learn to tolerate gaps between the imperatives of power and the romance of liberty. Veblen's view is quite different. For him, far from shunning power, Americans embrace it as the ulterior motive of their economic liberties. Cynicism evolves out of the pressure of living under a system of economic opportunities that is interwoven with stark economic inequalities, unbalanced powers, and much informal coercion.

77. David Brooks's (2006) description of the gritty style of Chicago's urban realist journalism exemplifies the naturalization of petty opportunism that Veblen identified with American ideology writ large: "the underlying message . . . was that human beings are selfish connivers, on the make in ways big and small, and since the powerful have the capacity to grab more than the powerless, they have to be challenged and opposed." But the reigning principle of challenge here is not democratic justice; it is "the hoodlum's ethic: where's mine?"

78. Riordon, 1963, 3.

79. Mamet, 1992.

80. Veblen, 1997, 158.

81. Ibid., 143, n. 1.

82. Ibid., 143, 142; 1954, 332–340.

83. Veblen, 1997, 157–158.

84. Ibid., 122–123.

85. Ibid. 158; 1954, 154. Cf. the scholarship of such historians as J. W. Hurst (1956) and Morton Horwitz (1977), which suggests that the evolution of nineteenth-century American law was less about the authoritative application of authority than the authoritative release of private energies; Lowi's (1969) critique of "interest group liberalism" demonstrates adaptation of the going ethos to an age of organized group power.

86. Veblen, 1997, 142, 158. The field of urban political economy is now filled with studies of the urban power implications of land development and speculation. But the originality of Veblen's insights into the country town roots of urban boosterism, much less the wider political culture, have yet to be credited by scholars in this burgeoning literature. See, e.g., Judd and Swanstrom, 2004; Logan and Molotch, 1987; Stone, 1989; Stone and Sanders, 1987; Mollenkopf, 1983; Feagin, 1988; Harvey, 1985, 1973; Peterson, 1981.

87. Veblen, 1997, 170–171. Veblen would surely be impressed by recent efforts among African-Americans for reparations, as well as Native Americans for return of tribal lands; but he would likely note that the businesslike proclivity of the Native American

gambling industry, corporate scandals, and financial collapse make for more headlines than reports of reparations.

88. Bacevich, 2008, 172.

89. Veblen, 1997, 34. As John Diggins notes, "In treating cultural ideas as the unconscious foundations of social life," Veblen anticipated the Gramscian notion of "hegemony . . . a phenomenon made all the more perplexing because it involves man's subjugation to ideas rather than to power and coercion." We disagree with Diggins' formulation only in this key respect: for Veblen, "subjugation to ideas" is precisely an expression of power (2000, 105).

90. Veblen, 1997, 140–141; 1919, 174–175.

8. Veblen and Politics

1. Veblen, 1979, 9.

2. Ibid., 99–100.

3. Peukert, 2001, 551.

4. On the other hand, Veblen's critique of teleology, a pervasive and crucial aspect of his evolutionary naturalism, finds no contradiction in his thought. On this score, Veblen was a ruthlessly consistent and effective opponent of teleological explanation. Much of his aversion to ideological thinking stems precisely from this aversion to teleology, for so much of ideology rests on different conceptions of a normal, natural, or historical trend toward some definite outcome.

5. Veblen, 1978, 287.

6. Veblen, 1979, 105.

7. Veblen, 1997, 9.

8. Veblen, 1969c, 397.

9. Veblen, 1969d, 441–442.

10. Veblen, 1979, 355–356.

11. Veblen, 1969a, 31.

12. MacFarquhar, 2009.

BIBLIOGRAPHY

Adorno, Theodore W. 1967. "Veblen's Attack on Culture," in *Prisms*. Foreword by Theodore J. Adorno. Introduction by Samuel M. Weber. Cambridge, Mass.: MIT Press.

Agamben, Giorgio. 2005. *State of Exception*. Trans. Kevin Attell. Chicago: University of Chicago Press.

Almond, Gabriel A. 1990. *A Discipline Divided: Schools and Sects in Political Science*. Thousand Oaks, Calif.: Sage.

Anderson, Margaret L. 2000. *Practicing Democracy: Elections and Political Culture in Imperial Germany*. Princeton, N.J.: Princeton University Press.

Anderson, Perry. 1979. *Lineages of the Absolutist State*. London: Verso.

Anonymous. 2004. *Imperial Hubris: Why the West Is Losing the War on Terror*. Washington, D.C.: Brassey's Inc.

Arendt, Hannah. 1972. *Crises of the Republic*. New York: Harcourt Brace Jovanovich.

Aristotle. 1946. *The Politics*. Trans. with Introduction and Notes by Ernest Barker. New York: Oxford University Press.

Arrighi, Giovanni, and Beverly J. Silver, eds. 1999. *Chaos and Governance in the Modern World System*. Minneapolis: University of Minnesota Press.

Atherton, Lewis E. 1952. "The Midwestern Country Town: Myth and Reality." *Agricultural History* 26 (July): 73–80.

Ayres, Clarence. 1937. Letter to Frank Knight, February 23. Papers of Frank Knight. Regenstein Library. University of Chicago.

Bacevich, Andrew J. 2002. *American Empire: The Realities and Consequences of U.S. Diplomacy*. Cambridge, Mass.: Harvard University Press.

———. 2005. *The New American Militarism: How Americans Are Seduced by War*. New York: Oxford University Press.

———. 2008. *The Limits of Power: The End of American Exceptionalism*. New York: Metropolitan Books, Henry Holt.

Bachrach, Peter, and Morton Baratz. 1970. *Power and Poverty: Theory and Practice.* New York: Oxford University Press.

Baer, John W. 1992. *The Pledge of Allegiance: A Short History,* http://history.vineyard.net/pledge.htm. Consulted 6 July 2006.

Banfield, Edward C. 1974. *The Unheavenly City Revisited.* Boston: Little Brown.

Baran, Paul. 1957. "The Theory of the Leisure Class." *Monthly Review* 9 (3–4): 83–91.

Baran, Paul, and Paul Sweezy. 1966. *Monopoly Capital: An Essay on the American Economic and Social Order.* New York: Monthly Review Press.

Barer, Schlomo. 2000. *The Doctors of Revolution: 19th-Century Thinkers Who Changed the World.* New York: Thames and Hudson.

Barnet, Richard. 1972. *Roots of War.* New York: Atheneum.

Barrow, Clyde W. 1993. *Critical Theories of the State: Marxist, Neo-Marxist, Post-Marxist.* Madison: University of Wisconsin Press.

Bartels, Larry M. 2008. *Unequal Democracy: The Political Economy of the New Gilded Age.* New York: Russell Sage.

Bartley, Russell H., and Sylvia E. Bartley. 2004. "Confessional and Pecuniary Codes of Conduct in the Life and Work of Thorstein Veblen." Delivered at meetings of the International Thorstein Veblen Association. Carleton College. Northfield, Minn.: 1–12.

———. 2007. "The Physical World of Thorstein Veblen." Paper presented to the International Conference on the 150th Anniversary of Veblen's Birth, Valdres, Norway.

Bartley, Russell H., and Sylvia E. Yoneda. 1994. "Thorstein Veblen on Washington Island: Traces of a Life." *International Journal of Politics, Culture, and Society* 7 (4): 589–613.

Bauer, Raymond A., Ithiel de Sola Pool, and Lewis A. Dexter. 1972. *American Business and Public Policy: The Politics of Foreign Trade.* Chicago: Aldine, Atherton.

Baumgartner, Frank R., and Bryan D. Jones. 1993. *Agendas and Instability in American Politics.* Chicago: University of Chicago Press.

Bell, Daniel. 1960. *The End of Ideology: On the Exhaustion of Political Ideas in the '50s.* Glencoe, Ill.: Free Press.

———. 1963. "Veblen and the New Class." *American Scholar* 32 (August): 616–638.

———. 1973. *The Coming of Post-Industrial Society.* New York: Basic Books.

———. 1978. *The Cultural Contradictions of Capitalism.* New York: Basic Books.

———. 1990. Introduction to *The Engineers and the Price System,* by Thorstein Veblen, 2–34. New Brunswick, N.J.: Transaction Publishers.

Benhabib, Selya, ed. 1996. *Democracy and Difference: Contesting the Boundaries of the Political.* Princeton, N.J.: Princeton University Press.

Bentley, Arthur F. 1949. *The Process of Government: A Study of Social Pressures.* Bloomington, Ind.: Principia Press.

Berkowitz, Peter, ed. 2005. *Terrorism, the Laws of War, and the Constitution: Debating the Enemy Combatant Cases.* Stanford: Hoover Institution.

Berle, Adolph A., and Gardiner C. Means. 1932. *The Modern Corporation and Private Property.* New York: Macmillan.

Bessel, Richard, and E. J. Feuchtwanger, eds. 1981. *Social Change and Political Development in Weimar Germany*. London: Croon Helm.

Black, Edwin. 2001. *IBM and the Holocaust: The Strategic Alliance Between Nazi Germany and America's Most Powerful Corporation*. New York: Three River's Press, Crown.

Block, Fred. 1984. "The Ruling Class Does Not Rule: Notes on the Marxist Theory of the State." In *The Political Economy: Readings in the Politics and Economics of American Public Policy*, ed. Thomas Ferguson and Joel Rogers, 32–46. Armonk, N.Y.: M.E. Sharpe.

Blum, William. 1995. *Killing Hope: U.S. Military and CIA Intervention Since World War II*. Monroe, Maine: Common Courage Press.

Bobbitt, Philip. 2008. *Terror and Consent: The Wars for the Twenty-First Century*. New York: Knopf.

Boggs, Carl, ed. 2003. *Masters of War: Militarism and Blowback in the Era of American Empire*. New York: Routledge.

Bollobás, Eniko. 2002. "Dangerous Liaisons: Politics and Epistemology in Post-Cold War American Studies." *American Quarterly* 54 (December): 563–580.

Bourdieu, Pierre. 1984. *Distinction: A Social Critique of the Judgment of Taste*. Trans. Richard Nice. Cambridge, Mass.: Harvard University Press.

Bowler, Peter J. 2003. *Evolution: The History of an Idea*. 3d ed. Berkeley: University of California Press.

Bowman, Scott R. 1996. *The Modern Corporation and American Political Thought: Law, Power, and Ideology*. University Park, Penn.: Pennsylvania State University Press.

Braudel, Fernand. 1973. *Capitalism and Material Life, 1400–1800*. Trans. Miriam Kochan. New York: Harper Colophon.

Braverman, Harry. 1975. *Labor and Monopoly Capital: The Degradation of Work in the 20th Century*. Foreword by Paul M. Sweezy. New York: Monthly Review Press.

Brooks, David. 2004. "For Iraqis to Win, the U.S. Must Lose." *New York Times*, 11 May, A23.

——. 2006. "Page One's Missing Characters." *New York Times*, 6 July, A21.

Burnham, James. 1941. *The Managerial Revolution*. New York: John Day.

Bush, George W. 2002. *The National Security Strategy of the United States of America*. Washington, D.C.: The White House.

Bush, Paul D. 1999. "Veblen's 'Olympian Detachment' Reconsidered." *History of Economic Ideas* 7 (3): 127–151.

Business Week. 2002. "Foreign Policy: Bush Is Half Right." 7 October, 46–47.

Buxton, William. 1985. *Talcott Parsons and the Capitalist Nation State*. Toronto: University of Toronto Press.

Carey, Alex. 1997. *Taking the Risk Out of Democracy: Corporate Propaganda Versus Freedom and Liberty*. Ed. Andrew Lohery. Foreword by Noam Chomsky. Urbana: University of Illinois Press.

Castells, Manuel. 1997. *The Information Age: Economy, Society and Culture*. Vol. 2, *The Power of Identity*. Malden, Mass.: Blackwell.

Ceasar, James. 2000. "The Great Divide: American Interventionism and Its Opponents." In *Present Dangers: Crisis and Opportunity in American Foreign and Defense Policy*, ed. Robert Kagan and William Kristol, 25–43. San Francisco: Encounter Books.

Chandler, Alfred D., Jr. 1977. *The Visible Hand: The Managerial Revolution in American Business*. Cambridge, Mass.: Harvard University Press.

Clarke, Richard A. 2004. *Against All Enemies: Inside America's War on Terror*. New York: Free Press.

Clawson, Dan, Alan Neustadtl, and Mark Weller. 1998. *Dollars and Votes: How Business Campaign Contributions Subvert Democracy*. Philadelphia: Temple University Press.

Collins, Randall. 1974. "Reassessments of Sociological History: The Empirical Validity of the Conflict Tradition." *Theory and Society* 1, no. 2 (Summer): 147–178.

Commager, Henry Steele. 1950. *The American Mind: An Interpretation of American Thought and Character since the 1880s*. New Haven: Yale University Press.

Commons, John R. 1968. *The Legal Foundations of Capitalism*. Madison: University of Wisconsin Press.

Corey, Lewis. 1937. "Veblen and Marxism." *Marxist Quarterly* 1 (January–March): 162–168.

Crook, Paul. 1994. *Darwinism, War and History*. Cambridge: Cambridge University Press.

Cummings, John. 1899. Review of *The Theory of the Leisure Class*, by Thorstein Veblen. *Journal of Political Economy* 7 (September): 425–455.

Cutler, Addison T. 1938. "The Ebb of Institutional Economics." *Science and Society* 2 (Fall): 448–470.

Dahl, Robert. 1961. *Who Governs? Democracy and Power in an American City*. New Haven: Yale University Press.

——. 2002. *How Democratic Is the Constitution?* New Haven: Yale University Press.

Dahrendorf, Ralf. 1969. *Society and Democracy in Germany*. Garden City, N.Y.: Doubleday.

Dandaneau, Steven P. 1996. *A Town Abandoned: Flint, Michigan Confronts De-Industrialization*. Albany: State University of New York.

Daniels, Roger. 2004. *Guarding the Golden Door*. New York: Hill and Wang.

Danner, Mark. 2003. *Torture and Truth: America, Abu Ghraib, and the War on Terror*. New York: New York Review of Books.

——. 2005. "The Secret Way to War." *New York Review of Books* 52 (10): 70–74.

Daugert, Stanley M. 1950. *The Philosophy of Thorstein Veblen*. New York: Crown Press.

Davis, Arthur. 1945. "Sociological Elements in Veblen's Economic Theory." *Journal of Political Economy* 53 (2): 132–149.

——. 1957. "The Postwar Essays." *Monthly Review* 9 (3): 91–97.

——. 1968. "Veblen, Thorstein." In *International Encyclopedia of the Social Sciences*, ed. David L. Sills, 16:303–308. New York: Macmillan and Free Press.

——. 1980. *Thorstein Veblen's Social Theory*. New York: Arno Press.

Debord, Guy. 1983. *Society of the Spectacle*. Detroit: Black and Red.

DeLeon, David. 1978. *The American as Anarchist: Reflections on Indigenous Radicalism.* Baltimore: Johns Hopkins University Press.

Dewey, Ernest W. 1959. "Thorstein Veblen: Radical Apologist for Conservatism." *American Journal of Economics and Sociology* 18 (January): 171–180.

Diamond, Sara. 1995. *Roads to Dominion: Right-Wing Movements and Political Power in the United States.* New York: Guilford.

Dickens, Charles. 1997. *A Tale of Two Cities.* With a new Introduction by Frederick Busch. New York: Signet, New American Library.

Diggins, John P. 1996. *Max Weber: Politics and the Spirit of Tragedy.* New York: Basic Books.

———. 2000. *Thorstein Veblen: Theorist of the Leisure Class.* Princeton, N.J.: Princeton University Press. Originally published as *The Bard of Savagery* (New York: Seabury Press, 1978).

Dobriansky, Lev E. 1957. *Veblenism: A New Critique.* Introduction by James Burnham. Washington, D.C.: Public Affairs Press.

Domhoff, G. William, and Hoyt B. Ballard, eds. 1968. *C. Wright Mills and the Power Elite.* Boston: Beacon Press.

Dorfman, Joseph. 1934. *Thorstein Veblen and His America.* New York: Viking.

Dos Passos, John. 1964. *U.S.A.: The Big Money.* Introduction by Alfred Kazin. New York: New American Library.

Dowd, Douglas. 2000. *Thorstein Veblen.* With a new Introduction by Michael Kearney. New Brunswick, N.J.: Transaction Publishers.

Draper, Hal. 1977. *Karl Marx's Theory of Revolution.* Vol. 1, *State and Bureaucracy.* New York: Monthly Review Press.

Drew, Elizabeth. 2005. "Selling Washington." *New York Review of Books* 52 (11): 24–27.

Drury, Shadia. 1988. *The Political Ideas of Leo Strauss.* New York: St. Martin's.

———. 1999. *Leo Strauss and the American Right.* New York: St. Martin's.

Dubber, Markus D. 2005. *The Police Power: Patriarchy and the Foundations of American Government.* New York: Columbia University Press.

Dugger, William M. 1984. "Veblen and Kropotkin on Human Evolution." *Journal of Economic Issues* 18 (4): 971–985.

———. 1989. *Corporate Hegemony.* Westport, Conn.: Greenwood.

———. 2006. "Veblen's Radical Theory of Social Evolution." *Journal of Economic Issues* 40 (3): 651–672.

Dugger, William M., and Howard J. Sherman. 2000. *Reclaiming Evolution.* London: Routledge.

Eby, Clare V. 1992. "Veblen's Anti-Anti-Feminism." *Canadian Review of American Studies.* Special Issue, Part 2: 215–238.

———. 1993. "Babbitt as Veblenian Critique of Manliness." *American Studies* 34 (2): 5–24.

———. 1998. *Dreiser and Veblen: Saboteurs of the Status Quo.* Columbia, Mo.: University of Missouri Press.

———. 2002. "Boundaries Lost: Thorstein Veblen, *The Higher Learning in America*, and the Conspicuous Spouse." Ed. Jack Salzman. *Prospects* (Cambridge: Cambridge University Press) 26:251–293.

Edelman, Murray J. 1964. *The Symbolic Uses of Politics*. Urbana, Ill.: University of Illinois Press.

Edgell, Stephen. 2001. *Veblen in Perspective*. Armonk, N.Y.: M. E. Sharpe.

Edsall, Thomas. 1984. *The New Politics of Inequality*. New York: Norton.

Ely, John Hart. 1993. *War and Responsibility: Constitutional Lessons of Vietnam and Its Aftermath*. Princeton, N.J.: Princeton University Press.

Evans, Judy. 1993. "Ecofeminism and the Politics of the Gendered Self." In *The Politics of Nature: Explorations in Green Political Theory*, ed. Andrew Dobson and Paul Lucardie, 177–189. New York: Routledge.

Ewen, Stewart. 1988. *All Consuming Images*. New York: Basic Books.

Feagin, Joe R. 1988. *Free-Enterprise City: Houston in Political-Economic Perspective*. New Brunswick, N.J.: Rutgers University Press.

Ferguson, Niall. 2004. *Colossus: The Rise and Fall of the American Empire*. New York: Penguin.

Ferguson, Thomas, and Joel Rogers. 1986. *Right Turn: The Decline of the Democrats and the Future of American Politics*. New York: Hill and Wang.

———. 1995. *Golden Rule: The Investment Theory of Party Competition and the Logic of Money-Driven Political Systems*. Chicago: University of Chicago Press.

Ferrarotti, Franco. 1992. "Some Observations on the American Reception of Thorstein Veblen." *International Review of Sociology* 3:101–124.

Fisher, Irving. 1909. "Capital and Interest." *Political Science Quarterly* 24 (3):504–516.

Fisher, Louis. 1995, 2004. *Presidential War Power*. 2d ed. rev. Lawrence, Kans.: University Press of Kansas.

———. 2005. *Military Tribunals and Presidential Power: American Revolution to the War on Terrorism*. Lawrence, Kans.: University Press of Kansas.

Fitzgerald, Francis. 2002. "George Bush and the World." *New York Review of Books* 49 (14): 80–85. Consulted at www.uni-muenster.de/PeaCon/global-texte/g-w/n/, 1 July 2006.

Flyvbjerg, Bent. 1998. *Rationality and Power: Democracy in Practice*. Chicago: University of Chicago Press.

Foner, Eric. 1998. *The Story of American Freedom*. New York: Norton.

Fordham, Benjamin O. 2007. "Paying for Global Power: Costs and Benefits of Postwar U.S. Military Spending." In *The Long War: A New History of U.S. National Security Policy Since World War II*, ed. Andrew J. Bacevich, 371–404. New York: Columbia University Press.

Foster, John Bellamy. 2002. "Imperialism Rediscovered." *Monthly Review* 54 (6): 1–16.

Foucault, Michel. 1979. *Discipline and Punish*. Trans. Alan Sheridan. New York: Vintage.

———. 1980. *Power/Knowledge: Selected Interviews and Other Writings 1972–1977*. Ed. Colin Gordon. Trans. Colin Gordon et al. New York: Pantheon.

———. 2007. *Security, Territory, Population: Lectures at the College de France, 1977–1978.* Ed. Michael Senellart. Trans. Graham Burchell. New York: Palgrave.

Frei, Christoph. 2001. *Hans J. Morgenthau: An Intellectual Biography.* Baton Rouge: Louisiana State University Press.

Friedberg, Aaron L. 2000. *In the Shadow of the Garrison State: America's Anti-Statism and Its Cold War Grand Strategy.* Princeton, N.J.: Princeton University Press.

Friedman, Milton. 1962. *Capitalism and Freedom.* With the assistance of Rose D. Friedman. Chicago: University of Chicago Press.

Friedmann, John. 1987. *Planning in the Public Domain: From Knowledge to Action.* Princeton, N.J.: Princeton University Press.

Fukuyama, Francis. 1992. *The End of History and the Last Man.* New York: Free Press.

———. 2006. *America at the Crossroads: Democracy, Power, and the Neo-Conservative Legacy.* New Haven: Yale University Press.

Fulbrook, Mary. 1990. *A Concise History of Germany.* Cambridge: Cambridge University Press.

Gabriel, Ralph H. 1956. *The Course of American Democratic Thought.* 2d ed. New York: Ronald Press Co.

Galbraith, James K. 2008. *The Predator State.* New York: Free Press.

Galbraith, John Kenneth. 1956. *American Capitalism: The Concept of Countervailing Power.* Boston: Houghton Mifflin.

———. 1958. *The Affluent Society.* Boston: Houghton Mifflin.

———. 1967. *The New Industrial State.* New York: New American Library.

———. 1973. *Economics and the Public Purpose.* New York: New American Library.

Gambs, John S. 1946. *Beyond Supply and Demand.* New York: Columbia University Press.

Gattone, Charles F. 2006. *The Social Scientist as Public Intellectual.* Lanham, Md.: Rowman and Littlefield.

Geuss, Raymond. 2008. *Philosophy and Real Politics.* Princeton, N.J.: Princeton University Press.

Gordon, Michael R., and General Bernard E. Trainor. 2006. *Cobra II: The Inside Story of the Invasion and Occupation of Iraq.* New York: Pantheon.

Gorz, Andre. 1985. *Paths to Paradise: On the Liberation from Work.* Trans. Malcom Imrie. Boston: South End.

Gowan, Peter. 1999. *The Global Gamble: Washington's Bid for World Dominance.* London: Verso.

Graham, Otis L. 1976. *Toward a Planned Society: From Roosevelt to Nixon.* New York: Oxford University Press.

Gramsci, Antonio. 1971. *Selections from the Prison Notebooks.* Ed. and trans. Quintin Hoare and Geoffrey Nowell Smith. New York: International Publishers

Greider, William. 1998. *Fortress America: The American Military and the Consequences of Peace.* New York: Public Affairs Press.

Griffin, Robert A. 1982. *Thorstein Veblen: Seer of Socialism.* Hampden, CT: Advocate Press.

Guerin, Daniel. 1970. *Anarchism: From Theory to Practice*. Introduction by Noam Chomsky. New York: Monthly Review Press.

Gumplowicz, Ludwig. 1980. *Outlines of Sociology*. Ed. with an Introduction and a new Preface by Irving Louis Horowitz. New Brunswick, N.J.: Transaction Publishers.

Habermas, Jurgen. 1970. *Toward a Rational Society: Student Protest, Science and Politics*. Boston: Beacon Press.

——. 1989. *The Structural Transformation of the Public Sphere: An Inquiry into a Category of Bourgeois Society*. Trans. Thomas Burger with the assistance of Frederick Lawrence. Cambridge, Mass.: MIT Press.

Halper, Stefan, and Jonathan Clarke. 2004. *America Alone: The Neo-Conservatives and the Global Order*. Cambridge: Cambridge University Press.

Hamilton, Alexander, James Madison, and John Jay. 1961. *The Federalist Papers*. Ed. Clinton Rossiter. New York: Mentor, New American Library.

Hamilton, Walton H. 1919. "The Institutional Approach to Economic Theory." *American Economic Review*, Supplement (March): 309–318.

Hammes, Col. Thomas X. 2006. *The Sling and the Stone: On War in the 21st Century*. St. Paul, Minn.: Zenith Press.

Hardach, Karl. 1980. *The Political Economy of Germany in the Twentieth Century*. Berkeley: University of California Press.

Hardt, Michael, and Antonio Negri. 2000. *Empire*. Cambridge, Mass.: Harvard University Press.

——. 2004. *Multitude: War and Democracy in the Age of Empire*. New York: Penguin.

Harris, Abram L. 1934. "Economic Evolution: Dialectical and Darwinian." *Journal of Political Economy* 42, no. 1 (February): 34–79.

Harvey, David. 1973. *Social Justice and the City*. Baltimore: Johns Hopkins University Press.

——. 1985. *The Urbanization of Capital: Studies in the History and Theory of Capitalist Urbanization*. Baltimore: Johns Hopkins University Press.

——. 2003. *The New Imperialism*. New York: Oxford University Press.

——. 2005. *A Brief History of Neoliberalism*. New York: Oxford University Press.

Hayden, Tom. 2006. *Radical Nomad: C. Wright Mills and His Times*. With contemporary reflections by Stanley Aronowitz, Richard Flacks, and Charles Lemert. Boulder, Colo.: Paradigm.

Hayek, Friedrich A. 1945. *The Road to Serfdom*. Introduction by John Chamberlin. Chicago: University of Chicago Press.

Hayward, Clarissa Rile. 2000. *De-Facing Power*. New York: Cambridge University Press.

Hearn, Frank. 1985. *Reason and Freedom in Sociological Thought*. Winchester, Mass.: Allen and Unwin.

Himmelfarb, Gertrude. 2001. *One Nation, Two Cultures*. New York: Vintage.

Hintze, Otto. 1975. *The Historical Essays of Otto Hintze*. Ed. with Introduction by Felix Gilbert, with assistance of Robert M. Berdahl. New York: Oxford University Press.

Hobbes, Thomas. 1968. *Leviathan*. Ed. with Introduction by C. B. MacPherson. Harmondsworth, U.K.: Penguin.

Hobson, John A. 1936. *Veblen*. London: Chapman and Hall.

Hodder, H. J. 1956. "The Political Ideas of Thorstein Veblen." *Canadian Journal of Economics and Political Science* 27 (3): 347–357.

Hodgson, Geoffrey M. 1992. "Thorstein Veblen and Post-Darwinian Economics." *Cambridge Journal of Economics* 16:285–301.

——. 1996. "Varieties of Capitalism and Varieties of Economic Theory." *Review of International Political Economy* 3 (3): 406–412.

——. 2001. "Darwin, Veblen and the Problem of Causality in Economics." *History and Philosophy of the Life Sciences* 23:385–423.

Horkheimer, Max. 1941. "The End of Reason." *Studies in Philosophy and Social Science* 9 (3): 366–387.

——. 1967. *Critique of Instrumental Reason*. New York: Seabury Press.

——. 1986. *Critical Theory*. New York: Continuum.

Horwitz, Morton J. 1977. *The Transformation of American Law, 1780–1860*. Cambridge, Mass.: Harvard University Press.

——. 1992. *The Transformation of American Law, 1870–1960: The Crisis of Legal Orthodoxy*. New York: Oxford University Press.

Hunt, E. K. 1986. *Property and Prophets: The Evolution of Economic Institutions and Ideologies*. 5th ed. New York: Harper and Row.

Huntington, Samuel P. 1968. *Political Order in Changing Societies*. New Haven: Yale University Press.

——. 1981. *American Politics: The Promise of Disharmony*. Cambridge, Mass.: Harvard University Press.

——. 1996. *The Clash of Civilizations and the Remaking of World Order*. New York: Simon and Schuster.

Hurst, James Willard. 1956. *Law and the Conditions of Freedom in the Nineteenth-Century United States*. Madison: University of Wisconsin Press.

Ignatieff, Michael. 2003. "The Burden." *New York Times Magazine*, 5 January, sec. 3, 22–27, 50–54.

Illich, Ivan. 1973. *Tools for Conviviality*. New York: Harper.

Jacobs, Wilbur R. 1978. "The Great Despoliation: Environmental Themes in American Frontier History." *Pacific Historical Review* 47 (1): 1–26.

Jacoby, Russell. 1999. *The End of Utopia: Politics and Culture in an Age of Anxiety*. New York: Basic Books.

Jessop, Bob. 1982. *The Capitalist State: Marxist Theories and Methods*. New York: New York University Press.

——. 1990. *State Theory: Putting the Capitalist State in Its Place*. University Park, Penn.: Pennsylvania State University Press.

Joas, Hans. 2003. *War and Modernity*. Cambridge: Polity Press.

Johnson, Chalmers. 2004. *The Sorrows of Empire: Militarism, Secrecy, and the End of the Republic*. New York: Henry Holt.

Jorgensen, Elizabeth Watkins, and Henry Irvin Jorgensen. 1999. *Thorstein Veblen: Victorian Firebrand*. Armonk, N.Y.: M. E. Sharpe.

Jouvenal, Bertrand de. 1949. *Power: Its Nature and the History of Its Growth.* Preface by D. W. Brogan. Trans. J. F. Huntington. New York: Viking.

Judd, Dennis R., and Todd Swanstrom. 2004. *City Politics: Private Power and Public Policy.* 4th ed. New York: Pearson Longman.

Kagan, Robert. 2004. *Of Paradise and Power: America and Europe in the New World Order.* New York: Vintage.

Kagan, Robert, and William Kristol. 2000. *Present Dangers: Crisis and Opportunity in American Foreign and Defense Policy.* San Francisco: Encounter Books.

Kalb, Don, et al., eds. 2000. *The Ends of Globalization: Bringing Society Back In.* Lanham, Md.: Rowman and Littlefield.

Kaplan, Lawrence F., and William Kristol. 2003. *The War Over Iraq.* San Francisco: Encounter Books.

Kaplan, Robert D. 2002. *Warrior Politics: Why Leadership Demands a Pagan Ethos.* New York: Vintage.

Kariel, Henry S. 1966. *The Promise of Politics.* Englewood Cliffs, N.J.: Prentice-Hall.

Kilpinen, Erkki. 2004. "How to Fight the 'Methodenstreit'? Veblen and Weber on Economics." Paper delivered at the meetings of the International Thorstein Veblen Association. Carleton College. Northfield, Minn.

King, Roger. 1986. *The State in Modern Society: New Directions in Political Sociology.* Chatham, N.J.: Chatham House.

Klare, Michael T. 2001. *Resource Wars: The New Landscape of Global Conflict.* New York: Henry Holt.

——. 2004. *Blood and Oil: The Dangers and Consequences of America's Growing Dependency on Imported Petroleum.* New York: Henry Holt.

Knight, Frank. 1920. Review of *The Place of Science in Modern Civilization,* by Thorstein Veblen. *Journal of Political Economy* 28 (June): 518–520.

——. 1941. "Anthropology and Economics." *Journal of Political Economy* 49 (April): 247–268.

——. 1956. *On the History and Method of Economics.* Chicago: University of Chicago Press.

——. 1960. *Intelligence and Democratic Action.* Cambridge, Mass.: Harvard University Press.

——. 1969. *Freedom and Reform.* Port Washington, N.Y.: Kennikat Press.

Knoedler, Janet, and Anne Mayhew. 1999. "Thorstein Veblen and the Engineers: A Reinterpretation." *History of Political Economy* 31 (2): 255–271.

Koh, Harold H. 1990. *The National Security Constitution: Sharing Power After the Iran-Contra Affair.* New Haven: Yale University Press.

Kropotkin, Peter. n.d. *Mutual Aid: A Factor in Evolution.* Foreword by Ashley Montagu. Boston: Porter Sargent.

Kuhn, Thomas S. 1970. *The Structure of Scientific Revolutions.* Chicago: University of Chicago Press.

Kushner, Tony. 1993. *Angels in America: A Gay Fantasia on National Themes.* Part One, *Millennium Approaches.* New York: Theatre Communications Group.

Landsman, Randolph. 1957. "The Philosophy of Veblen's Economics." *Science and Society* 21 (Fall): 333–345.

Lapham, Lewis H. 2005. "Pilgrims of Hope." Notebook. *Harper's Magazine* 310, no. 185 (February): 9–11.

Laslett, John, and S. M. Lipset. 1974. *Failure of a Dream? Essays in the History of American Socialism.* Garden City, N.Y.: Anchor Books.

Latham, Earl. 1952. *The Group Basis of Politics: A Study in Basing-Point Legislation.* Ithaca, N.Y.: Cornell University Press.

Leach, William. 1993. *Land of Desire.* New York: Vintage Books.

Lerner, Max. 1948. *The Portable Veblen.* Ed. and Introduction by Max Lerner. New York: Viking.

———. 2002. "Thorstein Veblen: Recipe for an American Genius." In *Veblen's Century: A Collective Portrait,* ed. Irving Louis Horowitz, 65–88. New Brunswick, N.J.: Transaction Publishers.

Liebel, Helen. 1965. "Thorstein Veblen's Positive Synthesis." *American Journal of Economics and Sociology* 24 (April): 201–216.

Lindblom, Charles E. 1977. *Politics and Markets: The World's Political Economic Systems.* New York: Basic Books.

———. 1984. "The Market as Prison." In *The Political Economy: Readings in the Politics and Economics of American Public Policy,* ed. Thomas Ferguson and Joel Rogers, 3–11. Armonk, N.Y.: M. E. Sharpe.

Lipset, Seymour Martin. 1960. *Political Man: The Social Bases of Politics.* Garden City, N.Y.: Doubleday.

———. 1996. *American Exceptionalism: A Double-Edged Sword.* New York: Norton.

Lloyd, Brian. 1997. *Left Out: Pragmatism, Exceptionalism, and the Poverty of American Marxism, 1890–1922.* Baltimore: Johns Hopkins University Press.

Loader, Colin, and Rick Tilman. 1995. "Thorstein Veblen's Analysis of German Intellectualism." *American Journal of Economics and Sociology* 54 (July): 339–355.

Logan, John R., and Harvey Molotch. 1987. *Urban Fortunes: The Political Economy of Place.* Berkeley: University of California Press.

Lovins, Amory. 1977. *Soft Energy Paths: Toward a Durable Peace.* San Francisco: Friends of the Earth International.

Lowi, Theodore J. 1969. *The End of Liberalism: Ideology, Policy and the Crisis of Public Authority.* New York: W. W. Norton.

Lowndes, Vivian. 2009. "New Institutionalism and Urban Politics." In *Theories of Urban Politics,* ed. Jonathan S. Davies and David L. Imbroscio, 2d ed., 91–105. London: Sage.

Lukes, Stephen. 1974. *Power: A Radical Analysis.* New York: Macmillan.

Lustig, R. Jeffrey. 1982. *Corporate Liberalism: The Origins of Modern American Political Theory, 1890–1920.* Berkeley: University of California Press.

Lynd, Robert S. 1956. "Power in American Society as Resource and Problem." In *Problems of Power in American Democracy,* ed. Arthur Kornhauser, 1–45. Detroit: Wayne State University Press.

——. 1968. "Power in the United States." In *C. Wright Mills and the Power Elite*, ed. G. William Domhoff and Hoyt B. Ballard, 103–115. Boston: Beacon Press.

MacFarquhar, Neil. 2009. "In Iran, Both Sides Seek to Carry Islam's Banner." *New York Times*, 22 June, A7.

Machiavelli, Niccolo. 1961. *The Prince*. Trans. with an Introduction by George Bull. Baltimore: Penguin Books.

——. 2003. *The Art of War*. Trans., ed., and with commentary by Christopher Lynch. Chicago: University of Chicago Press.

MacIver, Robert. 1947. *The Web of Government*. New York: Macmillian.

Macpherson, C. B. 1962. *The Political Theory of Possessive Individualism: Hobbes to Locke*. Oxford: Clarendon Press.

Mamet, David. 1992. *Glengarry Glen Ross*. Film. Directed by James Foley. New Line Cinema.

Mann, James. 2004. *Rise of the Vulcans: The History of Bush's War Cabinet*. New York: Viking.

Mann, Michael. 1988. *States, War, Capitalism*. New York: Basil Blackwell.

Mannheim, Karl. 1950. *Freedom, Power, and Democratic Planning*. New York: Oxford University Press.

Mansbridge, Jane. 1983. *Beyond Adversary Democracy*. Chicago: University of Chicago Press.

Marcuse, Herbert. 1941. "Some Social Implications of Modern Technology." *Studies in Philosophy and Social Science* 9 (3): 414–439.

——. 1964. *One-Dimensional Man*. Boston: Beacon Press.

Marx, Karl. 1967. *Capital: A Critical Analysis of Capitalist Production*. Vol. 1, unabridged. Ed. Frederick Engels. Trans. from the 3d German edition by Samuel Moore and Edward Aveling. New York: International Publishers.

——. 1988. *The Communist Manifesto*. Ed. Frederick L. Bender. New York: W. W. Norton.

Mason, Roger. 1981. *Conspicuous Consumption: A Study of Exceptional Consumer Behavior*. New York: St. Martin's.

——. 1998. *The Economics of Conspicuous Consumption: Theory and Thought since 1700*. Cheltenham, U.K.: Edward Elgar.

Mayhew, Anne. 2001. "Human Agency, Cumulative Causation, and the State: Remarks upon Receiving the Veblen-Commons Award." *Journal of Economic Issues* 35, no. 2 (June): 239–250.

McConnell, Grant. 1966. *Private Power and American Democracy*. New York: Knopf.

McNeill, William. 1982. *The Pursuit of Power: Technology, Armed Force and Society Since A.D. 1000*. Chicago: University of Chicago Press.

Mead, George Herbert. 1918. Review of *An Inquiry into the Nature of Peace and the Terms of Its Perpetuation*, by Thorstein Veblen. *Journal of Political Economy* 26 (7): 752–762.

——. 1964. *Selected Writings*. Ed. with Introduction by Andrew Reck. Indianapolis, Ind.: Bobbs-Merrill.

Mead, Lawrence M. 1986. *Beyond Entitlement: The Social Obligations of Citizenship*. New York: Free Press.

———. 1992. *The New Politics of Poverty: The Non-Working Poor in America*. New York: Basic Books.

Means, Gardiner. 1962. *The Corporate Revolution in America: Economic Reality vs. Economic Theory*. New York: Crowell-Collier Press.

Meier, Heinrich. 1996. *Carl Schmitt and Leo Strauss: The Hidden Dialogue*. Trans. J. Harvey Lomax. Foreword by Joseph Cropsey. Chicago: University of Chicago Press.

Meinecke, Friedrich. 1998. *Machiavellianism: The Doctrine of Raison d' Etat and Its Place in Modern History*. Trans. Douglas Scott. Introduction by Werner Stark. New Brunswick, N.J.: Transaction Publishers.

Melman, Seymour. 1970. *Pentagon Capitalism: The Political Economy of War*. New York: McGraw-Hill.

———. 1974. *The Permanent War Economy: American Capitalism in Decline*. New York: Simon and Schuster.

Merchant, Carolyn. 1991. "Women and Nature." In *The Green Reader: Essays Toward a Sustainable Society*, ed. Andrew Dobson, 258–261. San Francisco: Mercury House.

Meštrović, Stjepan. 2003. *Thorstein Veblen on Culture and Society*. London: Sage.

Michels, Robert. 1949. *Political Parties: A Study of the Oligarchical Tendencies of Modern Democracy*. Trans. and ed. Eden and Cedar Paul. Glencoe, Ill.: Free Press.

Mies, Maria. 2001. "Women, Nature and the International Division of Labor." Interview by Ariel Sahheh. In *There Is an Alternative: Subsistence, Worldwide Resistance to Corporate Globalization*, ed. Veronika Bennholdt-Thomsen, Nicholas Faraclas, Claudia Von Werlhof, 3–14. New York: Palgrave.

Miliband, Ralph. 1969. *The State in Capitalist Society: An Analysis of the Western System of Power*. New York: Harper Colophon.

———. 1977. *Marxism and Politics*. New York: Oxford University Press.

Mill, John Stewart. 1951. *Utilitarianism, Liberty, and Representative Government*. Introduction by A. D. Lindsay. New York: E. P. Dutton.

Miller, Joshua I. 2005. "Fashion and Democratic Relationships." *Polity* 37 (1): 3–23.

Mills, C. Wright. 1953. Introduction to *The Theory of the Leisure Class*, by Thorstein Veblen. New York: New American Library, Mentor Books.

———. 1956. *The Power Elite*. New York: Oxford University Press.

———. 2001. *The New Men of Power: America's Labor Leaders*. Introduction by Nelson Lichtenstein. Urbana, Ill.: University of Illinois Press.

Mitchell, Wesley C. 1936. *What Veblen Taught*. New York: Viking.

———. 2002. "The Place of Veblen in the History of Ideas." In *Veblen's Century: A Collective Portrait*, ed. Irving Louis Horowitz, 41–63. New Brunswick, N.J.: Transaction Publishers.

Mollenkopf, John H. 1983. *The Contested City*. Princeton, N.J.: Princeton University Press.

Montesquieu, Charles de Secondat. 1949. *The Spirit of the Laws*. Trans. Thomas Neugent. Introduction by Franz Neumann. New York: Hafner.

——. 1973. *Persian Letters*. Trans. with an Introduction and Notes by C. J. Betts. Baltimore: Penguin.

Moore, Barrington, Jr. 1966. *Social Origins of Dictatorship and Democracy: Lord and Peasant in the Making of the Modern World*. Boston: Beacon Press.

——. 1978. *Injustice: The Social Bases of Obedience and Revolt*. White Plains, N.Y.: M. E. Sharpe.

Morgenthau, Hans J. 1946. *Scientific Man vs. Power Politics*. Chicago: University of Chicago Press.

——. 1960. *The Purpose of American Politics*. New York: Knopf.

——. 1962a. *Politics in the Twentieth Century: The Decline of Democratic Politics*. Chicago: University of Chicago Press.

——. 1962b. *The Restoration of American Politics*. Chicago: University of Chicago Press.

——. 1967. *Politics Among Nations*. 4th ed. New York: Knopf.

Mumford, Lewis. 1931. "Thorstein Veblen." *New Republic* 67 (5 August): 314–316.

——. 1934. *Technics and Civilization*. New York: Harcourt, Brace.

——. 1964. *The Pentagon of Power: The Myth of the Machine*. New York: Harcourt Brace Jovanovich.

Murphey, Murray G. 1990. Introduction to *The Instinct of Workmanship and the State of the Industrial Arts,* by Thorstein Veblen. New Brunswick, N.J.: Transaction Publishers.

Murphree, Idus. 1959. "Darwinism in Thorstein Veblen's Economics." *Social Research* 26 (June): 311–324.

Murray, Charles A. 1984. *Losing Ground: American Social Policy, 1950–1980*. New York: Basic Books.

Nettlau, Max. 1996. *A Short History of Anarchism*. Trans. Ida Pilat Isca. Ed. Heiner M. Becker. London: Freedom Press.

Neumann, Franz L. 1944. *Behemoth: The Structure and Practice of National Socialism, 1933–1944*. New York: Oxford University Press.

——. 1956. *The Democratic and the Authoritarian State: Essays in Political and Legal Theory*. Ed. with Preface by Herbert Marcuse. Glencoe, Ill.: Free Press.

Neustadt, Richard E. 1964. *Presidential Power: The Politics of Leadership*. New York: New American Library.

Ngai, Mae M. 2004. *Impossible Subjects: Illegal Aliens and the Making of Modern America*. Princeton, N.J.: Princeton University Press.

Niebuhr, Reinhold. 1932. *Moral Man and Immoral Society: A Study in Ethics and Politics*. New York: Charles Scribner's.

Nietzsche, Friedrich. 1968. *The Will to Power*. Trans. Walter Kaufman and R.J. Hollingdale. Ed. with commentary by Walter Kaufman. London: Weidenfeld and Nicholson.

Nisbet, Robert. 1975. *The Twilight of Authority*. New York: Oxford University Press.

Nitzan, Jonathan. 1998. "Differential Accumulation: Towards a New Political Economy of Capital." *Review of International Political Economy* 5 (2): 169–216.

Noble, David W. 1968. "The Sacred and the Profane: The Theology of Thorstein Veblen." In *Thorstein Veblen: The Carleton College Veblen Seminar Essays*, ed. Carlton C. Qualey, 72–105. New York: Columbia University Press.

Norton, Ann. *Leo Strauss and the Politics of American Empire*. New Haven: Yale University Press.

O'Connell, Robert L. 1989. *Of Arms and Men: A History of War, Aggression, and Weapons*. New York: Oxford University Press.

O'Hara, Phillip Anthony. 1993. "Veblen's Analysis of Business, Industry and the Limits of Capital: An Interpretation and Sympathetic Critique." *History of Economics Review* 20 (Summer): 95–119.

O'Hara, Phillip Anthony, and Howard Jay Sherman. 2004. "Veblen and Sweezy on Monopoly Capital, Crises, Conflict, and the State." *Journal of Economic Issues* 38 (4): 969–987.

Oppenheimer, Franz. 1975. *The State*. Introduction by Charles H. Hamilton. Trans. John Gitterman. Montreal: Black Rose Books.

Orren, Karen. 1991. *Belated Feudalism: Labor, the Law, and Liberal Development in the United States*. New York: Cambridge University Press.

Orren, Karen, and Stephen Skowronek. 2004. *The Search for American Political Development*. New York: Cambridge University Press.

Özveren, Eyüp. 2007. "Veblen's 'Higher Learning': The Scientist as Sisyphus in the Iron Cage of the University." Paper presented to the International Conference on the 150th Anniversary of Veblen's Birth, Valdres, Norway, 2007. Cited with permission of the author.

Page, Benjamin I., and Robert Y. Shapiro. 1992. *The Rational Public: Fifty Years of Trends in Americans Policy Preferences*. Chicago: University of Chicago Press.

Parker, Geoffrey. 1996. *The Military Revolution: Military Innovation and the Rise of the West, 1500–1800*. New York: Cambridge University Press.

Parker, Richard. 2005. *John Kenneth Galbraith*. New York: Farrar, Straus and Giroux.

Parsons, Talcott. 1966. "On the Concept of Political Power." In *Class, Status and Power: Social Stratification in Comparative Perspective*, ed. Reinhard Bendix and Seymour Martin Lipset, 2d. ed., 240–265. New York: Free Press.

——. 1968. "Distribution of Power in American Society." In *C. Wright Mills and the Power Elite*, ed. G. W. Domhoff and Hoyt Ballard. Boston: Beacon Press.

Patsouras, Louis. 2004. *Thorstein Veblen and the American Way of Life*. Montreal: Black Rose Books.

Peacock, Alan T., and Jack Wiseman. 1961. *The Growth of Public Expenditure in the United Kingdom*. Assisted by Jindrich Veverkan. A study by the National Bureau of Economic Research. Princeton, N.J.: Princeton University Press.

Peterson, Paul E. 1981. *City Limits*. Chicago: University of Chicago Press.

Peukert, Helge. 2001. "On the Origins of Modern Evolutionary Economics: The Veblen Legend after 100 Years." *Journal of Economic Issues* 35, no. 3 (September): 543–555.

Phillips, Kevin. 2004. *American Dynasty: Aristocracy, Fortune, and the Politics of Deceit in the House of Bush*. New York: Viking.

Pichler, Hans-Karl. 1998. "The Godfathers of 'Truth': Max Weber and Carl Schmitt in Morgenthau's Theory of Power Politics." *Review of International Studies* 24:185–200.

Plant, Judith. 1991. "Ecofeminism." In *The Green Reader: Essays Toward a Sustainable Society*, ed. Andrew Dobson, forward by David Gancher, 100–103. San Francisco: Mercury House.

Plato. 1945. *The Republic of Plato*. Trans. with an Introduction and Notes by Francis M. Cornford. New York: Oxford University Press.

Plotkin, Sidney. 1987. *Keep Out: The Struggle for Land Use Policy Reform*. Berkeley: University of California Press.

——. 1991. "Community and Alienation: Enclave Consciousness and Urban Movements." In *Breaking Chains: Social Movements and Collective Action*, ed. Michael P. Smith, 5–25. New Brunswick, N.J.: Transaction Publishers.

——. 2010. "Veblen's *Higher Learning in America* and the Ambiguities of Academic Indpendence." In *Transforming Higher Education: Economy, Democracy, and the University*, ed. Stephen J. Rosow and Thomas Krieger, 37–63. Lanham, Md.: Rowman and Littlefield.

Plotkin, Sidney, and William E. Scheuerman. 1994. *Private Interest, Public Spending: Balanced-Budget Conservatism and the Fiscal Crisis*. Boston: South End.

Pocock, J. G. A. 1975. *The Machiavellian Moment: Florentine Political Thought and the Atlantic Republican Tradition*. Princeton, N.J.: Princeton University Press.

Polanyi, Karl. 1957. *The Great Transformation: The Political and Economic Origins of Our Times*. Introduction by Robert MacIver. Boston: Beacon Press.

Poulantzas, Nicos. 1978. *Political Power and Social Classes*. Trans. Timothy O'Hagan. London: Verso.

——. 1980. *State, Power, Socialism*. Trans. Patrick Camiller. London: Verso.

Putnam, Robert D. 2000. *Bowling Alone: The Collapse and Revival of American Community*. New York: Simon and Schuster.

Putnam, Robert D., with Robert Leonardi and Nanetti Y. Raffaella. 1993. *Making Democracy Work: Civic Traditions in Italy*. Princeton, N.J.: Princeton University Press.

Qualey, Carleton C., ed. 1968. *Thorstein Veblen: The Carleton College Veblen Seminar Essays*. New York: Columbia University Press.

Raskin, Marcus G., and A. Carl LeVan, eds. 2005. *In Democracy's Shadow: The Secret World of National Security*. New York: Nation Books, Avalon.

Ricci, David M. 1984. *The Tragedy of Political Science: Politics, Scholarship, Democracy*. New Haven: Yale University Press.

Rieff, David. 2003. "Liberal Imperialism." In *The Imperial Tense: Prospects and Problems of American Empire*, ed. Andrew J. Bacevich, 10–28. Chicago: Ivan R. Dee.

Riesman, David. 1953. *Thorstein Veblen: A Critical Interpretation*. New York: Charles Scribners Sons.

Riesman, David, and Staughton Lynd. 1960. "The Relevance of Thorstein Veblen." *American Scholar* 29, 4 (Autumn): 543–551.

Riordon, William L. 1963. *Plunkitt of Tammany Hall: A Series of Very Plain Talks on Very Practical Politics*. Introduction by Arthur Mann. New York: E. P. Dutton.

Ropp, Theodore. 1977. "Nineteenth-Century European Military-Industrial Complexes." In *War, Business, and American Society*, ed. Benjamin Franklin Cooling, 10–23. Port Washington, N.Y.: Kennikat Press.

Rosen, Stephen Peter. 2003. "Imperial Choices." In *The Imperial Tense: Prospects and Problems of American Empire*, ed. Andrew J. Bacevich, 211–226. Chicago: Ivan R. Dee.

Rosenberg, Bernard. 1956. *The Values of Veblen: A Critical Appraisal*. Foreword by Max Lerner. Washington, D.C.: Public Affairs Press.

Ross, Dorothy. 1991. *The Origins of Social Science*. Cambridge: Cambridge University Press.

Rumsfeld, Donald. 2005. *The National Defense Strategy of the United States of America*. Washington, D.C.: U.S. Department of Defense.

Russett, Cynthia Eagle. 1976. *Darwin in America: The Intellectual Response, 1865–1912*. San Francisco: W. H. Freeman.

Rutherford, Malcolm. 1992. "Thorstein Veblen and the Problem of the Engineers." *International Review of Sociology* 3:125–150.

Saint-Simon, Henri de. 1964. *Social Organization, the Science of Man, and Other Writings*. Ed. and trans. Felix Markham. New York: Harper.

Sale, Kirkpatrick. 1980. *Human Scale*. New York: Coward, McCann and Geoghegan.

Samuels, Warren J. 1979. "Thorstein Veblen: Heterodox Economist, In Retrospect." *Social Science Quarterly* 60 (3): 454–459.

Samuels, Warren J., and Arthur S. Miller, eds. 1987. *Corporations and Society: Power and Responsibility*. New York: Greenwood.

Sandilands, Catriona. 1999. *The Good-Natured Feminist: Ecofeminism and the Quest for Democracy*. Minneapolis: University of Minneapolis Press.

Schattschneider, E. E. 1960. *The Semisovereign People: A Realist's View of Democracy in America*. New York: Holt, Rinehart and Winston.

——. 1969. *Two Hundred Million Americans in Search of a Government*. New York: Holt, Rinehart and Winston.

Scheuerman, William E. 1997. *Between the Norm and the Exception: The Frankfurt School and the Rule of Law*. Cambridge, Mass.: MIT Press.

——. 1999. *Carl Schmitt: The End of Law*. Lanham, Md.: Rowman and Littlefield.

——. 2007. "Carl Schmitt and Hans Morgenthau: Realism and Beyond." In *Realism Reconsidered: The Legacy of Hans J. Morgenthau in International Relations*, ed. Michael Williams, 62–92. Oxford: Oxford University Press.

Schlesinger, Arthur M., Jr. 1973. *The Imperial Presidency*. Boston: Houghton Mifflin.

——. 2004. *War and the American Presidency*. New York: W. W. Norton.

Schmitt, Carl. 1985. *Political Theology: Four Chapters on the Concept of Sovereignty*. Trans. with an Introduction by George Schwab, with a new Introduction by Tracy B. Strong. Chicago: University of Chicago Press.

——. 1988. *The Crisis of Parliamentary Democracy*. Trans. Ellen Kennedy. Cambridge, Mass.: MIT Press.

——. 1996. *The Concept of the Political*. Trans. with an Introduction and Notes by George Schwab; With Leo Strauss' Notes on Schmitt's Essay, trans. Harvey Lomax. With a new Foreword by Tracy B. Strong. Chicago: University of Chicago Press.

——. 2007. *The Theory of the Partisan*. Trans. G. L. Ulmen. New York: Telos Press.

Schneider, Louis. 1948. *The Freudian Psychology and Veblen's Social Theory*. New York: King Crown's Press.

——. 1949. "Some Psychiatric Views on 'Freedom' and the Theory of Social Systems." *Psychiatry* 12:251–264.

Schor, Juliet. 1998. *The Overspent American*. New York: Basic Books.

——. 2004. *Born to Buy*. New York: Scribner.

Schor, Juliet, and Douglas B. Holt, eds. 2000. *The Consumer Society Reader*. New York: The New Press.

Schumacher, E. F. 1973. *Small Is Beautiful: Economics as if People Mattered*. London: Blond and Briggs.

Schumpeter, Joseph A. 1962. *Capitalism, Socialism and Democracy*. 3d ed. New York: Harper Torchbooks.

Scott, James C. 1985. *Weapons of the Weak: Everyday Forms of Peasant Resistance*. New Haven: Yale University Press.

——. 1998. *Seeing Like a State: How Certain Schemes to Improve the Human Condition Have Failed*. New Haven: Yale University Press.

Scott, Peter. 1996. "The New Alchemy: Veblen's Theory of Crisis and the 1974 British Property and Secondary Banking Crisis." *Journal of Economic Issues* 30 (March): 1–12.

Seckler, David. 1975. *Thorstein Veblen and the Institutionalists: A Study in the Social Philosophy of Economics*. With Foreword by Lord Robbins. Boulder: Colorado Associated University Press.

Seely, John Robert. 1886. *An Introduction to Political Science*. London: Macmillan.

Seidelman, Raymond. 1985. *Disenchanted Realists: Political Science and the American Crisis, 1884–1984*. With the Assistance of Edward J. Harpham. Foreword by Theodore J. Lowi. Albany: State University of New York Press.

Sennett, Richard. 1970. *The Uses of Disorder: Personal Identity and City Life*. New York: Knopf.

Shafer, Byron E., ed. *Is America Different?* Oxford: Clarendon Press, 1991.

Shannon, Christopher. 1996. *Conspicuous Criticism: Tradition, the Individual, and Culture in American Social Thought, from Veblen to Mills*. Baltimore: Johns Hopkins University Press.

Sherman, Howard J. 2003. "Evolutionary Economics from a Radical Perspective." *Journal of Economic Issues* 37, 1 (March): 75–83.

Shields, Currin V. 1952. "The American Tradition of Empirical Collectivism." *American Political Science Review* 46 (March): 104–120.

Shiva, Vandana. 2000. *Stolen Harvest: The Hijacking of the Global Food Supply*. Cambridge, Mass.: South End Press.

Skidlesky, Robert. 2006. "Hot, Cold and Imperial." *New York Review of Books* 53 (12): 50–55.

Sklansky, Jeffrey. 2002. *The Soul's Economy: Market Society and Selfhood in American Thought, 1820–1920*. Chapel Hill: University of North Carolina Press.

Sklar, Martin J. 1988. *The Corporate Reconstruction of American Capitalism, 1890–1916: The Market, Law and Politics*. New York: Cambridge University Press.

Skocpol, Theda. 1979. *States and Social Revolutions: A Comparative Analysis of France, Russia and China*. New York: Cambridge University Press.

Skocpol, Theda, and Edwin Amenta. 1985. "States and Social Policies." *Annual Review of Sociology* 12:131–157.

Skowronek, Stephen. 1982. *Building a New American State: The Expansion of National Administrative Capacities, 1877–1920*. New York: Cambridge University Press.

Sloterdijk, Peter. 1987. *Critique of Cynical Reason*. Trans. Michael Eldred. Foreword by Andreas Huyssen. Minneapolis: University of Minnesota Press.

Smith, Adam. 2002. *The Theory of Moral Sentiments*. Ed. Knud Haakonssen. New York: Cambridge University Press.

Smith, Mark A. 2000. *American Business and Political Power: Public Opinion, Elections, and Democracy*. Chicago: University of Chicago Press.

Smith, Merritt Roe. 1977. "Military Arsenals and Industry before World War I." In *War, Business and American Society*, ed. Benjamin Franklin Cooling, 24–42. Port Washington, N.Y.: Kennikat Press.

Smith, Rogers M. 1997. *Civic Ideals: Conflicting Visions of Citizenship in U.S. History*. New Haven: Yale University Press.

Smith, Steve. 1989. "The Fall and Rise of the State in International Politics." In *Democracy and the Capitalist State*, ed. Graeme Duncan, 33–55. New York: Cambridge University Press.

Sombart, Werner. 1976. *Why Is There No Socialism in the United States?* Ed. with Introduction by C. T. Husbands. Foreword by Michael Harrington. White Plains, N.Y.: M. E. Sharpe.

Sonn, Richard D. 1992. *Anarchism*. New York: Twayne.

Spengler, Joseph J. 1972. "Veblen on Population and Resources." *Social Science Quarterly* 52 (4): 861–878.

Spindler, Michael. 2002. *Veblen and Modern America*. London: Pluto Press.

Stabile, Donald. 1984. *Prophets of Order: The Rise of the New Class, Technocracy and Socialism in America*. Boston: South End Press.

Steel, Ronald. 2003. "The Missionary." *New York Review of Books* 50 (18): 26–35.

Steinfels, Peter. 1979. *The Neoconservatives: The Men Who Are Changing American Politics*. New York: Simon and Schuster.

Stone, Clarence N. 1989. *Regime Politics: Governing Atlanta, 1946–1988*. Lawrence, Kans.: University of Kansas Press.

Stone, Clarence N., and Heywood T. Sanders, eds. 1987. *The Politics of Urban Development*. Lawrence, Kans.: University of Kansas Press.

Strauss, Leo. 1953. *Natural Right and History*. Chicago: University of Chicago Press.

——. 1964. *The City and Man*. Chicago: University of Chicago Press.

——. 1968. *Liberalism Ancient and Modern*. Foreword by Allan Bloom. Chicago: University of Chicago Press.

Suskind, Ron. 2006. *The One Percent Doctrine: Deep Inside America's Pursuit of Its Enemies Since 9/11*. New York: Simon and Schuster.

Sweezy, Paul M. 1957. "The Theory of Business Enterprise and Absentee Ownership," in "Thorstein Veblen," special issue, *Monthly Review* 9 (July–August): 105–112.

——. 1958. "Veblen on American Capitalism." In *Thorstein Veblen: A Critical Appraisal*, ed. Douglas Dowd. Ithaca, N.Y.: Cornell University Press.

Teggert, Richard V. 1932. *Thorstein Veblen: A Chapter in the History of Economic Thought*. Berkeley: University of California Publications.

Therborn, Göran. 1977. "The Frankfurt School." In *Western Marxism: A Critical Reader*, ed. New Left Review. London: Verso.

Thompson, E. P. 1964. *The Making of the English Working Class*. New York: Pantheon.

——. 1975. *Whigs and Hunters: The Origin of the Black Act*. London: Alan Lane.

Tichenor, Daniel J. 2002. *Dividing Lines: The Politics of Immigration Control in America*. Princeton, N.J.: Princeton University Press.

Tilly, Charles, ed. 1974. *The Formation of National States in Western Europe*. Princeton, N.J.: Princeton University Press.

——. 1985. "Warmaking and State Making as Organized Crime." In *Bringing the State Back In*, ed. Peter B. Evans, Dietrich Rueschemeyer, Theda Skocpol, 169–191. New York: Cambridge University Press.

——. 1992. *Coercion, Capital, and European States, AD 990–1992*. Cambridge, Mass.: Blackwell.

Tilman, Rick. 1984. *C. Wright Mills*. University Park, Penn.: Pennsylvania State University Press.

——. 1992. *Thorstein Veblen and His Critics, 1891–1963*. Princeton, N.J.: Princeton University Press.

——. 1996. *The Intellectual Legacy of Thorstein Veblen: Unresolved Issues*. Westport, Conn.: Greenwood Press.

——. 1996a. "Veblen and the Industrial Republic: The Path to the Future." In *The Intellectual Legacy of Thorstein Veblen: Unresolved Issues*, 167–197. Westport, Conn.: Greenwood Press.

——. 1996b. "Veblen and American Pragmatism: The Case of John Dewey." In *The Intellectual Legacy of Thorstein Veblen: Unresolved Issues*, 109–141. Westport, Conn.: Greenwood Press.

——. 1996c. "Veblen and the New Deal." In *The Intellectual Legacy of Thorstein Veblen: Unresolved Issues*, 199–222. Westport, Conn.: Greenwood Press.

——. 2004a. "Veblen the Feminist and the Feminism of Dewey and Mills." In *Thorstein Veblen, John Dewey, C. Wright Mills and the Generic Ends of Life*, 33–60. Lanham, Md.: Rowman and Littlefield.

——. 2004b. "The Moralists and the Meaning of Sports and Games of Chance." In *Thorstein Veblen, John Dewey, C. Wright Mills and the Generic Ends of Life*, 81–91. Lanham, Md.: Rowman and Littlefield.

——. 2005. "Thorstein Veblen's Views on American 'Exceptionalism': An Interpretation." *Journal of Economic Issues* 39 (1): 1–28.

Tocqueville, Alexis de. 1945. *Democracy in America*. Ed. Phillips Bradley. 2 vols. New York: Knopf.

——. 1998. *The Old Regime and the Revolution*. Ed. with Introduction and Critical Apparatus by François Furet and Françoise Melanio. Trans. Alan S. Kahan. Chicago: University of Chicago Press.

Truman, David. 1951. *The Governmental Process: Political Interests and Public Opinion*. New York: Knopf.

Turner, Frederick Jackson. 1906. *Rise of the New West 1819–1829*. New York: Harper and Brothers.

——. 1920. *The Frontier in American History*. New York: Henry Holt.

——. 1932. *The Significance of Sections in American History*. New York: Henry Holt.

——. 1935. *The United States, 1830–1850: The Nation and Its Sections*. New York: Henry Holt.

Valelly, Richard. 2006. "Political Scientists' Renewed Interest in the Workings of Power." The Chronical Review, *The Chronical of Higher Education*, 11 August, B6–7.

Van Creveld, Martin. 1991. *The Transformation of War*. New York: Free Press.

Veblen, Thorstein. 1917. *An Inquiry into the Nature of Peace and the Terms of Its Perpetuation*. New York: MacMillan.

——. 1919. *The Vested Interests and the Common Man*. New York: Viking.

——. 1954. *Imperial Germany and the Industrial Revolution*. Introduction by Joseph Dorfman. New York: Viking. (Originally published in 1915.)

——. 1957. *The Higher Learning in America: A Memorandum on the Conduct of Universities by Business Men*. Introduction by Lewis Hacker. New York: Hill and Wang. (Originally published in 1918.)

——. 1964. *Essays in Our Changing Order*. Ed. L. Ardzrooni. New York: Augustus Kelley. (Originally published in 1934.)

——. 1964a. "The Army of the Commonweal." In *Essays in Our Changing Order*, ed. L. Ardzrooni. New York: Augustus Kelley. (Original essay published 1894.)

——. 1964b. "The Barbarian Status of Women." In *Essays in Our Changing Order*, ed. L. Ardzrooni. New York: Augustus Kelley. (Original essay published 1899.)

——. 1964c. "The Beginnings of Ownership." In *Essays in Our Changing Order*, ed. L. Ardzrooni. New York: Augustus Kelley. (Original essay published 1898.)

——. 1964d. "The Instinct of Workmanship and the Irksomeness of Labor." In *Essays in Our Changing Order*, ed. L. Ardzrooni. New York: Augustus Kelley. (Original essay published 1898.)

——. 1964e. "The Intellectual Pre-eminence of Jews in Modern Europe." In *Essays in Our Changing Order*, ed. L. Ardzrooni. New York: Augustus Kelley. (Original essay published 1919.)

——. 1964f. "Kant's Critique of Judgment." In *Essays in Our Changing Order*, ed. L. Ardzrooni. New York: Augustus Kelley. (Original essay published 1884.)

——. 1964g. "Mr. Cumming's Strictures on 'The Theory of the Leisure Class.' " In *Essays in Our Changing Order*, ed. L. Ardzrooni. New York: Augustus Kelley. (Original essay published 1899.)

——. 1964h. "Fisher's Rate of Interest." In *Essays in Our Changing Order*, ed. L. Ardzrooni. New York: Augustus Kelley. (Original essay published 1909.)

——. 1964i. "Dementia Praecox." In *Essays in Our Changing Order*, ed. L. Ardzrooni. New York: Augustus Kelley. (Original essay published 1919.)

——. 1964j. "The Opportunity of Japan." In *Essays in Our Changing Order*, ed. L. Ardzrooni. New York: Augustus Kelley. (Original essay published 1915.)

——. 1964k. "Editorials from the Dial: June 14, 1919." In *Essays in Our Changing Order*, ed. L. Ardzrooni. New York: Augustus Kelley. (Original essay published 1899.)

——. 1964l. "Christian Morals and the Competitive System." In *Essays in Our Changing Order*, ed. L. Ardzrooni. New York: Augustus Kelley. (Original essay published 1910.)

——. 1964m. "The Economic Consequences of the Peace." In *Essays in Our Changing Order*, ed. L. Ardzrooni. New York: Augustus Kelley. (Original essay published 1899.)

——. 1964n. "Bolshevism Is a Menace—To Whom?" In *Essays in Our Changing Order*, ed. L. Ardzrooni. New York: Augustus Kelley. (Original essay published 1899).

——. 1964o. "Menial Servants During the Period of the War." In *Essays in Our Changing Order*, ed. L. Ardzrooni. New York: Augustus Kelley. (Original essay published 1918.)

——. 1964p. "Farm Labor for the Period of the War." In *Essays in Our Changing Order*, ed. L. Ardzrooni. New York: Augustus Kelley. (Original essay published 1919.)

——. 1964q. "Farm Labor and the I.W.W." In *Essays in Our Changing Order*, ed. L. Ardzrooni. New York: Augustus Kelley. (Original essay written in 1918, published 1932.)

——. 1969. *Veblen on Marx, Race, Science and Economics*. New York: Capricorn Books. Originally published as *The Place of Science in Modern Civilization and Other Essays* (New York: B. W. Huebusch, 1919).

——. 1969a. "The Place of Science in Modern Civilization." In *Veblen on Marx, Race, Science and Economics*. New York: Capricorn Books. (Original essay published 1906.)

——. 1969b. "Why Is Economics Not an Evolutionary Science?" In *Veblen on Marx, Race, Science and Economics*. New York: Capricorn Books. (Original essay published 1898.)

——. 1969c. "Some Neglected Points in the Theory of Socialism." In *Veblen on Marx, Race, Science and Economics*. New York: Capricorn Books. (Original essay published 1892.)

——. 1969d. "The Socialist Economics of Karl Marx and His Followers," I and II. In *Veblen on Marx, Race, Science and Economics*. New York: Capricorn Books. (Original essays published 1906, 1907.)

——. 1969e. "The Limitations of Marginal Utility." In *Veblen on Marx, Race, Science and Economics*. New York: Capricorn Books. (Original essay published 1898.)

——. 1969f. "Industrial and Pecuniary Employments." In *Veblen on Marx, Race, Science and Economics*. New York: Capricorn Books. (Original essay published in 1901.)

——. 1969g. "The Preconceptions of Economic Science, I." In *Veblen on Marx, Race, Science and Economics*. New York: Capricorn Books. (Original essay published 1899.)

——. 1969h. "The Evolution of the Scientific Point of View." In *Veblen on Marx, Race, Science and Economics*. New York: Capricorn Books. (Original essay published 1908.)

——. 1978. *The Theory of Business Enterprise*. With a new Introduction by Douglas Dowd. New Brunswick, N.J.: Transaction Publishers. (Originally published 1904.)

——. 1979. *The Theory of the Leisure Class*. Introduction by Robert Lekachman. New York: Penguin Books. (Originally published 1899.)

——. 1983. *The Engineers and the Price System*. Introduction by Daniel Bell. New Brunswick, N.J.: Transaction Publishers. (Originally published 1921.)

——. 1990. *The Instinct of Workmanship and the State of the Industrial Arts*. With a new Introduction by Murray G. Murphey. New Brunswick, N.J.: Transaction Publishers. (Originally published 1914.)

——. 1997. *Absentee Ownership: Business Enterprise in Recent Times: The Case of America*. Introduction by Marion Levy, Jr. New Brunswick, N.J.: Transaction Publishers. (Originally published 1923.)

Viano, Francesca L. 2009. "Ithaca Transfer: Veblen and the Historical Profession." *History of European Ideas* 35:38–71.

Viereck, Peter R. E. 1949. *Conservatism Revisited: The Revolt Against Revolt, 1815–1849*. New York: Charles Scribner's Sons.

Vogel, David. 1989. *Fluctuating Fortunes: The Political Power of Business in America*. New York: Basic Books.

Voss, Kim. 1993. *The Making of American Exceptionalism*. Ithaca, N.Y.: Cornell University Press.

Waddoups, Jeffrey, and Rick Tilman. 1992. "Thorstein Veblen and the Feminism of Institutional Economists." *International Review of Sociology* 3:182–204.

Weber, Max. 1948. *From Max Weber: Essays in Sociology*. Trans., Ed., and with an Introduction by H. H. Gerth and C. Wright Mills. New York: Oxford University Press.

——. 1948a. "Politics as a Vocation." In *From Max Weber: Essays in Sociology*, trans., ed., and with an Introduction by H. H. Gerth and C. Wright Mills, 77–128. New York: Oxford University Press.

——. 1948b. "Science as a Vocation." In *From Max Weber: Essays in Sociology*, trans., ed., and with an Introduction by H. H. Gerth and C. Wright Mills, 129–156. New York: Oxford University Press.

——. 1948c. "Structures of Power." In *From Max Weber: Essays in Sociology*, trans., ed., and with an Introduction by H. H. Gerth and C. Wright Mills, 159–179. New York: Oxford University Press.

——. 1949. *The Methodology of the Social Sciences*. Trans. and ed. Edward A. Shils and Henry Finch. With a Foreword by Edward A. Shils. New York: Free Press.

——. 1978. *Economy and Society: An Outline of Interpretive Sociology.* Ed. Guenther Roth and Claus Wittich. 2 vols. Berkeley: University of California Press.

Webster's New World Dictionary of the American Language. 1968. Cleveland: The World Publishing Company.

White, Morton S. 1957. *Social Thought in America.* Boston: Beacon Press.

White, Ron D. 1978. "Growth versus Conservation: A Veblenian Perspective." *Journal of Economic Issues* 12 (2): 427–433.

Williams, Michael. 2004. "Why Ideas Matter in International Relations: Hans Morgenthau, Classical Realism, and the Moral Construction of Power Politics." *International Organization* 58 (Fall): 633–665.

Williams, William Appleton. 1957. "The Nature of Peace." *Monthly Review* 9 (3–4): 112–117.

Wills, Garry. 2003. *Negro President: Jefferson and the Slave Power.* Boston: Houghton Mifflin.

Wiltgen, Richard. 1990. "The Darwinian Evolutionary Perspectives of Engles and Veblen." *International Journal of Social Economics* 17 (4): 4–11.

Wolin, Sheldon. 1960. *Politics and Vision: Continuity and Innovation in Western Thought.* Boston: Little Brown.

——. 1996. "Fugitive Democracy." In *Democracy and Difference: Contesting the Boundaries of the Political*, ed. Selya Benhabib, 31–45. Princeton, N.J.: Princeton University Press.

——. 2008. *Democracy Inc.: Managed Democracy and the Specter of Inverted Totalitarianism.* Princeton, N.J.: Princeton University Press.

Wood, Gordon S. 2009. *Empire of Liberty: A History of the Early Republic, 1789–1815.* New York: Oxford University Press.

Yoo, John. 2005. *The Powers of War and Peace.* Chicago: University of Chicago Press.

Young, Iris Marion. 1996. "Communication and the Other: Beyond Deliberative Democracy." In *Democracy and Difference: Contesting the Boundaries of the Political*, ed. Selya Benhabib, 120–135. Princeton, N.J.: Princeton University Press.

Zweig, David, and Bi Jianhai. 2005. "China's Global Hunt for Energy." *Foreign Affairs* 84 (5): 25–38.

Pragmatism, 28–30, 67, 71, 74, 76–77, 197, 215n10, 216n13

Predation: and emulation, 9, 12, 152; origins of, 12, 72; and war, 15, 83, 136–144, 235n43; and power, 32, 71, 72–76, 84, 86, 106, 143–144, 164; continuation of, 44; and habit, 72, 85, 100, 202, 219n70; and politics, 83, 86, 110–113, 140, 155–156, 197; evolution of, 85, 93, 100; and resistance, 96; and exploit, 97–100, 105, 110; and charisma, 100–101; and class relations, 106, 139, 143–144, 146–147, 223n7; and handicraft era, 131; and barbarism, 136–137, 140–142, 159; and outsiders, 137–139, 155; and opportunism, 193

Price system, 46–47, 59–60, 161, 163–164, 189, 237n75

Private property, 130–131, 187–189

Production, 10, 60, 91, 98, 106, 108, 113

Prussia, 117, 134, 228n35

Public opinion: and government, 55; and democracy, 172–175, 179, 202–203; and expert opinion, 174, 234n21; and law, 175, 186–190; and illiberal habits, 179–186; and opportunism, 190–193, 237–238n76, 238n77

Purposive behavior: and freedom, 49, 79, 150; and humans as teleological agents, 49–50, 73, 86, 96, 149–150; exploit subverting, 97–99, 150–151; self-generated purpose, 97, 222n39

Racism, 180, 181, 193

Radicalism: and Veblen criticism, 24, 27–28, 38–39, 62–72, 76; and Veblen's critique of power, 55; political base of, 77

Radical realism, 39, 40, 62, 144, 148, 179, 220n85

Rationality: and modernity, 3–4; and commercial order, 46; and state, 47; and social science, 57; instrumental rationality, 59, 72; substantive rationality, 59; and radicalism, 62;

technical rationality, 66–67, 71; and self-interest, 80; and capitalism, 167, 233n6; and democracy, 174; of law, 176; and resistance, 207

Realism, 55, 60, 62–63, 84, 87–89, 93–94, 97, 100

Religion: Veblen's religious skepticism, 21, 34, 60; and fundamentalism, 53, 67; and Veblen criticism, 61, 74; and industry, 104; and pagan anarchy, 122; and exploit, 141; and class relations, 146–147; and power, 153–154, 229n53; and masterless men, 180; and public opinion, 182–183, 185; and politics, 207–208

Resistance: to change, 44, 170; and power, 96–97; and exploit, 99; and class relations, 148–149, 151; and democracy, 178, 202–208; and monarchy, 232n85

Responsibility: irresponsibility, 38, 44, 124, 128, 133, 136–137, 142, 168, 177, 179, 181, 183, 227n32; popular demands for, 143; and class relations, 148; and religion, 153; and patriotism, 154; and government, 176, 186

Riesman, David, 24, 28, 56, 58, 68, 212n29, 220n85

Roosevelt, Franklin D., 56, 227n32

Rosenberg, Bernard, 68–69, 219n46, 229n53

Ross, Dorothy, 37, 68, 217n42

Satire, 31, 32, 34, 48, 78, 229n52

Savagery: and anarchy, 11, 119; and Veblen's biography, 19; and barbarism, 52, 118; and community, 52, 63, 85; and power, 57, 102; and Veblen criticism, 60, 75; and conflict, 84–85, 113; and industry, 103–105, 202; and maternal anarchy, 108–116, 123, 125, 127, 132, 173, 224n48; and politics, 118–119, 132; democracy as form of, 172; evolutionary distinction in, 223n24; presuppositions about, 223n25

Schmitt, Carl, 138, 229n52